What is the Antichrist – Islam Connection?

Scripture quotations are from New International Version, © 1985 by Zondervan Bible Publishers; The Interlinear Bible, © 1986 by Jay P. Green; Holman Christian Standard Bible, © 2003 by Holman Bible Publishers; New American Standard Bible, © 1995 by the Lockman Foundation; and from direct translations made by Michael A. H. Back.

Map of the Babylonian Empire found in chapter one is courtesy of www.digitalbible.org, Maps of the Persian, Grecian, and Roman empires found in chapter one are courtesy of the Grolier Encyclopedia of Knowledge, © 1991 by Grolier Incorporated. American Eagle photograph courtesy of the American Eagle Foundation at www.eagles.org.

Manufactured and Published in the United States of America.

www.mystery-bablyon.us

e-mail: back@mystery-babylon.us

ISBN: 978-1-84728-504-1

ABOUT THE AUTHORS

Roland L. Back has been studying the end times and bible prophecy for over four decades. He is an ordained minister, and has served in the leadership of several churches in the mid-Michigan area over the years. He and his beloved wife and companion, Carolyn, had been married for 34 years when she passed away in February of 2001. The greatest testament to their ministry for the Lord is that all five of their children have continued to serve the Lord as adults, and to pass on that legacy to their own children.

Michael A. H. Back has been studying Greek for over twenty years. He started with Attic (Classical) Greek in college, and switched to Koine (the dialect of the Bible) Greek a few years later. He is very active in his local church where he regularly teaches Bible classes, and periodically, Biblical Greek. He studied world religions in college, where he spent several semesters studying Islam. He is a full time author, sometime computer consultant, and runs occasional martial arts classes for home schooled children (he holds a master's rank in the martial arts). He has been married for twenty-five years to the woman of his dreams, and they currently have four children, a daughter-in-law, a daughter in the faith, and two grandchildren.

Dedication

This is dedicated first and foremost to

The Lord Jesus Christ

May it be used for His glory.

We especially dedicate this book to

Carolyn Ann Back

for being a wonderful, loving wife and a great mother; and for her many hours spent in constant prayers to make these writings possible. She was truly a gifted handmaiden of the Lord for her extraordinary prophetic insights. Precious memories of her will always burn within our heart. We will miss her greatly.

Author's Foreword

It was the summer of 1976. I was 15 years old. I remember that moment clearly and distinctly. It seemed like one of those frozen moments in life, when time ceases to move, and everything stands still. A moment when you realize, in a peripheral sort of way, that something was happening that will change your world forever. A defining moment. A bit of history in the making. You know, something big like that.

I came into the house, and as I paused in the living room, I heard bits and pieces of conversation from the kitchen about Mystery Babylon. I wasn't really listening until something caught my attention.

"Roland, that's got to be it. I think you've found it."

What? In my soft, considerate, be-seen-and-not-heard, teenaged humility, I immediately interrupted.

"You figured it out?" I asked. "Did you figure out who the Great Prostitute is?"

I almost held my breath. Did he REALLY have an answer?

Now I realize that in most houses, this is not a regular topic of conversation between parents and teenagers, much less a burning question to which everyone in the household is eagerly awaiting an answer. But in our house, this was THE question. The one we (meaning dad) simply couldn't figure out. The mystery of all mysteries. The big one.

Dad had been studying this topic for years. The popular belief then, as it seems to be now, was that Mystery Babylon was Catholicism, but he had rejected that theory long ago. It simply didn't fit all the facts. A half dozen other theories were considered and discarded for exactly the same reason. They simply didn't fit all the facts. His was a long, and mostly frustrating search for the answer to that question.

But on that warm June afternoon, he had a different answer. Picking up a recent magazine with a mosque on the cover, he handed it to me.

"This." I stared at the magazine uncomprehending.

"This is the great whore. Islam."

I held the magazine in my hand, and searched the cover, taking in the information, processing it, rolling it around in my mind. This had been an unsolved mystery, a question perpetually awaiting an answer in my household for so long that I guess I had gotten used to hearing, "I don't know." Actually having an answer felt strange.

Islam?

Even when he was considering or researching other answers, he always said, "I don't know." He had never actually given a definite answer before. So I paused, and considered his answer. And then dismissed it.

Actually, I didn't just dismiss it, I violently rejected it. My mind reeled away from this possibility. Maybe it was because after so many years of searching, the question had grown to such huge proportions in my mind that no "earthly" religion could fill the shoes. Maybe it was that Islam seemed far too mundane. After so much time and suspense, I was expecting the answer to be ominous and exotic, looming and dark, sinister and evil. Kinda like Darth Vader. Or maybe I had simply gotten used to the idea of not having an answer to that question. But whatever the reason, I simply couldn't accept it. I didn't actually say anything, but I was certain, with that all-knowing, rock solid, absolutely positive kind of certainty that only teenagers can have, that he was wrong.

Over the next year, however, I listened very carefully as he painstakingly took people through the steps to show them that Islam had to be, and in point of fact, was the ONLY choice for the identity of the Great Prostitute. The understanding that **I** had been the one who was wrong (gasp!) when I dismissed his statement slowly overtook me. Then I realized it had been there all along. Staring all of us in the face. There was only one choice – one possibility – one religion that actually fit all the facts: Islam.

But for various reasons, whether it be prejudice, or old church doctrine, or ignorance, or lack of knowledge, or stubbornness, or in my case, almost all of the above, we simply hadn't seen it.

Over the next few years, dad taught and taught and taught on this topic. But there were too many people to teach, and not enough Dad to go around. Examining all the evidence for this theory took time – time most people simply did not have, or were unwilling to commit to a teaching session about a topic that simply sounded too far fetched.

And so, the idea of writing a book started to surface.

I went away to college, got married, and came back with my family.

In the winter of 1984, I started helping Dad on the book. He already had a rough draft manuscript. Over the next ten years, I wrote and re-wrote, and re-wrote the book. All the while seeking a publisher. And got one rejection after another. Then, in the late 80's and early 90's, so many of our predictions about world events started happening (such as the collapse of the USSR, and the independence of the southern Muslim republics of the USSR), that I had to rewrite it several more times. I think I re-wrote that entire book five times. And still, the rejections kept coming. It just didn't seem like the time was right, so we put the book away.

More years passed, a new millenium arrived, and we picked it up again. New technology, new programs, and new connections made this time quicker, smoother, and much more successful. And even though we discovered that the only copy still in existence was on paper (the disk copies were all damaged), which meant scanning, editing, and re-writing all over again, the time was finally right.

And so, twenty-five years after Dad first told me that Islam was the religion symbolized by Babylon the Great, the Mother of Prostitutes, the first edition of this book was finally published. I printed and bound each book myself, and we distributed several hundred copies through our web site, www.mystery-babylon.us.

Now, four years after that first laser printed, home bound book lay on my kitchen table ready to be mailed, the second edition is being professionally published and globally distributed through lulu.com. With a new name (the original title was "Mystery Babylon Revealed: Islam") and additional charts and information, the dream that started when I was a teenager is being fully realized as I enter my second year with a new and wonderful title: grandfather.

My name is on the cover along side his, but this is really my Dad's book, his "revelation," his discovery. I am the helper, the apprentice, the sounding board, the typist and editor, but he is the author.

Along with that, there are a number of people that I need to thank.

First is my dear wife. This book simply wouldn't exist without her patience, help, advice, input, prayers, support, editing, typing, scanning . . . and of course, her love and companionship. She keeps me sane, makes me laugh, encourages me when I am discouraged, overlooks my many, many faults, and . . . . well . . . is a more incredible and precious wife than I deserve (or even dreamed existed)! She means more to me than I have the words to express. I love you, dear.

Next there are my oldest daughter, who created the drawings inside and the cover of the book, as well as my daughter-in-law, who patiently and painstakingly proofread the book with laser accurate eye. Thanks Sweeties.

Then there are my three cousins, Gary, Jeff and Brian. Gary and Jeff were invaluable in my research of ancient history, particularly ancient races (Jeff) and ancient religions (Gary). In particular, they helped me understand the empires of the Babylonians and Grecians. Brian not only created many of the charts and graphs, but he also taught me how to create some of my own so I could expand the number of charts in the second edition. Thanks guys.

I also want to thank Debbie, who volunteered to take over as the Web Master of our web page (www.mystery-babylon.us), and turned it into a professional site. Thanks Debbie, we couldn't have done it without you.

Finally, there are the many family and friends that have been a tremendous help and support throughout this process. At the top of the list are my beloved children and grandchildren. And of course, my sisters and brother. I love all you guys. There is also Linda Smalley, Elizabeth

Avens, and many, many others. The full and complete list of people who deserve thanks is simply too long to specifically name them all, but I want each and everyone to know how much I appreciate their help, encouragement, and prayers.

It was partly because of these people, and the visionaries who created lulu.com, that you can now read this book. Thanks everyone.

It was a long road getting this book into your hands. Treat it gently, and with a more open mind than I did all those years ago.

I promise it will be worth it.

Michael Back

CONTENTS

Introduction

Are there "rules" for interpreting prophecy?
Did we study the teachings of any other authors?
What are some of the popular beliefs about the end times?
What will you find in this book?
Why did we write this book?
Why should you read this book?

"See, I lay in Zion a chosen and precious cornerstone, and the one who trusts in him will never be put to shame.' Now to you who believe, this stone is precious. But to those who do not believe, 'The stone the builders rejected has become the capstone,' and, 'A stone that causes men to stumble and a rock that makes them fall'."
I Peter 2:6-8

Bible scholars, Bible teachers, and theologians have been struggling with the seventeenth chapter of Revelation for hundreds of years. Who is the Great Harlot? What is Mystery Babylon? What is the beast with seven heads and ten horns? What are the seven mountains? As Daniel said, "There is a God in Heaven who reveals mysteries," and now, that same God has finally revealed the answers to these mysteries.

We are not more intelligent or more perceptive than all other students of scripture, nor have we done some great work for the Lord that caused Him to decide we deserve to receive this insight into His word. We are merely recipients of His Grace who hope and pray that our handling of the rhema He has entrusted to us will meet with His approval. As such, we dedicate this book to our Lord and Savior, Jesus Christ. May it be used for his glory.

We have employed a few rules as guidelines to help us interpret the prophecies we will be examining in this book. Those guidelines work equally well for interpreting prophesies, parables, and allegories in other sections of the Bible as well.

1. *Wherever possible, let the Bible provide the interpretations of the prophecy.* For example, let the scriptural use and meaning of the word "mountain" determine what the seven mountains in Revelation must mean, not a popular tag placed on a city by men.

2. *If at all possible,* **REMAIN CONSISTENT**. A symbol frequently means the same thing throughout the Bible. The meanings of most Biblical symbols, such as mountains, clay, wheat, sheep, and so on, are remarkably uniform throughout the Old and New Testament. Where we need to be careful is when two symbols SEEM to be the same, but they are not. For example, there are two separate and distinct beasts (a leopard and a dragon) in Revelation with seven heads and ten horns, and they do not represent the same thing. On the other hand, the allusions to a lion, a bear, and a leopard in Revelation are intentional references to the dream described in the seventh chapter of Daniel.

3. *Be careful when mixing separate prophecies and allegories.* If you mix Jesus' allegories about sheep and wolves with his parables about sheep and goats, you may conclude there are three classes of people (Sheep, Goats, and Wolves), which is NOT what Jesus intended. There are not three classes of people here, but two; the goats and wolves represent different aspects of the SAME class of people. Likewise we need to be careful about mixing the symbols from two separate dreams or visions (for example: mixing Daniel's vision of the ram and goat with his vision of the lion, leopard, bear, and strange beast should NOT lead us to the conclusion that these six separate beasts represent six separate kingdoms; closer examination reveals that the ram and goat from one vision represent the same kingdoms as the leopard and bear from another).

4. ***Most importantly****: Do not let current events decide the interpretation of scripture.* Figure out what scripture means strictly from the evidence contained in the Bible, THEN look around and find out if any current (or historical) events fit what scripture says will happen. For example, don't let the rumor that China might have about two hundred and fifty million men in its army cause one to interpret the two hundred and fifty million demon locust in Revelation as an army from China. If no one had told you that China may have that many people in its army, would you have concluded from the scriptural evidence alone that it must be an army from the east? We think if you examine the scriptures closely, you will find no such evidence in that passage.

During our studies, we have taken ample opportunity to review the works of numerous other scholars and teachers concerning the writings in Daniel and Revelation. Among those whose works we studied are Gaebelein, Ladd, Bauer, Scofield, Larkin, and the currently popular works of Pat Robertson, Hal Lindsey, Jack Van Impe, and Tim LaHaye, as well as those of a few more recent and lesser known writers. Of the more than two dozen authors reviewed, we retain the most respect for the scholarship and faith evidenced in the works of Charles Larkin, who published his books in the range from 1910 to 1920.

Charles Larkin exhibited extreme faith in the scriptures, practiced rule number four throughout his books, ignored the current state of world affairs (World War I took place in that span), and resisted the temptation to attach unwarranted eschatological significance to the world changing events unfolding in Europe. Time has proven the validity of his approach; he predicted many events that would take place in Europe and the Middle East long after he died, and avoided attaching untrue "end times" significance to the events of his lifetime. While we do not agree with all of his conclusions, what impressed us the most is that, when it came to the end times, his errors were not due to sensationalizing current events, to vain and wild imaginations, nor to a lack of faith in the literal fulfillment of scripture, but primarily to the era in which he lived (we firmly believe that some mysteries in scripture have been kept hidden by God until He deems it time to reveal them).

Many people have the view that there are hundreds, or even thousands of theories and doctrines about the events in Revelation. The eschatological information in Daniel, Ezekiel, and Revelation is not so vague that everyone who has carefully studied them has a different point of view. As is the case with most events in human endeavor, a person's doctrines and theories about the end times are determined largely by one's initial assumptions and the amount of time and effort they are willing to put into the study. Their initial assumptions, coupled with the sheer number of hours they are willing to put into research and study, will help form their conclusions as much as the subtleties of symbolic language.

There are four major approaches to eschatological texts in scripture, which we will call (1) the secular view; (2) the "historical" or "amillennial" view; (3) the spiritual view; (4) the futurist view.

The secular view is that the book of Revelation is primarily a political document, disguised as theology, attacking the Roman authorities. This view is prominent among "religion" professors at secular universities, but has very few followers outside the darkened halls of secular academia. We reject the secular view completely, since the foundation of that framework is that scripture is not the inspired work of God, but was written by men with no input from the Spirit.

The historical view is similar to the secular view in that it believes Revelation to be an attack on the historical Roman Empire, with no real reference to future events. The gigantic difference between the two rests solely on the historical view's acceptance of the inspiration of the scripture. This view has a fair following among "religion" professors in both secular and Christian colleges, and in some of the older, mainline denominations (Catholic, Lutheran, United Methodist, Episcopalian, etc.). We also cast aside this view outright, since it rests almost exclusively on the belief that prophecy, if there is such a thing, does not relate to any events beyond the first century.

One of the chief, some could say fatal, flaws of this approach is that it demands that virtually everything written in Revelation had ALREADY HAPPENED by the time the book was actually written (in Revelation 1:9, John reveals that he wrote the book while on the Island of Patmos. His exile to Patmos occurred sometime during the reign of Domitian, between 81-96 AD). Revelation can, from this point of view, be described as a historical book that deceptively appears to be, and even claims to be about future, end times, prophetic events. This, we believe, is not in keeping with the nature of our God, or the Spirit of His Word. While scripture can be difficult to understand at times, it is NEVER deceptive.

The historical view is also called the amillennial[1] view. There are numerous versions of this, but the most common deny the literal return of our Lord Jesus in the last days. This theory seems to have started with Augustine in the fourth century, and is prominent in the Catholic Church today. In amillennialism almost everything in the scriptures is symbolic of something else: Israel is the church, Jerusalem is Rome, the temple is a believer, and so on. Under this approach, nothing in a prophetic section is literal, and any word can represent almost anything except itself.

The spiritual view insists that the eschatological texts in scripture are also symbolic of powerful spiritual truths that apply to Christians in their daily walks right now. There truly are great spiritual truths which apply to daily life hidden within the end times texts, but we need to be careful not to assume that this is the ONLY thing to be found within these prophesies. We uphold that much of what we have heard

---

[1] Amillennial literally means "no millenium." The millenium is a period described in Revelation that is directly connected to the return of Jesus at the end of this age. Opposed to amillennialism is pre-millennialism and post-millennialism. Briefly stated, a pre-millennialist believes Christ will literally return before the millennium, and a post-millenialist believes he will return after the millennium. Postmillennialism largely died out after World War II.

preached from this view is of the Spirit of our Living God, but it is not the purpose of this book to delve into this particular approach.

One variant of the spiritual view is that the prophecies will be fulfilled spiritually, not literally (and that they already have been fulfilled). In this view the beast symbols primarily represent eras in the history of the church, and almost all of it has already happened (including the second coming of Christ). This approach is very similar to the historical view.

The futurist view maintains that large portions from Daniel, Isaiah, Ezekiel, and Revelation (among others) point to the end of the world as we know it, and to the Second Coming of our Lord Jesus Christ. This is the most popular view among Protestant, evangelical Christians. We hold to this perspective.

Among the futurists, the primary differences center on when the "rapture" will take place (before the tribulation, sometime during the tribulation, or after the tribulation), where the Antichrist will come to power (Europe, Russia, the Middle East, or North America), and the meaning of "Israel" (the literal, Jewish nation of Israel, or symbolic of the church). Hand in hand with where the Antichrist will arise is the identity of the Mother of Harlots, Babylon the Great (Catholicism, Apostate Christianity, New Age Movement, or U.S.A.). The most popular views among evangelicals today are a pre-tribulation rapture, a European Antichrist, and either Catholicism or Apostate Christianity as Babylon. Popular opinion appears to be somewhat evenly split on whether or not "Israel" in prophecy is the literal nation, or symbolic of the church.

Since we firmly believe the secular and historical views to be without merit, we focused almost exclusively on the works of those authors espousing a futurist approach to scripture. During our review of the works of these various men we began to realize our book would challenge some popular and long held theories concerning the end-times. For those of you who have not read extensively on the end times, and because we will refer to these doctrines throughout our book, here are the primary teachings found in the evangelical church today that conflict with a clear understanding of the end times, and hinder the Body of Christ from preparing for this "insane" age which is even now upon us. We believe these doctrines are in error.

POPULAR DOCTRINES ABOUT END TIMES

1. The Ten Toed and Ten Horned Kingdoms are the Common Market.

2.   The Antichrist comes out of the Common Market and is a European king.
3.   The Antichrist literally rules the WHOLE world, and establishes one world government.
4.   Babylon the Great, the Mother of Harlots (in Revelation 17) is the Catholic Church, apostate Christianity, the U.S.A., or the New Age movement.
5.   All references to "Israel" in prophecy are NOT about the literal nation of Israel, nor about the Jews, but are exclusively symbolic of the Church.
6.   Israel accepts the Antichrist as the Messiah.
7.   Russia invades Israel.
8.   The Church will escape the tribulation, and thus does not need to prepare for it (pre-tribulation rapture).
9.   "Gomer'" is Germany, "Meshech" is Moscow, and "Gog and Magog" are Russia.
10. The Wrath of God falls on the United States.
11. Rome is the center of all end times activity.
12. The Antichrist will be a Jew, a Russian, a German, an Italian (or Catholic), or an American.

We do not challenge these doctrines lightly, nor just to add a new voice to those already shouting in churches and on television. **Our primary motivation is for the Church to fully understand and prepare for the coming events, that the bridegroom's arrival not catch her sleeping and unprepared.** That is why we have written this book, and why you should read it.

As it turns out, simply determining exactly where the Antichrist shall arise can eliminate most of these erroneous beliefs. In fact, the main thrust of this book, proving that the woman symbol in Revelation called "Mystery Babylon, the Mother of Harlots" (the "religious tool" the Antichrist uses to come to power) represents Islam in the last days, cannot be supported until the country that shall spawn the Antichrist is clearly and definitively identified. Thus, the first section of this book focuses on the evidence, which we believe is clear and easily understood, needed to answer that question.

As happens with prophetic mysteries, the answers to the puzzles in the seventeenth chapter of Revelation are not particularly difficult to understand or comprehend. On the other hand, they are not short and simple, nor are they always straightforward. If they were, so many learned men and women would not have struggled for so long to understand them.

Just as it would be difficult to build a house without first learning carpentry (and a few other skills), it will be almost impossible to understand most of the book of Revelation (chapter Seventeen in particular) without first understanding portions of the book of Daniel. Daniel could be described as the "foundation" for which Revelation is the house.

The distinguished Jewish historian, Josephus, wrote:

> *"I have only undertaken to describe things past or present, but not things future: yet if any one be so very desirous of knowing truth, as not to wave such points of curiosity, and cannot curb his inclination for understanding the uncertainties of the future, and whether they will happen or not, let him be diligent in reading the book of Daniel, which he will find among the sacred writings."*[2]

With that in mind, let us move first to Daniel.

---

[2] The Works of Josephus, William Whiston, trans. (Peabody, MA: Hendrickson Publishers, 1985), p. 224.

THE MULTI-METALLIC IMAGE
Introduction to the Players

In about the year 604 BC King Nebuchadnezzar II of the Babylonian Empire had a dream that bothered him so much he decided it must have a deeper meaning. The king was well aware that anyone could make up an interpretation, particularly if the person's life were on the line, so he devised a plan to ensure that any interpretation he received would be the truth.

His plan was simple; instead of telling the dream to his wise men, only the one that could first tell the king what he had dreamed would be trusted to tell the truth about the interpretation. Why? Because he knew only a god could give a man a dream, and thus, only a god could interpret it accurately. His puzzle would be no trouble for a wise man truly in contact with the divine. If no one could do it they were not really wise men, but liars and cheats, and the royal executioner would considerably shorten their life expectancy. The wise men, predictably, were somewhat uncomfortable with this arrangement.

They begged the king to tell them the dream. They tried to explain to the king that, although they were very wise, no man, no matter how wise, could tell the interpretation of a dream when he didn't know the details. Even though Nebuchadnezzar really was asking the impossible, and he knew it, he became so furious that he ordered the deaths of all men acting in the capacity of "supernatural" advisors.

By acknowledging that none of them could tell the king what he had dreamed, that no mortal man could, the "wise men" of Babylon were simply admitting none of them were truly in contact with God. When Daniel heard he and his friends were about to die because pagan diviners were not hearing from God (something that was no surprise to him), he went to the king and asked for time to seek God for an answer. Since this was what the king had wanted in the first place, Nebuchadnezzar honored his request, and the Lord answered Daniel's prayers. (Daniel 2:1-26).

Daniel returned to king Nebuchadnezzar and told him the dream and its interpretation.

THE DREAM

"No wise man, Enchanter, magician or diviner can explain to the king the mystery he has asked about, but there is a God in heaven who reveals mysteries. He has shown King Nebuchadnezzar what will happen in days to come. Your dream and the visions that passed through your mind as you lay on your bed are these:

"As you were lying there, 0 King, your mind turned to things that will come, and the revealer of mysteries showed you what is yet going to happen. As for me, this mystery has been revealed to me, not because I have greater wisdom than other living men, but so that you, 0 King, may know the interpretation and that you may understand what went through your mind.

"You looked, 0 King, and there before you stood a large statue--an enormous, dazzling statue, awesome in appearance. The head of the statue was made of pure gold, its chest and arms of silver, its belly and thighs of bronze, its legs of iron, its feet partly of iron and partly of baked clay.

While you were watching, a rock was cut out, but not by human hands. It struck the statue on its feet of iron and clay and smashed them. Then the iron, the clay, the bronze, the silver and the gold were broken to pieces at the same time and became like chaff on a threshing floor in the summer. The wind swept them away without leaving a trace. But the rock that struck the statue became a huge mountain and filled the whole earth.

"This was the dream, and now we will interpret it to the king. You, 0 King, are the King of kings. The God of heaven has given you dominion and power and might and glory: in your hands he has placed mankind and the beasts of the field and the birds of the air. Wherever they live, he has made you ruler over them all. You are that head of Gold. After you, another kingdom will rise, inferior to yours. Next a third kingdom, one of bronze, will rule over the whole earth. Finally, there will be a fourth kingdom, strong as iron--for iron breaks and smashes everything--and as iron

breaks things to pieces, so it will crush and break all the others. Just as you saw that the feet and toes were partly of baked clay and partly of iron, so this will be a divided kingdom: yet it will have some of the strength of iron in it, even as you saw iron mixed with the clay. As the toes were partly iron and partly clay, so this kingdom will be partly strong and partly brittle. And just as you saw the iron mixed with baked clay, so the people will be a mixture and will not remain united, any more than iron mixes with clay.

"In the time of those kings, the God of heaven will set up a kingdom that will never be destroyed, nor will it be left to another people. It will crush all those kingdoms and bring them to an end, but it will itself endure forever. This is the meaning of the vision of the rock cut out of a mountain, but not by human hands--a rock that broke the iron, the bronze, the clay, the silver and the gold to pieces.

"The great God has shown the king what will take place in the future. The dream is true and the interpretation is trustworthy." (Daniel 2:27-45)

Recap

The king dreamed about a multi-metallic statue of a man and an aggressive rock produced without hands. The image consisted of five materials, with five body parts separated accordingly: Gold (head), silver (chest and arms), bronze (belly and thighs), iron (legs), and a section of iron mixed with clay (feet and toes). The supernaturally produced rock struck the statue on the feet and toes of iron and clay, and the whole statue crumbled into dust and the wind blew it away. The rock then became a mountain that filled the whole earth.

THE BODY PARTS

After telling Nebuchadnezzar his dream, Daniel went on to explain that the head represented Nebuchadnezzar himself, and through him, the Babylonian empire. Daniel did not name the empire represented by the chest and arms of silver, but merely said it was another empire (a different empire from Babylon) that would come after Nebuchadnezzar's empire, and was inferior to Babylon. He also did not identify the third or fourth empires, although he did mention the fourth empire would be as strong as iron, and it would crush and break all the others. It is worth noting he did not specifically enumerate a fifth

empire, but he did describe a fifth body section with feet and toes of iron and clay.

The best place to start is to identify each empire represented by a section of the multi-metallic statue. According to Daniel, the head represents Nebuchadnezzar and his empire, Babylon, so we can move on to the second empire. Daniel identifies the next empire when he narrates the overthrow of the Babylonian Empire by the Medes and Persians (chapter five of Daniel). So the Medio-Persian Empire, or more specifically, the rulers of the Medio-Persian Empire, must be the chest and arms of silver. The Medio-Persian Empire eventually fell to Alexander the Great (the belly and thighs of bronze). His empire, after dividing into smaller sections, eventually fell to the invading armies of the Roman Empire (the legs of iron). The Roman Empire did not fall to one new empire; it split in half, with the West gradually being beaten down by repeated attacks,[3] and the East lasting until 500 years ago.

---

[3] 476 AD is the accepted date for the fall of the Western Roman Empire, as that is the date in which the last "Western Roman Caesar" ended his rule. The secular political structure did not completely collapse for another two centuries, however,

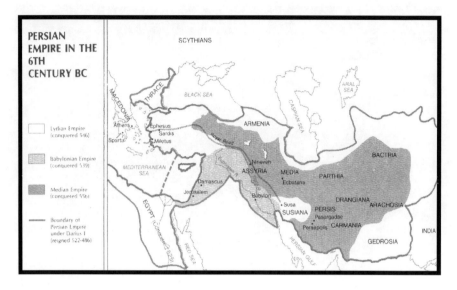

Medes and Persians

The Medio-Persian Empire consisted of two peoples, the Medes and the Persians, who ruled the empire and conquered new lands together. Initially, the Medes were dominant, and the Persians were forced to pay tribute to Media. Cyrus the Great, a Persian, believed the Medes and Persians to be two arms of the same race, so he swept into Media,

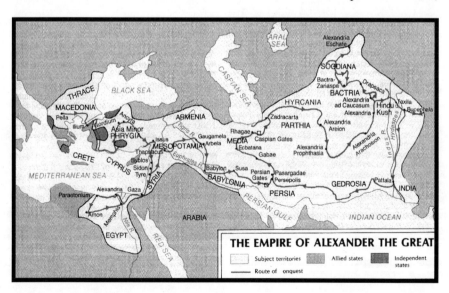

after which the church stepped in and set up a "theocratic" government, and what would become the Catholic Church of today began to emerge.

captured their capitol, and united them under one empire. After "conquering" the Medes, Cyrus did not subjugate them, he elevated them to equal position within the empire as the Persian people. The Medes were happy to join as equals, and their leaders became royalty and military leaders under Cyrus. The two kingdoms pooled their resources to conquer the rest of what became the Medio-Persian Empire (because the Persians were dominant from the beginning of the primary expansion period until it fell to the Greeks, some history books simply call it the Persian Empire). Thus, there are two arms of silver.

Greece and Rome

The Lord did not divulge much about the empire represented by the belly and thighs of bronze (Grecian Empire) at this point, but he did reveal a considerable amount about the legs of iron (Roman Empire). First, God uses TWO LEGS of iron to represent the empire. Since the two arms of silver represented two kingdoms who were working together, we might suspect the two legs symbolize the same thing, namely, two different kingdoms working together as one unit. But there was only one kingdom within the Roman Empire, and Rome was not even in league with any other kingdom, as the Medes and Persians

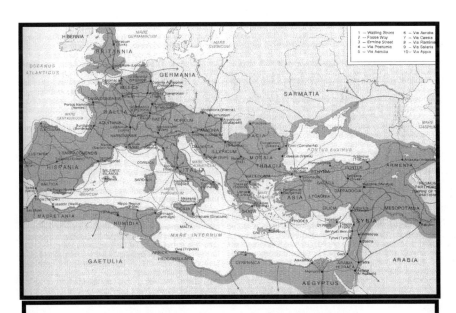

THE ROMAN EMPIRE
At its greatest extent (about 117 AD)

were. While it is true that the Romans were alone in establishing their empire, the empire was not one united kingdom; on several levels and at various times, it consisted of two very different kingdoms.

The separation between these "two kingdoms within the empire" is subtler than with the Medio-Persian Empire. There were at least three splits within the Roman Empire symbolized by the legs: an east and west cultural split, a built-in political schizophrenia, and ultimately, the empire actually split into two distinct and separate kingdoms.

The cultural split included such things as language and political differences in the daily life of the people. In the west everyone could speak their native tongue and Latin while in the east it was their native tongue and Greek. Western people preferred democratic style governments, and turned more to the senate as the focus of power while in the east, the governments had always been monarchies, and the people looked more to Caesar as the supreme authority (most Easterners didn't even understand the purpose or meaning of a senate). As one traveled further from Rome, Caesar was more powerful and the Senate less.

Politically, Rome could never really decide who was in authority: was it Caesar or the Senate? They even divided the Empire into Imperial and Senatorial provinces. In the Imperial provinces Caesar ruled supreme, and in the Senatorial provinces the Senate made the rules. The Caesars considered to have been the best by most historians were the ones who rarely tested their authority, and involved themselves in empire politics the least. Rome literally had two separate rulers: Caesar and the Senate.

Eventually, the empire actually split into two separate kingdoms: The Western Roman Empire, and the Eastern Roman Empire. For about a hundred years there were two separate capitols (Rome and Constantinople), two rulers, and two senates. In 476 AD the Western Roman Empire collapsed,[4] but the Eastern (which had solved the political schizophrenia by making Caesar supreme, reducing the senate to little more than a rubber stamp assembly, or aristocratic club) lasted another thousand years.

It is worth noting that no other vision in Daniel or Revelation depicts the split within the Roman Empire. Why? Because except for a brief period of about a hundred years (out of fifteen hundred years of

---

[4] After the "official" end of the Western Empire in 476 AD, when Romulus Augustus, the last leader to call himself "Caesar," or "emperor," was forced to abdicate, Rome suffered through many tribulations, and exchanged hands a few times, but it did continue to exist. For a brief period (541-565), it was even owned again by the Eastern Roman Empire.

existence), there were not two distinct, physical "Roman" empires, and the other subtle differences between the eastern and western portions of the empire are not distinct enough to warrant illustration in succeeding visions. In other words, although the split is important enough to be mentioned, it will not play a major role in the end times. From a prophetic standpoint, the key element is not that there was a division within the Roman Empire, but that the capitol shifted to the East (into modern Turkey) for the last two thirds of its existence.

Bigger is Better

Another point from history worth noting is each succeeding empire ultimately occupied more land than the empire they destroyed. The Babylonian empire stretched from the northern tip of the Persian Gulf, west to Palestine (including what is now Jordan and Syria), north from the tip of the Persian Gulf through the western edge of Iran, and back to the northeast encompassing modern Iraq, and the eastern half of Turkey. The Medio-Persian empire stretched from nearly the eastern borders of Greece all the way to the Indus river in Pakistan (Including what is now Turkey, Syria, Jordan, Palestine, Iraq, Iran, Afghanistan, Armenia, Azerbaijan, Georgia, Turkmenistan, Uzbekistan, and Tajikistan), and south into northern Egypt. The Grecian Empire included the entire Medio-Persian empire (except what is now the southern republics of the Soviet union) plus Greece, and more of Egypt. The Roman Empire eventually covered the WHOLE coast of the Mediterranean (including the whole north African coast), and most of Southern Europe (including Great Britain), although it only penetrated into the former Grecian Empire as far as the western edge of Iraq. So each succeeding empire grew larger than the one just before it.

Governments

Daniel also says the empire that arises after Babylon will be inferior to Babylon. The decreasing value of each metal, from the very rare and precious gold to the very common and not so precious iron, represents the decrease in power of each successive king in each empire.

Nebuchadnezzar was the absolute, unchallenged ruler of Babylon. If the law said he couldn't do something, he would change the law. He was the ultimate authority. Daniel says, "those the king wanted to put to death, he put to death: and those he wanted to spare, he spared." (Daniel 5:19).

The Medio-Persian rulers were just as subject to the law as any other citizen of the Persian empire (as illustrated in Daniel's forced visit to a lion's den by a very reluctant Medio-Persian king, and in the story of

Esther, where a Persian king unknowingly orders the death of his beloved wife and her people, and unable to repeal the law, must find a way around it). Unlike Nebuchadnezzar, they were not a law unto themselves. If the law said they couldn't do something, there was almost nothing they could do about it.

The Grecian Empire was primarily a military monarchy, which is only as strong as the loyalty of the military (as illustrated every day in South America and Africa). In a military monarchy, while a ruler is feared by the masses, has the loyalty of his troops, and keeps the standard of living tolerable, he has pretty good job security. One problem, though, is the real power ultimately rests with the generals. When Alexander died, his empire did not go to his son or wife, but to his four generals, who divided it among themselves.

Finally, there was the unstable, schizophrenic government of the Romans. The Romans were never able to determine who was really in charge, and this built-in weakness, which almost guaranteed a constant struggle for power at the very foundation of the Roman governmental system, eventually brought about the downfall of the Western Roman Empire. Like rotting at the core of a wooden beam, the Roman Empire was doomed to eventually fall in on itself. The Eastern Roman Empire solved the struggle by establishing Caesar as the outright ruler (and lasted another thousand years).

Military Might

Daniel points out that just as iron (especially as steel) is the strongest of these metals, so the Roman Empire will be the strongest of these empires. In line with Daniel's interpretation the strength of the metal must represent the military might of each empire. Since each successive metal is stronger, each successive empire must be militarily superior to those before it. From history we find that each was also more enduring than the ones before it (each conquering empire reigned longer before falling to invading armies than the one before it).

The Babylonians used their chariots, particularly with archers inside, as an ancient version of the armored "blitzkrieg" tactics later employed by the Nazis. They were fast, powerful, and in the ancient world, nearly unstoppable in the open field. They struck with frightening speed, and crushing force. If there was one thing the other kingdoms feared, it was Nebuchadnezzar's chariot charges.

The Medes and Persians were unrelenting, ruthless fighters, and occasionally employed "creative" tactics. One such example is the way they conquered the city of Babylon, which the Babylonians thought to be so impregnable they were throwing a big party in the midst of the

Medio-Persian siege. They had plenty of food storage, and they had access to the Euphrates River, which ran directly through the city, to supply water. You couldn't scale the walls, which slanted outward and were roughly fifteen feet wide. You couldn't come up the river in boats because the Babylonians had barred the river entrances. With a handful of men, the Babylonians could hold off a whole army of invaders indefinitely. Or so they thought.

The invading Medes and Persians realized very quickly the futility of trying to conquer the city through conventional methods, so they became unconventional. Withdrawing from the city to a point far enough away that the Babylonians could not observe their actions, they began to dig a huge canal. Beyond the limits of curious Babylonian eyes, the canal eventually stretched from a point far upstream of Babylon, all the way around the city to a point far downstream. During the evening famous for the appearance of God's hand, which wrote a message of judgment on the wall (Daniel 5:1-30), the invading army knocked out the two barriers between the canal and the river, re-routing the river into the canal. The old riverbed provided an open road right into the city, and Babylon fell that night without any fighting.

Grecian military tactics and strategy far surpassed those of the Persian's; so much so that some military historians consider Alexander the Great to be the greatest military genius that ever lived. In almost every battle he ever fought (most of which were against the Medes and Persians) his enemies outnumbered him, sometimes as much as ten to one, and yet he always won. With exceptional strategic ability, excellent battlefield communication, and well trained, loyal troops that could shift their formations with lightning speed, it was not until long after his death that the Grecian armies lost their first battles to an invading army: The Romans.

Modern generals still employ strategies developed by the Roman military leaders. One technique that worked so effectively against the Greeks (and one of many borrowed from Alexander) was the phalanx; a tight, rectangular, nearly unstoppable formation of roughly a hundred men with shields, swords, and spears. With precision formations, advanced tactics, extreme discipline, and superior weapons, the Romans developed the most powerful military of any empire to that age and possibly to the age of modern weapons.

The Rock

The Rock produced without hands" represents Jesus and, as Daniel points out, the mountain that fills the earth is His kingdom on earth. A Rock "cut out without hands" shows the supernatural nature of the destruction of the last empire and establishment of this new kingdom. In other words, man must use his hands to build something while God moves through the power of His Word and His Spirit.

Some have suggested that this has already happened, and that the Kingdom of God represented by this Rock is spiritual in nature. There is one major problem with this view: the Rock DESTROYS the old empire, and the spiritual Kingdom of God established by Jesus during the Roman Empire DID NOT destroy the Roman Empire (which lasted hundreds of years after the establishment of the church, and was completely destroyed only about 550 years ago). There is nothing within this dream to suggest that God's Kingdom will be anything other than a literal one. When Jesus returns, it will be to establish a permanent, physical world government on the Earth. The Rock in this dream is our Lord and Savior, who is symbolized by a rock or stone throughout the Bible, as illustrated by the following scriptures:

> *"You are built upon the foundation of the apostles and prophets with Jesus Christ Himself the chief* **CORNERSTONE**.*"* (Ephesians 4:20)

> *"'See. I lay in Zion a chosen and precious* **CORNERSTONE**, *and the one who trusts in him will never be put to shame. Now to you who believe, this* **STONE** *is precious. But to those who do not believe, 'the* **STONE** *the builders rejected has become the* **CAPSTONE'** *and 'a* **STONE** *that causes men to stumble and a* **ROCK** *that makes them fall'."* (I Peter 2:6-8)

> *"Therefore, thus says the Lord God, 'Behold, I am laying in Zion for a foundation a* **STONE**, *a tried* **STONE**, *a precious* **CORNERSTONE**, *a sure foundation: he that believes shall not make haste'."* (Isaiah 28:16)

> *"And who falls on this* **STONE** *will be broken to pieces, but he on whom it falls will be crushed."* (Matthew 21:44)

A Problem

The Rock struck the feet of the statue, demolishing the statue and establishing the Kingdom of God. This seems to suggest God would overthrow the Roman Empire, but we know the Roman Empire has vacated its Earthly residence, and the literal kingdom of God has not yet arrived. Each empire conquered the one before it, yet the Roman Empire died before God's Kingdom arrived and destroyed it. Jesus did not overthrow the Roman Empire on His first visit. We seem to have a sudden break, right at the ankles so to speak, in the flow of this prophecy.

There are four possible explanations. First, there is no specific significance to WHERE the Rock struck the statue (the place it struck the statue is an accident of the symbolism). Second, the feet and toes DO represent the same thing as the legs, and somehow God SPIRITUALLY overthrew the Roman Empire. Third, the legs do not represent the Roman Empire, and this section has a different meaning. Fourth, the feet and toes represent a fifth empire after the Roman Empire that God does not specifically enumerate.

In answer to the first possibility, it would be dangerous to assume that anything in a prophecy is unimportant. The third possibility does not fit the flow of the information provided by Daniel (if Babylon is the head of gold, the next three empires MUST be Medio-Persia, Greece, and Rome, since each of these conquered the preceding empire). The real options are that God spiritually overthrew the Roman Empire, or there is a fifth empire after Rome in this vision.

A huge and possibly fatal objection to the "spiritual overthrow" theory is that the rock thoroughly destroys all traces of the previous empires, leaving nothing of them behind. There is no way to make claim that the introduction of Christianity with the death and resurrection of Jesus did anything even remotely close to a complete obliteration of all previous empires. This claim cannot even be made spiritually, as evidenced by the number of people throughout the Middle East, and the world, who remain committed to a religion other than Christianity. If we are to remain even marginally consistent in interpreting the symbols within this dream, there is simply no way we can squeeze the "spiritual kingdom of God" into a narration about physical empires conquering each other.

That leaves us with the fourth explanation, an interpretation that demands five empires. This choice hinges upon one key point: can we find any evidence to support the idea that the feet and toes do NOT represent the exact same empire as the legs.

Daniel enumerates, one by one, the first four empires in this prophecy. He lists Babylon as the first, then says there will be another empire, and then a third, and after that, a fourth. He never actually enumerates a fifth empire. In addition, there seems a kind of connection between this supposed fifth empire and the Roman Empire. God represents the Roman Empire with iron, and there is iron in the representation of the fifth empire. Foremost, the words "another kingdom" or "a fifth kingdom" do not appear to separate the fifth empire from the Roman empire, while the word "finally" does appear as an introduction to the fourth empire (implying the fourth empire is the last). So, in order for this to make sense, we must first establish that we have valid grounds for assuming there really are five empires in this vision, not just four.

As it turns out, this is not nearly as difficult as it might seem. First, as we previously mentioned, there are five body parts and five different materials denoted on the statue. Further, Jesus crushes the empire represented by the feet and toes, yet He did NOT overthrow the Roman Empire. We know the feet and toes are an empire since Daniel says the feet and toes are a "divided kingdom" (Daniel 2:41) and the kingdom will be "partly strong and partly brittle." (Daniel 2:42).

There is no other explanation that fits all the facts; the feet and toes must be a separate empire from Rome to exist at the time of the Lord's return. If this is true, then why did God not enumerate the empire, or at least mention that another empire would arise after the fourth? And why do both the fourth and fifth empires contain the same metal, while none of the empires before the fourth share a common substance? Is there some kind of "connection" between the fourth and fifth empires that could span nearly five hundred years?

Yes, there IS a special connection between the Old Roman Empire and the empire represented by the feet and toes. First, there is a pattern the first four empires follow that the fifth does not. The first empire, Babylon, is militarily overthrown by Medio-Persia, which is destroyed by Grecia, which is conquered by Rome. But before a new empire could arise to dislodge the fourth, the age of Grace intervened. The progression ended. Why did the progression not continue with the fifth empire vanquishing the fourth? Because during the fourth empire, a unique event in the history of mankind took place: Jesus.

Something you will notice if you spend much time studying prophecy, there are almost no prophecies dealing with the era from about seventy years after Jesus' resurrection to our century. There is practically nothing in the whole Bible that refers specifically to that period. It is a time-out in the whole progression of Biblical events; a blank in the "prophetical history" of the earth. A final "period of Grace" during which God can build His church before the end arrives. The second reason the fifth empire resembles the fourth so closely is when the world took a prophetical time-out, Rome held the Middle East in its power; when the time-out ends, we will need a new empire to "represent" Rome so the "conquering cycle" can continue. So this fifth empire will represent the Roman Empire, but it will not really BE the old Roman Empire. There are some very definite and important differences between the old Roman Empire and this new "symbolic" Roman Empire. In the dream, the old Roman Empire consisted of two legs of pure iron while the new symbolic Roman Empire emerges as ten toes of iron mixed with clay. Daniel intentionally directs our attention to the ten toes; the toes are vital to understanding this fifth empire (Notice that he did not mention the ten fingers in his description of the Medio-Persian Empire, because ten fingers make no sense as symbols of the Medes and Persians).

What do they represent? Well, if the TWO arms and the TWO legs both represent TWO different "kingdoms" within one empire, then the ten toes must denote ten kingdoms within one empire. Daniel strongly supports this interpretation with the words (about the ten toes), "in the time of those KINGS, the God of heaven will set up a kingdom that will never be destroyed." (Daniel 2:44). *Kings*, not *king*. Plural. Ten kings ruling simultaneously.

This group of kingdoms will band together to form one huge "pseudo-empire," but they will not have much unity between them, as Daniel said, "the people will be a mixture and will not remain united, any more than iron mixes with clay." (Daniel 2:43). In what way will the people be a mixture? Daniel does not say, but it could be a combination of different nationalities, ethnic groups, political coalitions, languages, and moral codes. One thing is clear though; they will ultimately exist as a squabbling confederacy of independent little kingdoms. Since there will be ten rulers, not one, and this is not really an empire in the strictest sense, we will refer to this future, symbolic "Roman Empire" as the Mediterranean Confederacy of Ten Kingdoms,[5] and the historic Roman Empire will be christened the Old Roman Empire.

Although the Mediterranean Confederacy of Ten Kingdoms represents the Old Roman Empire, there is no evidence that modern day Rome will get involved in any way. Other than being within the same area, and a spiritual issue we will address later, THERE IS NO DIRECT CONNECTION BETWEEN THE OLD ROMAN EMPIRE AND THE

---

[5] This confederacy, symbolic of the Old Roman Empire, will be within the same area as that empire, which extended around the whole coast of the Mediterranean Ocean (thus the designation "Mediterranean"). There are almost thirty countries within the area once controlled by Rome. Of these, ten will band together to form this new confederacy, some of the thirty may be absorbed into the ten in wars prior to the formation of the Confederacy, while others will remain independent.

MEDITERRANEAN CONFEDERACY OF TEN KINGDOMS.[6] By this we mean that, contrary to some of the more popular theories:

1) The Mediterranean Confederacy of Ten Kingdoms is NOT a literal revival of the Old Roman Empire.
2) A Roman politician will NOT control it.
3) Satan will NOT raise an old Roman Caesar from the dead to rule it.
4) There will not be any connection between this confederacy and the Roman Catholic Church.

Granted, we have yet to produce a single bit of proof for any of these claims, but hang in there. All of these statements will be proven as we progress through the visions in Daniel and Revelation.

The Toes consist of iron mixed with clay. The iron suggests this confederacy will have the same kind of crushing military power in the future the Old Roman Empire had in the past. Still, Daniel saw clay mixed with this iron, and as he said, this clay shows weakness and division. Daniel says,

> "*Just as you saw that the feet and toes were partly of baked clay and partly of iron, so this will be a divided kingdom: yet it will have some of the strength of iron in it, even as you saw iron mixed with the clay. As the toes were partly iron and partly clay. So this kingdom will be partly strong and partly brittle.*" (Daniel 2:41-42)

Strong and Brittle

Notice Daniel did not say there are five iron toes and five clay toes, so that five of the kingdoms within the Mediterranean Confederacy of Ten Kingdoms are as strong as iron and five are as brittle as clay. We find the iron and clay, the strength and weakness, intermixed within all ten kingdoms. Granted, no two kingdoms are exactly alike, so some will be stronger than others, but this scripture does not mean exactly five will be strong and five will be weak. All the toes are partly of iron and partly of clay. If all ten countries have clay (weakness and division), what kind of weakness does the clay suggest?

---

[6] There is one extremely significant connection that we address briefly at the end of this chapter, but deal with it in greater detail later as it is crucial to understanding the symbols in Revelation: both empires will be ruled by the exact same satanic spirit.

The mixture of iron and clay is a continuation of the pattern that each new empire is militarily mightier, but governmentally weaker than those before it. Adding further to this internal governmental weakness will be the inherent instability of a confederacy held together by political and diplomatic maneuvering, treaties, promises, and possibly intermarrying. This is not one united confederate "empire," but ten separate, independent kingdoms, and these kingdoms, as Daniel said, " . . . *will be a mixture and will not remain united*." (Daniel 2:43). The military might, coupled with the glaring governmental weakness and diplomatic instability is so important Daniel went to extra lengths to explain the paradox of an empire both mighty and weak, both strong and brittle.

Each material in the statue is a metal, except clay. God could have used a rusted or brittle metal to allow the statue to consist only of metal, so it must be important that the material used to symbolize weakness be something other than a different metal. But why clay?

At various places throughout scripture, clay symbolizes mankind, or more exactly, it represents people, and usually in contrast with God (as a clay potter, for instance). Daniel lends further evidence to this theory by mentioning that the inclusion of the clay means "*THE PEOPLE will be a mixture*." (Daniel 2:43)

The citizens of the first four empires were not important. In the fifth empire, though, the people will play an important role none of the people in the first four empires played. The indication that the people play such an important role in the Mediterranean Confederacy of Ten Kingdoms merely emphasizes the weakness of the governments of the kingdoms. The people will have more of a say in these little kingdoms than their forerunners in Babylon, Persia, Greece, or Rome. In addition, because God uses clay to represent people from His perspective, this is the first real indication we get that religion (the interactions between people and their god) plays an important role in this empire. All this will become much clearer when we get to Mystery Babylon in Revelation.

In what way will the "people be a mixture"? There are several. First, they will be a mixture of many races, classes, educational levels, and political ideologies. The constant struggle between these various view points within these kingdoms will keep the workings and efficiency of the governments off balance, somewhat unstable and, as Daniel said, "brittle." Remember, unlike the empires of the past, in this new age of "human rights" and "democratic governments," the people will play an important role in the governance of these kingdoms.

There is another element to the people being a mixture that we should mention, and that is the mixture of light and darkness. Within these kingdoms will be believers and unbelievers, and the two cannot mix. This mixture of light within these kingdoms of darkness will cause Satan continuous spiritual problems, and will act as a type of "thorn in the side" of his plans. It is but one of the many reasons that the final kingdom, that of the Antichrist himself, will not be powerful enough to conquer the entire planet. We shall address the extent of his empire in much more detail later.

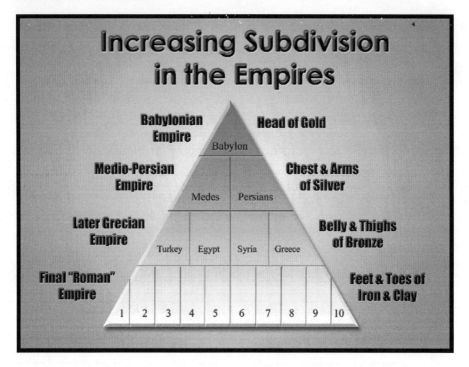

More is Less, Until it is One

Another element within the progression that further illustrates the increasing governmental fragility of each successive empire is subdivision. Babylon is one united kingdom. Medio-Persia has two cooperating kingdoms, the Grecian Empire split into four divisions after Alexander's death, and the final version of the Roman Empire is a confederacy of ten kingdoms. This pattern shows the sinful decay governmentally (and in all other areas of human interaction), that the establishment of God's kingdom will halt.

There is one interesting point about the statue that will become even more glaring when we get to Daniel's two visions of beasts: the statue is a whole when the Rock strikes the feet. As each empire replaced the empire before it, the statue remained. Nebuchadnezzar did not see just a head of gold, which crumbled away to be replaced by a chest and arms of silver, which in turn, crumbled away to be replaced by the belly and thighs of brass, and so on. The statue seems to suggest that as each new empire gained dominance, all the empires before it remained. This is important. This is not just a fluke, nor is it an accident within the symbolism. Later we will be looking at these empires from the perspective of wild beasts, and again, we find when God judges the final beast, it is specifically noted that the previous beasts are still in existence. As with the beasts, it is important that each body section on the statue remains.

When the stone hits the feet of the statue, which is symbolic of the Mediterranean Confederacy of Ten Kingdoms (the only one of the five empires in existence then), not just the feet crumble, but the whole statue crumbles to dust and God blows the dust away. What possible connection could there be between the destruction of the Mediterranean Confederacy of Ten Kingdoms by the Lord, and the crumbling of the portions of the statue that represent previous empires? We know the head of Gold, Nebuchadnezzar and Babylon, ceased to exist about twenty-five hundred years ago, and we know the Greeks, Medes, Persians, and old Romans also perished long ago. It seems all we should have left are the feet, but we don't; we have the whole statue, still "in existence" at the time of the return of Christ.

If portions of the statue represent empires, or more specifically, the kings of those empires, then might the whole statue represent something also? Is there something else happening in this vision that Daniel does not really address? What else might there be?

There are five empires illustrated in this vision (Daniel does not specifically enumerate the fifth, although he does call it a kingdom), and a sixth which is almost hidden within the symbolism. Each body section represents a consecutive empire, on down to the feet, which represent the fifth. So where is this sixth empire?

The whole statue is the sixth empire. The whole multi-metallic image, including Babylon, Medio-Persia, Grecia, Rome, and the Mediterranean Confederacy of Ten Kingdoms, represents the sixth, and final, gentile empire that shall rule the earth before Christ returns. [7]

---

[7] Corresponding to the EIGHTH Empire in Revelation. Revelation lists more empires because it includes two empires that existed prior to Babylon. Daniel and Nebuchadnezzar only desired to know what was going to happen in the future, so their visions started with Babylon. Knowledge of those two empires is necessary to understand the full end times narrative, so they are included in Revelation.

While the fifth empire, the Mediterranean Confederacy of Ten Kingdoms, will still be in existence when the stone hits the feet, it is NOT the last gentile empire that will arise before Christ's return (this will become clearer in later chapters). There is another empire that will arise AFTER this confederacy that will TAKE CONTROL of the fifth empire. The sixth will not destroy the fifth, it will dominate and control it while still allowing it to exist. In this manner the sixth will not follow the pattern of totally destroying the preceding empire. So when the stone strikes the feet, it destroys the fifth Empire, represented by the feet, and also the sixth empire, which is the whole statue.

	Body Part	Metal	Empire	Government Style (metal value)	Military Might (metal strength)
1st	Head	Gold	Babylon	Complete Dictatorship	Speed with Power
2nd	Chest & Arms	Silver	Medio-Persian	Monarchy & Law Equal	Numbers & Tactics
3rd	Belly & Thighs	Bronze	Grecian	Military Dictatorship	Superior Speed & Strategy
4th	Legs	Iron	Roman	Republic	Superior Weapons, Training & Discipline
5th	Feet & Toes	Iron & Clay	Future Symbolic "Roman"	Confederacy	??????
6th	Whole Statue	All Elements	Last Empire	Theocratic Dictatorship	All of the Above

The whole statue represents a sixth empire? Isn't this something of a stretch? WHY would God use the whole statue to represent the sixth empire, instead of adding another part to the statue? He could have put sandals on the feet and said something like, "just as the sandals cover the feet, so the sixth empire will not destroy the fifth, but will cover it, and control it."

God didn't do that because sandals would not have been an appropriate representation of the last empire. The "whole statue" reference is not an accident of the symbolism. Another part added to the statue (such as sandals) would have missed some very important facts about the last empire, particularly as they relate to spiritual power and authority.

The first important fact illuminated by the use of the whole statue to represent the sixth empire is that it will include elements of the territory, power, and authority from all five previous empires combined. These elements might encompass such aspects as the absolute authority of Nebuchadnezzar, the huge massing armies of the Persians, the tactical and strategic genius of Alexander, and the military might of Rome.[8] Aside from any of these physical characteristics though, the sixth will be the complete summation of the spiritual power, authority, and evil contained within all five of the previous empires.

This takes us to the second important fact illustrated by using the whole statue to represent the last empire.[9] The second reason is a little more involved, and to make it more understandable, we must first set the stage.

Hell hath No Fury like Satan Scorned

Satan's whole ambition, throughout the Old Testament, has been to wipe out the nation of Israel. His first reason was to prevent the first deliverer, Moses, from showing up to rescue Israel and provide the beginnings of the Bible. That failed. Then he tried to wipe them out to prevent the ultimate deliverer, the Messiah, the Son of God, Jesus from arriving on the scene and providing salvation for the world.

That also failed.

---

[8] The sixth empire will consist of Gold, Silver, Bronze, Iron and Clay. As with the fifth empire, the clay in the sixth empire indicates the importance of the people within this empire, that there will be division within the empire, and that a religion or religions will play an important part in the Empire.

[9] There is a third lesson to be gleaned from the existence of all the elements and all the body parts on the image in the end times: "How close are we to the return of Christ?" A full explanation of how this question relates to and is answered by the vision of the mulitmetallic image would be a serious distraction from the primary purpose of this chapter (which is to introduce us to the foundational principles and the key players that will help us to understand end times prophesies in the Bible). Therefore, we have chosen to postpone that discussion until later. For now, follow along as we build our arguments from chapter to chapter. After that, you will find this issue addressed in detail in the First Special Supplement at the end of this book (page 207).

So now Satan wants a "son" of his own, the Antichrist (remember, Satan is the ultimate counterfeiter) to finish the annihilation of Israel. His motivation this time? Revenge.

They are God's chosen people and God thwarted him twice through them, so Satan, being full of every petty little sin any person has, except in greater degree, is trying to "strike back at God" by destroying the people God loves. If he can't beat God, he will at least hurt God. Satan's master plan then, through the progression of these empires, is the ultimate, final destruction of Israel, and one final shot at the throne in Heaven.

The REAL Power Behind the Throne

An interesting tidbit about the spiritual realm revealed in the book of Daniel, and in various other places in scripture, is a satanic or holy angel rules each Earthly kingdom or empire. The archangel Michael, for example, is in charge of protecting and guiding Israel. A satanic angel, identified simply as the Prince of Grecia, ruled the Grecian Empire, another called the Prince of Persia ruled the Medio-Persian Empire, and a satanic angel probably called the Prince of Rome had the real authority in the Roman Empire (Daniel 10:12-13; Daniel 10:21-11:1; Ezekiel 28:1-19).

The destruction of each empire in Nebuchadnezzar's dream, from a spiritual perspective, means the demon in control of that empire has had his authority or dominion taken away. Unlike the Earthly form of the empire, when a satanic angel loses his authority to another demon, the new demon in control does not destroy the old one. Each "prince" is still around, scheming to regain his authority, and the most important satanic ruler, as we shall discuss later in detail, is the Prince of Grecia. So each body part, as well as the whole statue, actually represents THREE things: the satanic prince in control of the empire, the king of the empire, and the empire itself. Any given symbol may place more emphasis on one or two of these meanings[10], but all three are always present. This is true of every "kingdom" symbol we shall encounter in Daniel and Revelation.

---

[10] For example, in Daniel's vision of four beasts, the actions of the lion emphasize one king in the empire (Nebuchadnezzar). The whole multi-metallic statue and the leopard beast in Revelation place more emphasis on the satanic prince of the empire, and then on one king in the empire (the Antichrist). The bear in Daniel's vision of four beasts illustrates the actions of the first three of eleven kings in the empire. The legs of iron illustrate the first third of "Roman" history, focusing on the empire itself (rather than a specific king or satanic prince). The fourth beast in Daniel's vision of four beasts illustrates the fullest extent of "Roman" history, and alternately places the emphasis on the empire, one or more of the kings, and the satanic prince, and so on.

At its deepest level, each body section on the statue represents the power or authority of a satanic angel. The whole statue itself represents the satanic authority or power of Satan himself, or you might say, it represents the full satanic authority and power of all the previous empires, that is, the satanic princes, combined. During the final years of our age, Satan is bringing everything to a climax, so his power is the greatest for his final thrust at Israel and the throne of God. Another way of describing it is the statue represents the "body of Satan" or the "body of the Antichrist" (in a mimicry of how the church is the "body of Christ")[11]

This means that for the first time in history the satanic princes behind these different empires (who have been "jockeying" with each other for power up to now) will actually "unite" their efforts. They will finally combine their spiritual power under the authority of a final empire's prince toward the ultimate goal of accomplishing Satan's plan.

Upon the completion of the "Body of the Antichrist," when the ten toes come into existence as an empire, Satan will have gathered enough authority to usher in his ultimate empire, which is the sixth empire: represented by the whole statue. In this sixth empire the Antichrist will be, in effect, the "son" of Satan almost like Christ is the Son of God. There is one major difference: Christ is also God, where the Antichrist will not be Satan, but merely a man to whom Satan gives all his power and authority. Most of the detail concerning the Antichrist and this sixth empire will be covered in Revelation, but it is important to see that from the very first vision relating to these empires, there arises the aroma of the Antichrist and his empire.

Finally, Daniel tells us the supernatural rock struck the feet of the statue, destroyed the whole statue, and then became a mountain that filled the whole earth. This shows, as Daniel later explains, that in the times of these ten kings, the God of heaven will set up His Kingdom that will last forever. The important thing to note here is God uses a *mountain* to represent His kingdom. This does NOT mean a mountain always represents a Godly kingdom, but in various places in scripture, God uses mountains and hills as a type of generic symbol for kingdoms, and in Revelation, they will again represent kingdoms.

A considerable amount of other crucial actions, events and interactions do not appear in this dream, because God gave this dream

---

[11] This is what God means when he says our real battle is not with flesh and blood, but with "principalities and powers." Our battles are not with the men and women throughout the world who happen to be in positions of earthly authority, but rather, with the real authorities in our world, the spiritual "powers behind the throne."

to Nebuchadnezzar, a pagan king who wanted to know what was going to take place in the future. What is Nebuchadnezzar's perspective? Nebuchadnezzar believed human empires are great things (particularly if you happen to be the king). In effect, Nebuchadnezzar saw empires as precious metals; a perspective that leaves a considerable amount about the nature of empires beyond his comprehension. A few pages later in Daniel, God describes these same empires as wild ravaging beasts, but this time, the vision was to Daniel, not to Nebuchadnezzar, and this time, we find out how God views the empires of men.

Summary

Nebuchadnezzar's dream of a multi-metallic image is a vision of the empires that shall arise after Babylon from a man's perspective. The golden head represents Babylon, the chest and arms of silver represent the empires of the Medes and Persians, the belly and thighs of brass represent the Grecian Empire, the legs of iron represent the Roman Empire, and the feet and toes of iron and clay represent a confederacy of ten kingdoms that shall exist in the end times. The whole statue represents a sixth empire, ruled by the Antichrist, which shall gain control of the confederacy while allowing it to continue to exist. The Rock represents Jesus who will physically conquer the fifth and sixth empires, including all the spiritual power of the other four, at his return and establish an eternal, Godly Kingdom.

QUESTIONS FROM CHAPTER ONE

1) Who had the dream of the Multi-Metallic Statue, and why is the identity of the dreamer important?

2) What three things does the golden head represent?

3) What three things do the chest and arms of silver represent?

4) What three things do the belly and thighs of bronze represent?

5) What three things do the legs of iron represent?

6) What three things do the feet and toes of iron and clay represent, and how do we know they are separate from the legs of iron?

7) What three things does the whole statue represent, and how do we know it represents anything at all?

8) What does the rock represent?

9) What does the mountain represent?

10) What is the significance of two arms?

11) What are the three primary reasons for two legs? Why is this the only prophetic depiction of this empire anywhere in the Bible that depicts the "dual" aspect of this empire?

12) What does the clay represent?

13) Why are all the body parts included in the representation of the final empire?

14) How many empires are represented in this dream?

15) What is the significance of the decreasing value of each metal on the statue?

16) What is the significance of the increasing strength of each metal on the statue?

17) What is the significance of increasing subdivision in the empires?

18) Which empires are literally in existence when the rock strikes?

19) How much of this dream has been fulfilled?

THE FOUR BEASTS
Introduction to the Antichrist

Daniel had this next dream after the death of Nebuchadnezzar, during the reigns of Nabonidus and Belshazzar, who ruled Babylon jointly. In later years Nabonidus would occasionally leave Babylon in the hands of Belshazzar while away in Tema (in modern Saudi Arabia), where he spent a considerable amount of his time. During the first year of Belshazzar's reign, Daniel had a dream about four beasts:

THE DREAM

"In my vision at night I looked, and there before me were the four winds of heaven churning up a great sea. Four great beasts, each different from the others, came up out of the sea. The first was like a lion, and it had the wings of an eagle. I watched until its wings were torn off and it was lifted from the ground so that it stood on two feet like a man, and the heart of a man was given to it.

"And there before me was a second beast, which looked like a bear. It was raised up on one of its sides, and it had three ribs in its mouth between its teeth. It was told, 'Get up and eat your fill of flesh!' "After that, I looked, and there before me was another beast, one that looked like a leopard. And on its back it had four wings like those of a bird. This beast had four heads, and it was given authority to rule.

"After that, in my vision at night I looked, and there before me was a fourth beast--terrifying and frightening and very powerful. It had large iron teeth: it crushed and devoured its victims and trampled underfoot whatever was left. It was different from all the former beasts, and it had ten horns.

"While I was thinking about the horns, there before me was another horn, a little one, which came up among them: and three of the first horns were uprooted before it. This horn had eyes like the eyes of a man and a mouth that spoke boastfully.

"As I looked, thrones were set in place, and the Ancient of Days took his seat. His clothing was as white as snow: the hair of his head was white like wool. His throne was flaming with fire, and its wheels were all ablaze. A river of fire was flowing out from before him. Thousands upon thousands attended him: ten thousand times ten thousand stood before him.

"The court was seated and the books were opened. "Then I continued to watch because of the boastful words the horn was speaking. I kept looking until the beast was slain and its body destroyed and thrown into the blazing fire. (The other beasts had been stripped of their authority, but were allowed to live for a period of time.)

"In my vision at night I looked, and there before me was one like a son of man, coming with the clouds of heaven. He approached the Ancient of Days and was led into his presence. He was given authority, glory and sovereign power; all peoples, nations and men of every language worshipped him. His dominion is an everlasting dominion that will not pass away, and his kingdom is one that will never be destroyed.

"I, Daniel, was troubled in spirit, and the visions that passed through my mind disturbed me. I approached one of those standing there and asked him the true meaning of all this.

"So he told me and gave me the interpretation of these things: 'The four great beasts are four kingdoms that will rise from the earth. But the saints of the Most High will receive the kingdom and will possess it forever—yes, for ever and ever.'

"Then I wanted to know the true meaning of the fourth beast, which was different from all the others and most terrifying, with its iron teeth and bronze claws the beast that crushed and devoured its victims and trampled underfoot whatever was left. I also wanted to know about the ten horns on its head and about the other horn that came up, before which three of them fell, the horn that looked more

imposing than the others and that had eyes and a mouth that spoke boastfully. As I watched, this horn was waging war against the saints and defeating them, until the Ancient of Days came and pronounced judgment in favor of the saints of the most High, and the time came when they possessed the kingdom.

"He gave me this explanation: 'The fourth beast is a fourth kingdom that will appear on earth. It will be different from all the other kingdoms and will devour the whole earth, trampling it down and crushing it. The ten horns are ten kings who will come from this kingdom. After them another king will arise, different from the earlier ones: he will subdue three kings. He will speak against the Most High and oppress His saints and try to change the set times and the laws. The saints will be handed over to him for a time, times and half a time.

"'But the court will sit, and his power will be taken away and completely destroyed forever. Then the sovereignty, power and greatness of the kingdoms under the whole heaven will be handed over to the saints, the people of the Most High. His kingdom will be an everlasting kingdom, and all rulers will worship and obey him.'

"This is the end of the matter. I, Daniel, was deeply troubled by my thoughts, and my face turned pale, but I kept the matter to myself." (Daniel 7:2-28)

RECAP

Daniel saw four strange beasts rise out of a churning sea (the churning came from the four winds of heaven). The first looked like a lion with wings, the second beast was a mighty bear with three ribs in his mouth, the third was a type of leopard with four wings and four heads, and the fourth was unlike any beast Daniel had ever seen before. The fourth beast had teeth of iron, claws of bronze, and ten horns on his head. One standing nearby told him the four beasts represent four kingdoms that will rule over mankind. The beasts rise out of a churning, wind tossed sea. In the Bible, seas almost universally represent mankind as a whole. The churning of the sea shows the violence, strife, and turmoil in the interactions of mankind that sets the stage for each of these empires to arise. The churning is being caused by the four winds of heaven ("winds of heaven" can be translated "spirits of the air"), indicating that the human violence and strife is being caused or "driven" by a spiritual catalyst. That is, it is the push of the demonic spirits who rule over these empires to gain and hold authority that is the real cause of the human warfare that brings rise to these empires. The most important item to note here is these kingdoms arise from mankind, from the violent interactions between different nations; they do not come down from heaven, and God does not bring them to power. These are not godly kingdoms, they are wild, ravaging, human birthed empires. The international upheavals of man do not create a godly kingdom: God establishes it by the power of His Spirit.

THE FIRST BEAST

The first beast is a lion with two wings, and corresponds perfectly with the head of gold: Babylon. Everything about the lion fits Babylon, or more specifically, it fits what we know about one king of Babylon, Nebuchadnezzar (remember, Daniel did not say the head of gold was Nebuchadnezzar's country, he said it was Nebuchadnezzar). Nebuchadnezzar was the fierce warrior king of Babylon who, with his feared chariots which allowed him to strike with lightning speed, burst through the enemy lines, sending them into instant disarray and confusion, and then crushing them before they had a chance to regroup. Nebuchadnezzar was the general who conquered almost all the land ruled by the Babylonian Empire. After Nebuchadnezzar quit expanding the empire, Babylon didn't annex any more land.

Just as many consider the lion the king of beasts, Daniel called Nebuchadnezzar the king of kings. A lion is a fierce, kingly beast of prey, and this lion, with the added speed of two wings, was to be more feared than most. Daniel said he watched until the lion had his wings torn off, which fits Nebuchadnezzar's "retirement" from conquering new land shortly after he became the sole regent in Babylon (when his father died). Nebuchadnezzar ceased being a bloodthirsty general of conquest, but he was still the feared, at times ferocious, emperor of

Babylon. Though he is no longer swooping in on new countries to overthrow them, he is still very much a beast of prey who is fully capable of doing so.

Daniel next says God lifted the lion up on two feet like a man, and gave him the heart of a man. What happened to Nebuchadnezzar? He walked out onto his court one day and began to boast about how great he was. He had already received a warning, in a dream about a tree, to humble himself before the Lord (Daniel 4:4-27). He didn't listen, and after his boast on the terrace, God struck him with insanity. After seven years of believing he was an animal, his mind cleared, he looked up into heaven, praised God, and began saying of God the very things said of Nebuchadnezzar previously. We have every indication Nebuchadnezzar experienced a genuine heart conversion and became a believer at that point. The hardened, wild, ravaging beast of prey had changed into a man with a soft heart of compassion (Daniel 4:28-37).

THE SECOND BEAST

The next beast was a bear. This bear's legs were longer on one side than the other, giving the appearance that one side of his body was higher than the other. It also had three ribs in its mouth, and was told to go and devour much flesh. If the first beast was Babylon, it is only logical to presume the second beast is the next kingdom after Babylon, Medio-Persia. The bear is a good symbol of Medio-Persia as a bear is a very powerful and ferocious beast (as the Medio-Persian armies were). However, a bear is not fast enough to depend on speed when fighting or hunting (unlike Babylon, the Medes and Persians did not usually strike quickly; they tended to lay siege to cities or overpower an enemy through the sheer strength of superior numbers). One side of the bear is higher than the other, which shows that one kingdom within the Medio-Persian empire exercised dominance over the other (through most of the empire's existence, the Persians were dominant). The three ribs in the bear's mouth represent the three primary kingdoms overthrown by the Medes and Persians: Babylon to the west, Egypt to the south, and Lydia to the north. The command to the bear to eat its fill of flesh is a reference to the huge expansion of this empire over the previous one. The Medes and Persians established an empire more than three times the size of the Babylonian Empire.

THE THIRD BEAST

The third beast looked like a leopard, except it had four wings and four heads. A leopard is not as powerful as a lion or a bear, but it is no less feared in the jungle, because a leopard is sneaky. A leopard rarely attacks its prey head-on, preferring to drop on prey much larger than itself from the branch of a tree, and the prey, with a leopard on its back, is essentially defenseless. This fits Alexander the Great, the Grecian conqueror who established the Grecian Empire, because he did not have a large army to work with, and usually found himself engaged in battle with armies much larger than his. Alexander never faced those armies head-on, preferring maneuvers that would give the advantage to his smaller, quicker armies. He won all his battles against Persia, usually opposite armies that outnumbered him by as much as ten to one.

Just as the two wings on the lion suggested the power and speed of Nebuchadnezzar's armies, so the four wings of a bird represent similar characteristics. The leopard has four wings, not two, suggesting extreme speed, which fits Alexander; military historians believe Alexander had the quickest moving army in the ancient world. To this day, Alexander probably moved more men over more ground in less time than any other general in history. Still, these four wings are of a bird, not an eagle. The overwhelming power of Nebuchadnezzar's army (because of his powerful chariots) is not evident in Alexander's attacks, since the Grecian army did not have the strength or size to overwhelm an opponent. The power of the Grecian army lay completely in its speed and crafty tactics.

The leopard also had four heads and was given authority to rule. This is the first example of a pattern for interpretation of prophecies in Daniel and Revelation that we will use time and again throughout this book. The beast itself represents the kingdom as a whole, in all forms: past, present, future. The head of the beast depicts the future, or last form of the kingdom, and the actions on the head illustrate the changes the kingdom goes through as it evolves from its early version to later forms of the same kingdom.

So the leopard represents the whole Grecian empire from the time Alexander was just beginning to establish it, to its final overthrow by Rome, while the four heads symbolize the last forms of the empire. This fits the history of the Grecian empire very nicely, since after the death of Alexander, his generals could not agree on a new ruler, and eventually split his kingdom into four divisions, with each general crowning himself the emperor of one kingdom. Those partitions are the Turkish division (covering approximately the area of modern Turkey), the Grecian division (covering everything west of Turkey), the Syrian or Persian division (covering modern Syria, Iraq, Iran, and portions of Afghanistan and Pakistan), and the Egyptian division (covering most of modern Egypt). Palestine became a disputed area between the Syrian and Egyptian divisions.

After dividing Alexander's kingdom into four parts, the four generals began to make war on each other trying to consolidate back into one empire again, with the winning general to be the new emperor. The primary push behind this drive to consolidate is the demonic spirit who rules the Grecian Empire, the prince of Grecia. This demonic prince wants his whole kingdom back, so when they divided the empire, he commenced trying to unite it again. The point that these generals fought with each other is not merely to expand your understanding of ancient history; this fighting is an essential element that will allow us, in chapter four, to piece together the puzzle concerning which country is responsible for the Antichrist.

THE FOURTH BEAST

The fourth beast was unlike any of the previous beasts. There is no animal on the earth that could adequately symbolize the aspects about this fourth kingdom God wanted to bring out, so He uses a fictional beast. It is terrifying and powerful, and after the lion and the bear, only an imaginary beast would effectively show the awesome strength of this unmatched fourth kingdom, which, as you might suspect, is the Roman Empire. Most notably, to suggest its unsurpassed might, it doesn't just have big teeth and claws, it has iron teeth and bronze claws.

THE GRECO-ROMAN CONNECTION

The choice of iron and bronze here is to symbolize two things: first, the power of this fourth kingdom is as far above the previous kingdoms as iron and bronze are above regular teeth and claws. Second, part of the overwhelming military power attributed to the Roman legion came from borrowed Grecian tactics. So their might was a combination of superior Roman training and weaponry, coupled with revised and updated Grecian ideas (the iron and bronze being intentional references back to the multi-metallic statue from Nebuchadnezzar's dream, representing the Grecian and Roman Empires).

This is also the first hint suggesting some kind of link, association, or connection between the Roman and the Grecian empires. This connection is not at all clear, out front, or straightforward, and we do not have enough information to explore it yet. The vision of the two beasts, which we shall cover in the next chapter, and Revelation chapter seventeen, in chapters six and seven of this book, contain a considerable amount that will be helpful in our pursuit of more information about the "Greco-Roman connection," or to be more precise, "prophetic link between Rome and Greece." Discussion on this topic shall wait until then.

Notice there is nothing about this beast suggesting speed. The Romans had revised Alexander's tactics to fit their preferred type of fighting, which was to attack the opponent head-on and overwhelm them with superior fighting and numbers. The Romans never really used swift surprise attacks, primarily because it was never necessary.

This beast crushed and devoured its victims, trampling underfoot whatever remained. This shows the thoroughness of the Roman conquest. They didn't just overthrow a country, they crushed it, intent on destroying the very deepest roots of rebellion. A good example of this is the destruction of Jerusalem in 70 AD. When the Jews rebelled, the Romans did not just defeat the rebels, they crucified, killed, or enslaved every person who had contributed to the rebellion. They also destroyed the temple, since standard Roman procedures dictated eliminating any symbol around which a rebellious country could rally. Josephus says one million, one hundred thousand Jews died in the siege and destruction of Jerusalem, while the Romans enslaved another ninety-five thousand.[12] With the destruction of the temple in 70 AD, the Jewish state ceased to exist.

Fifty-two years later the Jews again rose in defiance of the Romans. Bar Kochba led the rebels and his early success even caused some to proclaim him the Messiah. For three long years the Jews fought for independence and freedom, but in the end, the Romans again crushed the rebels. Once again, in line with Roman military doctrine, the Romans destroyed any symbol around which the natives could rally; the city of Jerusalem was completely leveled. On top of the ruins of Jerusalem the Romans built the city Aelia Capitolina. Jews were not even allowed to enter the city.

---

[12] Josephus, p. 587.

With both the temple and the holy city of Jerusalem gone, the Jews had nothing around which to rally, and were dispersed throughout the world. That they were even able to maintain an ethnic identity during the ensuing two thousand years is a testimony to God's faithfulness. Roman military strength had crushed their will to fight, but not their will to live.

THE TEN HORNS

In our analysis of the multi-metallic statue, we discovered two "Roman" empires: the Old Roman Empire and the future Mediterranean Confederacy of Ten Kingdoms (symbolized by ten toes of iron and clay). Just as Nebuchadnezzar's dream does, Daniel's dream ties the two "Roman" empires closely together. As with the leopard and the Grecian Empire, the whole beast represents the past and future forms of the Roman Empire, while the head, and the actions on the head denote the final events and forms of the Roman Empire. As we mentioned in the first chapter, the age of grace is a "time-out" in prophetic history, and if you remove the age of grace, the old Roman Empire runs directly into the Mediterranean Confederacy of Ten Kingdoms without a break.

On the head are ten horns, which correspond to the ten toes on the statue, and represent the Mediterranean Confederacy of Ten Kingdoms. Daniel tells us the ten horns are ten kings who will come from this kingdom. These are not ten consecutive kings during the Old Roman Empire, they are the ten concurrent kings of the Mediterranean Confederacy of Ten Kingdoms, each king having his kingdom within the confederacy, all ruling simultaneously. When the stone strikes the statue, it strikes all ten toes at the same time, indicating that all ten are in existence at the time of the Second Coming.

The idea the ten horns could be ten consecutive kings, either in the Old Roman Empire, or in the new version of the "Roman" empire, rests upon a very precarious foundation, since it violates the continuity of every vision in Daniel. On the statue, the two arms represent two SIMULTANEOUS kingdoms working together, and the two legs represent two SIMULTANEOUS "kingdoms" within the Roman Empire. In this vision, the four heads on the leopard represent four SIMULTANEOUS divisions from the Grecian Empire. In the next vision we shall see two horns on a ram (the SIMULTANEOUS kingdoms of the Medes and Persians), and four horns on a goat that again represent four SIMULTANEOUS divisions from the Grecian Empire. Within each division there arose several consecutive kings, yet God does not show the rise and fall of each individual king within a division (except that of the Antichrist) since it never changed that basic structure of four SIMULTANEOUS kingdoms within the old Grecian Empire.

Whenever a consecutive progression must be illustrated it is due to a major structural change within the kingdom, and God illustrates that change through the removal of the old horn so a new horn or horns might take its place. We can see this in the next vision by Daniel (of two beasts) in which one horn breaks off to be replaced by four horns (to illustrate the drastic change that took place in the Grecian Empire when Alexander died: his generals divided the kingdom among themselves). God illustrates consecutive progression through ACTION on the head of the beast.

We do not see the ten horns on the head of the fourth beast, and the ten toes on the feet of the statue rising to power one after another. Since we see the ten horns on the head and the ten toes on the feet simultaneously they can only depict ten simultaneous divisions in the kingdom of the fourth beast. To ensure a proper interpretation of the symbols of this, and every other vision, we must remain consistent when examining each element. If we should change the uniformity of our approach when interpreting a specific vision, it will be clear from context (usually in the interpretation given by an angel).[13]

THE LITTLE HORN

Daniel says, "While I was thinking about the horns, there before me was another horn, a little one, which came up among them . . ." This "little horn" was not one of the original ten, as shown by the word "another." Later, while seeking an interpretation, Daniel says, "I also wanted to know about the ten horns on its head and about the other horn that came up . . ." Once again, Daniel distinguished between the first ten horns and the little horn. There are NOT ten horns including the little one, making a total of ten, but ten horns and another one, making a total of eleven. Not ten kings: eleven kings. This "little horn" is not an original member of the ten kings, he is another king who rises "among" them after the original ten have already established the Mediterranean Confederacy of Ten Kingdoms.

Does the little horn represent another kingdom from outside the confederacy, a new eleventh kingdom within the confederacy, or a "new" king within one of the original ten kingdoms. There is not

---

[13] In Revelation, for example, the angel clearly explains that of the seven heads, five have fallen, one still is, and one is yet to come, showing that a progression is intended in the symbols on the beast. If the angel does not indicate a progression, do not assume one.

enough information here to make a definitive determination, but as we shall prove later, the little horn is actually a new "religious" leader who rises to prominence within one of the original ten kingdoms. Instead of overthrowing the old king, however, he will appear to rule simultaneously with that country's original king (similar to Iran during most of the 1980's when the Ayatollah was the real leader, but the "official" leader was the president). The primary support for our conclusion will be presented when we get to Daniel's vision of two beasts.

For now, note that he is definitely a type of "king," and unlike the other horns, he is depicted "doing" things. Note that he rises "in the midst of" the other kings (not from somewhere else, "outside" of the group, but from within their midst, indicating he comes from within the existing Confederacy), and that he is a "little" horn (indicating a type of king that is different in some way, or seemingly "smaller," than the others). The "little" aspect is obviously not an indication of his power, as he uproots three of the other horns, but it does indicate that he is somehow different.

The little horn that rises among the ten has the eyes of a man. There must be a special significance to the illustration of eyes on this little horn, since ALL the horns represent kings, and ALL kings have eyes (not just the one symbolized by the little horn). The implication is that this king can see things that no other king could see. The scriptural meaning of eyes and sight usually signifies either the ability to see into the spiritual realm (i.e., Elisha and his servant, II Kings 6:8-23), or spiritual insight and understanding into what is seen. The king shown by the little horn probably will be able to see directly into the spiritual realm, or will have a unique understanding of the true meaning and spiritual significance of the events going on around him. Possibly he will understand that the real battles are being fought in the spiritual realm (thus, his direct blasphemy of God).

The little horn also is mentioned speaking boastfully. As far as most "non-royal" people are concerned, ALL kings speak boastfully. Each king in the confederacy probably will speak boastfully, but Daniel only mentions the little horn's boasting. God does not mention, in this dream or Nebuchadnezzar's, the boasting of any other king, including Nebuchadnezzar, yet we know Nebuchadnezzar boasted, because God cursed him with insanity as punishment for his boasts.

So what makes the boasting of this little horn so different from Nebuchadnezzar and the other kings that it merits direct illustration within the symbols of this dream? Why is his boasting unique? Unlike the boasts of Nebuchadnezzar, this king doesn't just boast about how great he thinks he is, his boasts include speaking directly against the Most High (God the Father) and declaring himself to be a god in the same way the Most High is God. His boasts are a form of very personal attack, not just against Israel, but against the Ancient of Days Himself. Considering his blasphemy and boasting, his war against the saints, his desire to change the set times (which Daniel 2:21 says only God can do), and to change the laws, there is only one person he could be: the Antichrist.

Daniel does not call him the Antichrist, because Daniel doesn't know anything about the Christ he is against, or what He will do. Nor does he know that the "Son of Man" in his dreams is the Messiah who will bring salvation, not just to Israel, but to all who seek the True God in every land.

FROM CONFEDERACY TO EMPIRE

Daniel explains that after the Antichrist comes to power, he promptly subdues three of the ten kings. He arrives on the scene after the Mediterranean Confederacy of Ten Kingdoms is already in existence, attacks and uproots three of the ten kings, and as will become clearer in Revelation, the other kings within the confederacy then capitulate without a fight. At that point, he is in complete control of the confederacy; he has conquered it, and is the unchallenged, ultimate ruler of the whole empire. He has not destroyed it, but has taken control of each country, and now rules supreme, changing the confederacy, or "pseudo-empire" into a real empire, with one unchallenged ruler.

Since the scripture states the little horn "uproots" three of the horns, yet it also says ALL TEN kings are alive when the God of Heaven establishes His kingdom, we can only assume that after "uprooting" three horns, the Antichrist actually "re-plants" three new horns (so there will be ten again). In concrete terms, the Antichrist probably kills the original kings in those countries, and then installs new kings, loyal to him, to govern them. In any event, it is clear from Nebuchadnezzar's dream and from Revelation that all ten kings, not seven, are ruling with the Antichrist when Jesus returns at the very end. Since we also know any uprooting or replanting of horns means a major structural change has taken place within the empire, it must mean more than just the deaths of three kings. The only logical explanation is the Antichrist initially absorbs the three kingdoms into his own. We know all ten kings are present when Christ returns (the statue has TEN toes when the rock strikes it, not seven), the Antichrist must reestablish the kingdoms he previously uprooted. His motivation for this could be anything from governmental practicality (it is much easier for a ruler to control an empire if he keeps the kingdom divided into sections and sets up "governors" to handle the daily details of running each province), to appeasement of the other seven kings in his empire. Either way, it is clear he recreates the three missing kings.

A valid question at this point would be: if the Antichrist really does "replant" the three horns he previously uprooted, why is this action not illustrated in the dream? And if the action is not illustrated, how can we be sure he actually does it? Well, since we know from this chapter he uproots three horns rising to power, and in Nebuchadnezzar's dream as well as chapter seventeen of Revelation, all ten horns are present AFTER he has consolidated his power, he MUST have replanted the three he pulled out. Obviously, since God does not illustrate the act of replanting the three horns in prophecy, He does not feel the action of reestablishing those kingdoms is important for a clear understanding of end times events (i.e. how it is done and the Antichrist's motivations for doing it are not important). It is apparently enough to know it will happen.

Since the Antichrist only subdues three of the ten kings in the Mediterranean Confederacy of Ten Kingdoms, you may be wondering if his conquest of exactly three kingdoms is significant. Why not four? Why not all ten? Which three does he attack and overthrow? Why do the other unconquered kingdoms just give up without a fight? Does it matter?

Yes, it does matter. It would be a very dangerous practice to assume that anything in any of these dreams or visions is unimportant. There is a specific reason that the Antichrist subdues exactly three of the ten kingdoms, and the Lord reveals the identities of those three . . . in the next vision of Daniel. Since our explanation will make more sense when coupled with the new information in chapter eight of the book of Daniel, we will wait until the next chapter to answer these questions. Be patient, it will be worth the wait.

He does not destroy the Mediterranean Confederacy of Ten Kingdoms, but after defeating three of the ten in battle he takes control of the empire. Each kingdom still has its own king (including the uprooted three, although it is most likely three new kings), while the Antichrist is the emperor of the whole empire. Here we see, a little clearer than in the dream of the statue, the establishment of the strange kingdom after the Mediterranean Confederacy of Ten Kingdoms; a kingdom that will not destroy the confederacy, but absorb it without drastically changing it.

The symbolism in this dream has caused considerable problems for students of scripture. The fourth beast, unlike the others, represents not one, but three empires (one in the past and two in the future): the Old Roman Empire, the Mediterranean Confederacy of Ten Kingdoms, and the Antichrist's Kingdom (the Antichrist can be viewed as the last king of the Mediterranean Confederacy; from that perspective, this is only one future empire). If that statement just confused you, be patient. This will become clearer as we go along.

Why does God use the same beast to illustrate all three empires? We have already explained the close connection between the Old Roman Empire and the Mediterranean Confederacy of Ten Kingdoms, which don't fight each other, and actually represent the same kingdom. But the Antichrist's kingdom attacks the kingdoms of the confederacy, so why not a different beast?

There are two very important reasons: The Antichrist's kingdom starts from a kingdom within the Mediterranean Confederacy of Ten Kingdoms, and he maintains the Mediterranean Confederacy of Ten Kingdoms exactly as it existed before he attacked (with the obvious exception that there is now one person in charge of the whole empire, not a council of ten). In no other instance did the attacking empire leave the former kings in power, since they would be viewed as too much of a danger to the new empire (they might try to raise a rebellion against the new rulers and reestablish their former empire again). Additionally, no new empire started from a country or region already under the control of a previous empire. The Antichrist will not have a separate empire before he attacks the confederacy, he will be part of the confederacy, and will rise from within. From this perspective he does not conquer the Mediterranean Confederacy of Ten Kingdoms, he unites it.

Additionally, the satanic spirit in control of the Antichrist's kingdom does not attack the Mediterranean Confederacy of Ten Kingdoms to overthrow it, but to reestablish a previous empire that ceased to exist over two thousand years ago. After subduing three of the ten kings in the Mediterranean Confederacy of Ten Kingdoms, he will have re-established this former empire. That the rest of the confederacy voluntarily submits to him is mere icing on the global cake.

So you see, the Antichrist does not destroy the fourth beast, he merely gains control of the empire it represents while reestablishing a former beast. Note that God, while being fully aware that the spirit behind the Antichrist is attempting to revive a former empire, considers the Antichrist another horn on the same beast, not a new beast (remember, God deals with people, not "governmental structures," and the ten kings are still alive and ruling).

In this dream, God presents the Antichrist as another king in the same Empire as the original ten. In the next vision we will find the Antichrist depicted as a king who arises in a completely different empire, while in Nebuchadnezzar's dream and later, in Revelation, He

	Empire	Symbol Detail	Symbol Meaning
Winged Lion	Babylonian	Eagle Wings	Crushing Chariot charges
		Heart of Man	Nebuchanezzar's Conversion
Lopsided Bear	Medio-Persian	Legs different Lengths	Two races working together
		Three ribs in mouth	Three major conquests
Four Headed & Winged Leopard	Grecian	Four heads	Four later divisons
		Four bird wings	Extreme military speed
Strange Beast	Three Empires: 1) Old Roman 2) Future Confederacy 3) Future Antichrist	Beast itself	Old Roman Empire
		Ten horns	Mediterranian Confederacy
		Little horn	Antichrist
		Iron teeth, bronze claws	"Greco-Roman Connection"

depicts the Antichrist's kingdom separately from all previous kingdoms but somehow containing elements of them all. All three views are correct.

Why? Because his empire can be viewed each way: since he radically changes the empire by uniting it under one rule, is controlled by a different spirit from the one who controlled the Mediterranean Confederacy of Ten Kingdoms, and contains elements of ALL the former empires, he can be viewed as a completely different empire.

Since (as we shall explore in the next chapter) he is attempting to establish an old empire that perished long ago, he could be seen as the leader of a revived former empire which had ceased to exist.

Since he rises from within the current empire and leaves the former kings in power, his empire could be viewed as a structural change within the current empire (as in the case of the Grecian' Empire when it split into four divisions). As God suggests by using all three approaches, neither view is right or wrong, it just depends on which points you are stressing at the time.

There is not enough information in this dream to figure out the exact identity of the kingdom the Antichrist is trying to "revive" (there is not even enough information in this dream to decide whether the "revival theory" is a valid assumption about the Antichrist's motivations), so we shall wait until the next vision to prove this point.

There is one point, related to the Antichrist's desire to "revive" an old empire we must deal with here. There is a long-standing belief that the Antichrist will rule the entire planet. The Antichrist, or more accurately, the spirit behind the Antichrist, is NOT trying to conquer or rule the world; the spirit in control of the Antichrist's kingdom wants only two things: its former kingdom back, and only THEN, when it has regained its former position of physical and spiritual might, it wants ISRAEL in a kingdom-sized coffin. As we shall see, the Antichrist simply doesn't have enough time to conquer the whole world. And finally, scripture actually lists the boundaries of the Antichrist's empire, and names some of the kingdoms that escape his clutches.

The scripture does not actually say that the Antichrist will rule the whole planet. Even the places that refer to the "whole earth" or "all men" in Revelation do not actually mean the whole planet any more than the ancient empire of Greece ruled the whole planet ("*Next, a third kingdom, one of bronze, will rule over THE WHOLE EARTH.*" Daniel 2:39). It simply means "the whole known earth at the time of this writing."

Saying the "whole earth" when only a part of the literal earth is meant is a figure of speech called a "synecdoche." That is, when the "whole" represents a part, and is well recognized by many Bible scholars as occurring here.[14] We do this in common speech all the time ("the law has arrived" when one policeman shows up; "Everyone was at the game" when obviously, no stadium is large enough to hold "everyone"; etc.). You could say it is a means of using slight

---

[14] Companion Bible, Page 12.

exaggeration to emphasize the effect, ramification, influence, or importance of the event or action.

As we shall see later, the Antichrist's reign lasts about seven years. During the first three and a half years of his reign, he is conquering the Mediterranean Confederacy of Ten Kingdoms (which is inside the borders of the Old Roman Empire), "reinterpreting" the religion, and establishing himself as a god. At the mid-way point, he attacks and conquers Israel. For the last three and a half years he is fighting and conquering some countries to the north and east of his empire. After winning his fight with the countries in the north and east, he returns to Israel, where he meets his end at Armageddon. He lacks the time to conquer the whole earth. He never goes further north than the southern edge of Russia, he stops just short of India, he never rules south of Ethiopia, and he never invades anyone across a major ocean.[15]

Of course, a mere glance at current events should be enough to convince most people that he will EFFECT the whole world (imagine ONE MAN controlling most of the world's oil), but that will be more economically than politically or militarily.

THE SAINTS

As Daniel continued to watch, the little horn made war against the saints, and was winning, until the Ancient of Days, God the Father, held court and gave a judgment favorable of the saints. God then destroyed the little horn, and God gave the kingdom to the saints to rule forever. It is worth noting at this point that when Daniel refers to the saints, he is NOT referring to the church, as he lacked any knowledge of the church, or its role in the last days. God reserved that portion for John, who was a part of the church, to reveal. Every time Daniel refers to the saints, he means the Jews, God's natural chosen people. Though the Antichrist will be persecuting Christians also, it is primarily against the Jews that the Antichrist wages war.

Daniel tells us that the saints will be handed over to (i.e., will be persecuted by) the Antichrist for "a time, times, and half a time." (Daniel 7:25). This phrase is just an idiom for "a year, two years, and half a year," which is three and a half years.[16] So for three and a half

---

[15] Among the many nations listed escaping the control of the Antichrist are the modern countries of Jordan (Edom, Moab, and Dedan), Yemen (Sheba), Spain (Tarshish), and all the countries south of Ethiopia ("Ethiopia at his feet"). Daniel 11:41; Ezekiel 38:13; Daniel 11:43. Additionally, in Revelation 16:13-16, three evil spirits are sent out to deceive the nations of the world into joining the Antichrist at Armageddon, which would be unnecessary if the Antichrist already controlled all the kingdoms of the Earth.

[16] This will be during the LAST three and a half years of his seven-year reign.

years the Antichrist will have the power to persecute and kill the Jews. There are, of course, other things happening during this three and a half years, most of which God covers in the book of Revelation.

Daniel kept watching the little horn until God destroyed the beast from which the little horn had sprouted, and cast it into the blazing fire. Daniel makes a note here that the other beasts were present, and that they had not been destroyed, but were stripped of their authority and allowed to live for a short time. This scene is the great judgment of nations that Christ mentioned in Matthew chapter 25 in his parable of the sheep and goats at the judgment. Just as Christ will be separating individuals, so He also will be separating nations. The sheep nations will be blessed, while the goat nations will be punished.

In this dream God reveals He will not just strip the Antichrist's kingdom, the fourth beast in its final form, of its authority, but will utterly destroy it. After the judgment, the kingdom of the Antichrist will no longer exist and the people will be ruled by other nations. The other kingdoms will still exist as nations, but without their former rulers. So after the return of Christ, the country of Greece (or Macedonia) and some countries identified with Babylon (probably a newly independent Iraq), and Medio-Persia (most likely Iran) will exist as nations; that is, they will have governmental structures in existence, but their military power and as well as their prestige and authority on an international scale will have been stripped away. In fact, many of these nations will still exist in the millennial reign of Christ. In the nation that birthed the Antichrist and his empire, however, the entire ruling structure from the Antichrist on down will be destroyed and cast into the lake of fire, and a new one will NOT be sent in to replace it. The people of that country will be ruled by some other nation.

THE KINGDOM OF GOD

After the destruction of the fourth beast, in its final form as the Antichrist's kingdom, all the power, greatness, and authority of the kingdoms on Earth will be handed over to the saints, the people of the Most High. The Kingdom of God, which shall last forever, shall be under the authority of the people of God. We shall rule the whole Earth in Christ's kingdom. Granted, Daniel is speaking about the Old Testament Saints here (remember, the focus of all of this is the literal nation of Israel), but the New Testament reveals that these saints are not simply those who are Jewish by birth, but rather, those who believe in and follow the Messiah (Messianic Jews), and that those Jewish believers are joined by their Messiah following brothers, the Gentile Christians.[17]

SUMMARY

This dream, given directly to Daniel, is God's perspective on the same kingdoms first seen in Nebuchadnezzar's dream. Instead of precious metals, God describes them as wild, ravenous, destructive beasts.

The first beast, a lion with eagle's wings, represents Nebuchadnezzar and Babylon. The second beast, a lopsided bear, represents the kingdoms of the Medes and Persians. The third beast, a four-headed, four-winged leopard, represents the Grecian Empire. The last beast represents the Old Roman Empire, the Mediterranean Confederacy of Ten Kingdoms, and the Antichrist's kingdom. The ten horns stand for the Mediterranean Confederacy of Ten Kingdoms portion of the beast, while the little horn signifies the Antichrist's rise to power.

The little horn (the Antichrist) speaks boastfully, attempting several things only God can do, and makes war against the saints of God. The saints are under the power of the little horn for three and a half years, when the Ancient of Days (the Father in Heaven) passes judgment against the little horn. The Son of Man (Christ) then destroys the Antichrist and his kingdom, and establishes the Kingdom of God on Earth, which shall be ruled by the saints forever.

KEEP IN MIND

In the next chapter, Daniel narrows his focus to two of the five kingdoms we have been examining up to now, with the ultimate goal of revealing some important information about the sixth, the Antichrist's empire. The points from this chapter you might want to keep in mind are that God uses a little horn to represent the Antichrist, and that the Antichrist subdues exactly three of the ten kings in the Mediterranean Confederacy of Ten Kingdoms.

---

[17] "Messiah" and "Christ" are the same title. Messiah is derived from the Hebrew word "Meshiach," while Christ is derived from the Greek word "Christos." Both mean the same thing ("anointed one"), and reference the same individual. In Hebrew He is *Yeshua Ha Meshiach*; in Greek, *Iesous ho Christos*; in English, Jesus Christ.

QUESTIONS FROM CHAPTER TWO

1) What kingdom does the lion represent?
2) What kingdom does the bear represent?
3) What kingdom does the leopard represent?
4) What do the four heads on the leopard represent?
5) What three kingdoms does the fourth beast represent?
6) What do the ten horns represent?
7) What does the little horn represent?
8) Who are the "saints?"
9) How long does the little horn have power over the saints?
10) Why did the Lord show Nebuchadnezzar these kingdoms as precious metals, while in Daniel's dream He used wild beasts?
11) Why does the last beast represent THREE different empires?
12) Why is the little horn the only one depicted with eyes, and speaking boastful words?
13) Are the ten horns consecutive or simultaneous, and how do we know?

THE RAM AND THE GOAT
Narrow the field to four

People have speculated for centuries about the identity of the kingdom where the Antichrist shall originate. Among the candidates are the United States, Russia, Italy, The Vatican, Germany, China, Great Britain, France, and the European Common Market. Most of these countries were added to the list because the scholars involved failed to follow one or more of the four rules for interpreting scripture outlined in the introduction to this book.

Along with grossly violating the fourth rule in the introduction, the primary mistake made by the scholars advocating the previous countries in their theories centered on not considering the second half of the book of Daniel. The specific identification of the kingdom from which the Antichrist will arise is actually quite simple, and Daniel covers it in great detail in chapters eight and eleven of his book.

The purpose of Daniel's vision of the ram and goat in chapter eight is to narrow our search for the Antichrist's kingdom from all the countries in the old world to FOUR, and to provide some vital information concerning those four kingdoms and the role they will play in the end times.

Two years after Daniel's vision of the four wild beasts in chapter seven of his book, he had another vision. In his vision he was standing beside a canal, observing the actions of a ram and goat:

THE VISION

"In my vision I was beside the Ulai Canal. I looked up, and there before me was a ram with two horns standing beside the canal, and the horns were long. One of the horns was longer than the other but grew up later. I watched the ram as he charged toward the west, the north, and the south. No animal could stand against him, and none could

rescue from his power. He did as he pleased and became Great.

"As I was thinking about this, suddenly a goat with a prominent horn between his eyes came from the west, crossing the whole earth without touching the ground. He came toward the two-horned ram I had seen standing beside the canal and charged at him in Great rage. I saw him attack the ram furiously, striking the ram and shattering his two horns. The ram was powerless to stand against him: the goat knocked him to the around and trampled on him, and none could rescue the ram from his power. The goat became very great, but at the height of his power his large horn was broken off, and in its place four prominent horns grew up toward the four winds of heaven.

"Out of one of them came another horn, which started small but Grew in power to the south and to the east and toward the Beautiful Land. It grew until it reached the heavens, and it threw some of the starry hosts down to the earth and trampled on them. It set itself up to be as great as the Prince of the host: it took away the daily sacrifice from him, and the place of his sanctuary was brought low. Because of rebellion, the host of the saints and the daily sacrifice were given over to it. It prospered in everything it did, and truth was thrown to the ground.

"Then I heard a holy one speaking and another holy one said to him. 'How long will it take for the vision to be fulfilled--the vision concerning the daily sacrifice, the rebellion that caused desolation, and the surrender of the sanctuary and of the host that will be trampled underfoot?'

"He said to me, 'It will take 2,300 evenings and mornings: then the sanctuary will be reconsecrated.'

"While I, Daniel, was watching the vision and trying to understand it, there before me stood one who looked like a man. And I heard a man's voice from the Ulai calling, 'Gabriel, tell this man the meaning of this vision.'

"As he came near the place where I was standing, I was terrified and fell prostrate. 'Son of man,' he said to me; 'understand that the vision concerns the time of the end.'

"While he was speaking to me, I was in a deep sleep, with my face to the ground. Then he touched me and raised me to my feet.

"He said, 'I am going to tell you what will happen later in the time of wrath, because the vision concerns the appointed time of the end. The two-horned ram that you saw represents the kings of Media and Persia. The shaggy goat is the king of Greece, and the large horn between his eyes is the first king. The four horns that replaced the one that was broken off represent four kingdoms that will emerge from his nation but will not have the same power.

"'In the latter part of their reign, when rebels have become completely wicked, a stern-faced king, a master of intrigue, will arise. He will become very strong, but not by his own power. He will cause astounding devastation and will succeed in whatever he does. He will destroy the mighty men and the holy people. He will cause deceit to prosper, and he will consider himself superior. When they feel secure, he will destroy many and take his stand against the Prince of Princes. Yet he will be destroyed, but not by human power.

"'The vision of the evenings and mornings that has been given you is true, but seal up the vision, for it concerns the distant future.'" (Daniel 8:2-26)

RECAP

First, Daniel notices a ram with two horns. One horn was longer than the other, but it came up later. The ram charged toward the west, the north, and the south. While Daniel was thinking about the ram, a shaggy goat with a large prominent horn between his eyes came from the west, crossing the whole earth without touching the ground. The goat struck the ram and shattered its two horns, then trampled the ram underfoot. At the height of the goat's power, the great horn between his eyes is broken off, and four prominent horns, facing four different directions, rose up in its place.

Out of one of these four large horns came a little horn, which grew in size and strength toward the south, the east and the Beautiful Land. This "little horn" grew until it reached the heavens, where it threw down some heavenly hosts and trampled them. It also defiled the sanctuary, threw truth to the ground, and prospered against the saints.

THE RAM

Since there are only two beasts in this vision, we can't just automatically assume the first beast represents the Babylonian Empire.

Fortunately, the Lord interprets most of the vision for us, identifying the Ram as the kings of the Medes and Persians.

Notice God again identifies a kingdom through the RULERS of that land. He punishes or rewards each kingdom, not because of what the citizens of the country want, believe, say, or do, but according to the actions of the king; "unto whom much is given, much is expected." Besides a certainty that the people probably couldn't agree on any one issue anyway, God views authority very seriously, often placing the lives and livelihoods of millions of people upon the heads of those in authority (note the whole nation of Israel frequently paid for the sins of their king).

Likewise, we see each kingdom in the dreams and visions in scripture identified through, represented by, and judged according to the actions of the king of that country.

The Ram had two long horns, but the younger horn had grown to be longer than the older horn. The horns represent the individual kings of the Medes and Persians. Initially, for a short time, the Median kings were dominant (before the actual establishment of the empire), but the Persians soon became the dominant force (under Cyrus the Great), and although the two races continued to work together, the Persians kings retained dominance throughout the remainder of the empire.

The Ram charged toward the west, the north, and the south, none could stand against him or rescue anyone from him, he did as he pleased, and became very great. The Medio-Persian empire started in what is now Iran, to the north they conquered Lydia (modern Turkey in the Northwest) and what is now the small, southern Muslim republics (northeast) that were once a part of the former Soviet Union, to the west, Babylon (modern Iraq, Syria, Jordan, and Palestine), and to the south, Egypt.

THE GOAT

While Daniel was still watching the ram, a goat with one large horn between his eyes came charging out of the west, crossing the whole Earth without touching the ground, and slammed into the ram. The goat, we are told, is the king of Greece, and the prominent horn is the first king of that empire, Alexander. Notice that the goat is called the "king of Greece," not the "kingdom of Greece," while the large horn on the goat is the "first king." Since it makes no sense to have the "first king" of Greece on the head of the "king of Greece," we see once again that the whole empire is illustrated through the KING of the empire. That is, the goat represents the Grecian Empire through all the kings that will rule in the empire, and the large horn is specifically the first king. Later, when there are four horns, they are the four simultaneous kings in the four divisions.

After conquering the Medio-Persian Empire, Alexander's kingdom became large and powerful. At the height of the goat's power, Daniel saw the great horn on the goat broken off (Alexander died of fever shortly after conquering Egypt), and in its place four large horns rose facing north, south, east, and west. After the death of Alexander, his four generals divided the empire into four sections (as covered in our previous chapter).

THE LITTLE HORN

Out of one horn came another horn, which started small but grew in power to the south and east and toward the beautiful land (Israel). As will become clear, this new horn can only represent the Antichrist. The south and east are most likely references to other countries to the south and east of the Grecian Empire, although at this point, we don't really have enough information to identify which countries those might be. It should be noted that the little horn does NOT grow in power to the North (the primary country North of the area of the Old Grecian Empire in modern times would be Russia) or to the West (Europe and America are the primary powers West of the Old Grecian Empire). This is our first major indication that the Antichrist does not even try to rule the entire planet, but limits his attentions to countries within the area of the Grecian Empire, and the countries to the east and south of that region.

The little horn grew until it reached up to heaven, where it threw some of the stars down to Earth and trampled on them. The little horn (which is not so little anymore) represents the Antichrist. What does it mean that he, a mere man, reached into heaven, and what do the stars represent?

Our first choice might be the angels in heaven, who, just before God cast him to Earth, chose to follow Satan. The problem with this interpretation rests on our point of reference, which is the Antichrist, NOT Satan. In addition, when Gabriel gives Daniel the interpretation, he does not mention angels, just mighty men and holy people (another term for saints).

From the angel's interpretation of the vision, and from the descriptive language used almost everywhere in the Old Testament (particularly Psalms) we can conclude that the host of the saints are the priests in the temple (remember, the saints refer to Israel, not the church). The prince of the host is the high priest, and the daily sacrifice refers to the sacrifices being offered in the temple on a daily basis (which at the time of this writing has not yet been rebuilt) as described in the law. The sanctuary is the Holy of Holies inside the temple. In line with this, the starry Host of Heaven probably refers to believers in Israel, who, as we learned earlier, will be under the power of the Antichrist for three and a half years.

Daniel tells us the host of the saints and the daily sacrifice are handed over to the Antichrist because of rebellion. Some saints will be deceived by the Antichrist, because truth has been thrown to the ground, and will rebel against the leaders of Israel. This apparently sets the stage for the Antichrist to move in and take control of the temple.

Daniel heard two "holy ones" speaking about how long the vision concerning the desolation of the sanctuary, the loss of the daily sacrifice, and the trampling of the host would last. As Daniel listened, a holy one told him it would take two thousand, three hundred evenings and mornings until the sanctuary would be restored into the hands of Israel again.[18] Twenty-three hundred evenings and mornings, or more accurately, eleven hundred and fifty evenings and eleven hundred and fifty mornings is three years, two months and ten days according to the Jewish calendar, or just a little under three and a half years.[19]

LITTLE HORN: ROMAN OR GRECIAN?

In Daniel's previous dream, about the four beasts that came out of the sea the little horn came up among the ten horns on the fourth beast, the Old Roman Empire. Here, in the dream of the ram and goat, the

---

[18] All of these times can only be referenced to the Jewish calendar, since our current calendar did not exist at the time of these prophecies. On the Jewish calendar, each month has exactly thirty days, and a year has three hundred and sixty days.

[19] Some translations read "2,300 days," which is an incorrect translation of the manuscript. The Hebrew word for "day" does not appear, while the actual words "morning" and "evening" are in the text. This is clearly 1,150 days.

little horn appears on the goat, which represents the same thing as the third beast in the previous dream: The Grecian Empire. So which is it? Does the little horn rise on the third beast or the fourth beast? Is it connected to the Old Roman Empire, or the Grecian Empire?

The answer is, of course, that there is a connection between the Antichrist's kingdom and both beasts. We have already described the type of association that will exist between the fourth beast (as the Mediterranean Confederacy of Ten Kingdoms) and the Antichrist in the previous chapter. The Antichrist will rule the Mediterranean Confederacy of Ten Kingdoms while allowing them to continue to exist as they did before the Antichrist took over. But what is the link between the Grecian Empire and the Antichrist? If you recall, we also mentioned that the iron and bronze on the fourth beast indicated a relationship of some sort between the Grecian and Roman Empires. The connection, as we shall see, IS the Antichrist.

The interpretation given by Gabriel says that in the later part of the reign of the kings in the four kingdoms from the Grecian Empire, a stern-faced king will rise to power. Now we know this humorless king represents the Antichrist, but we also know the kings from the Grecian Empire are gone; over two thousand years have passed since the Grecian Empire fell to the Romans. So how can the Antichrist arise in the latter part of their reign?

Actually, he already has, or more to the point, a man who is the primary symbol for the Antichrist has already done many things the Antichrist will do. In the latter part of the Grecian Empire, after it had dissolved into four separate kingdoms, shortly before the Romans decided to go a-conquering, a man came to power in one division by the name of Antiochus Epiphanes. He attained his throne through deceit, attempted to wipe out Judaism, took control of the temple and the sanctuary for about eleven hundred and fifty days, set up an altar to his own god in the sanctuary, and ultimately lost to an army led by Judas Maccabeus, who drove him out of Israel. Judas Maccabeus rededicated the temple to the Lord on the twenty-fifth of Kislev (Kislev corresponds roughly to December), and Israel started the feast of Hanukkah to celebrate his victory and the rededication of the temple. We will examine Antiochus Epiphanes in more detail in the next chapter.

This is a perfect example of a "rule" about prophecy that will help your understanding of scripture considerably: almost every prophecy has a minor and a major fulfillment. The "minor" fulfillment fits some portions of the prophecy, and becomes a symbol of the "primary" or "major" fulfillment, which will fit all portions of the prophecy. For example, Antiochus did not take a stand directly against the Prince of Princes, and his strength lay in his powers of deception and intrigue (the Antichrist WILL take a stand directly against the Prince of Princes, and his strength will not come from himself, but from the direct supernatural intervention of Satan).

The purpose of this vision is not to create a paradox concerning whether the Antichrist should be connected to the third or fourth beast, but to narrow our search for the country from which he will arise, and to fill in a few of the blanks concerning some of the key players in this little drama.

The reference to the existence of the Grecian kings will also be fulfilled during the days when the real Antichrist rises to power. There will be four kings ruling in countries roughly corresponding to the four divisions of the Grecian Empire in the last days, one of whom, as we shall see, will be the Antichrist himself. What about the other three kings? There will be kings in lots of countries, and if these countries exist in the last days, they will obviously have leaders, so why are they even mentioned in relation to the rise of the Antichrist? Because these three kings will play a special, central role in the events that lead the Antichrist to a position of world domination. What role? Read on.

THE GRECIAN KING

In Daniel's vision of four beasts, the little horn rises among ten horns, showing he is not one of the original ten kings, but he has a very close relationship with the ten kings (he did not rise up NEXT to them, but AMONG them). The nature of the relationship between the ten horns and the little horn is not explained in the vision of the four beasts, but in the vision of the ram and goat, we get more clues.

In Daniel's vision of the ram and goat the little horn rises OUT OF one of the four horns, not among them. This gives us a definitive bit of information: the Antichrist comes to power in one of the four divisions of the Old Grecian Empire. In narrowing the list of possible countries to only those within the Grecian Empire, this eliminates many popular contenders, including Italy and the vast majority of Europe, America, Russia and any other modern country that is not at least partly in the area of one of those divisions. This means that, despite the popularity of the theory, unless he comes to power in Greece, the Antichrist will NOT, in fact he CANNOT arise in a country within the European Union.

We know each horn represents a king in a division of the Grecian Empire, so when the little horn rises out a horn, we suddenly have TWO horns representing that division (the old horn was not broken off to have a little horn rise in its place): the original horn and the little horn. Two kings in one division.

As will become even clearer in Revelation, the Antichrist is a religious leader who, due to the nature of the religion in the area where he rises to preeminence, will become the ultimate ruler in all matters,

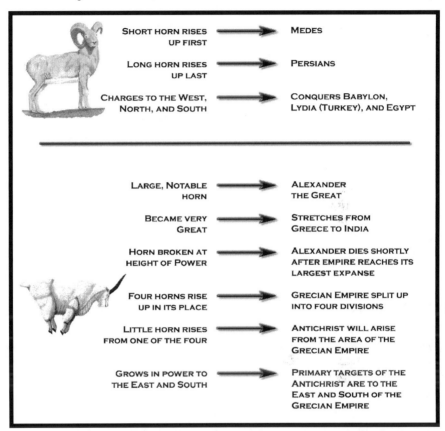

SHORT HORN RISES UP FIRST	→	MEDES
LONG HORN RISES UP LAST	→	PERSIANS
CHARGES TO THE WEST, NORTH, AND SOUTH	→	CONQUERS BABYLON, LYDIA (TURKEY), AND EGYPT
LARGE, NOTABLE HORN	→	ALEXANDER THE GREAT
BECAME VERY GREAT	→	STRETCHES FROM GREECE TO INDIA
HORN BROKEN AT HEIGHT OF POWER	→	ALEXANDER DIES SHORTLY AFTER EMPIRE REACHES ITS LARGEST EXPANSE
FOUR HORNS RISE UP IN ITS PLACE	→	GRECIAN EMPIRE SPLIT UP INTO FOUR DIVISIONS
LITTLE HORN RISES FROM ONE OF THE FOUR	→	ANTICHRIST WILL ARISE FROM THE AREA OF THE GRECIAN EMPIRE
GROWS IN POWER TO THE EAST AND SOUTH	→	PRIMARY TARGETS OF THE ANTICHRIST ARE TO THE EAST AND SOUTH OF THE GRECIAN EMPIRE

both religious and secular (similar to, but even more powerful than the late Ayatollah in Iran).

From this vision we know the Antichrist will not arise in Europe or the European Union (excepting Greece), Russia, North or South America, Asia, Africa, or Australia; he will come to power in the MIDDLE EAST, in one of only four possible areas. Those areas (the four divisions of the Grecian Empire) are the Grecian Division (roughly the area of modern Greece), the Turkish Division (a little less than the area of modern Turkey), the Egyptian Division (a little less than the area of modern Egypt), and the Syrian or Persian Division (the maximum extent is roughly the area of modern Syria, Iraq, Iran, Afghanistan, and half of Pakistan).

Which will he arise from? We don't really have enough information yet, which is why an angel later came to Daniel to further discuss the history of the kings in the Grecian Empire (found in Daniel chapter eleven); we will cover it in our next chapter.

We mentioned in chapter two that it is not a primary goal of the Antichrist, or at least the spirit behind the Antichrist, to overthrow the Mediterranean Confederacy of Ten Kingdoms when he attacks and uproots three horns. His biggest priority is to re-establish a previous empire. The remaining kingdoms of the Mediterranean Confederacy of Ten Kingdoms are of secondary concern. Which empire is he attempting to re-establish? Who are the three horns?

There are really only three candidates for the three horns the little horn uproots: the other three divisions of the Grecian empire. The Antichrist rises from one horn on the goat and we are told he rises to power during the LATTER REIGN OF THE GRECIAN KINGS REPRESENTED BY THE FOUR HORNS. So the existence of the other three divisions is vital to this vision, and their identification with the Grecian Empire is a key element in the end-times production.

All four will be a part of the Mediterranean Confederacy of Ten Kingdoms. The Antichrist will arise in one division and attack the other three. After subduing all three, the demonic spirit of Grecia will finally have reestablished his empire. This "resurrected" Grecian Empire, plus the other kingdoms in the confederacy that voluntarily submit to the Antichrist, result in a "new and improved" Grecian Empire, which is the sixth empire in our progression.

VOLUNTARY SUBMISSION

The "voluntary submission" of the rest of the Mediterranean Confederacy of Ten Kingdoms raises an interesting question: WHY do the rest of the kingdoms of the confederacy give up without a fight? There are probably several reasons. First, the Antichrist might guarantee the lives of the rest of the kings if they surrender without a fight while executing the kings of the captured kingdoms for emphasis. Second, all ten kings will probably send troops to protect the invaded countries, so the Antichrist may have completely crushed the troops of every country in the confederacy when he uproots three of them. If the fighting continued, he would eventually win anyway, so they quit.

Finally, every empire has a capitol, and you usually can not rule the empire until you control the capitol. Even an empire that is really a confederacy must have a capitol, if for no other reason than to have a neutral place for all ten kings to get together for their "council of ten" meetings. For practical and symbolic (one capitol would go a long way as a "symbol" of unity to the people of the confederacy) reasons, there needs to be one location to conduct the business of the empire, and that one place should not be the capitol of any of the ten kingdoms (it would make that kingdom seem more powerful or prestigious than the rest, a situation to which none of the squabbling members of this not-so-unified group would agree).

So in conquering three of the kingdoms, the Antichrist will most likely have captured the capitol of the confederacy (which, since confederate forces would defend the capitol fiercely, would result in the destruction or demoralization of a large chunk of the confederate fighting force), and after the capitol falls, complete surrender is usually inevitable. Where might this capitol be located? At first, this might seem like a wild guessing game, with almost any city as likely as any other, but it is not. We have some very strong clues that narrow down to just one city.

First, if the Antichrist rises to power in one division of the Grecian Empire, and while attacking the other three divisions captures the capitol, the capitol must be in one of those defeated divisions. This narrows our search to whichever countries happen to make up the Grecian, Turkish, Egyptian, and Persian divisions of the Grecian Empire in the last days. You might not think this really narrows the search much, since a search for a needle seems just as difficult when presented with four haystacks as when presented with ten. The number of possibilities still seems endless.

The task is not as difficult as it might seem. It is not so important who is left; who was eliminated? Remember, this confederacy is symbolic of the Old Roman Empire, will be within the boundaries of the Old Roman Empire, and will be enough like the Old Roman Empire to be directly connected with it in two separate visions. So what is the most likely capitol of an Empire that is symbolic of the Old Roman Empire and may be ruled by the same satanic spirit as the Old Roman Empire? What was the capitol of the Old Roman Empire? A city still considered the capitol of many human endeavors: Rome.

Wow! That must be it, right? Wrong. Rome is in Italy, which was NOT a division of the Grecian Empire. This may seem to take us back to the beginning, but it does exactly the opposite: it narrows the search to one city. If you will recall from the first chapter, the Old Roman Empire split in half. In the west, Rome remained the capitol, but in the east a new city was chosen: Constantinople (originally called Byzantium, and currently called Istanbul).

Istanbul is in Turkey (one of the four divisions), is NOT the capitol of Turkey (Ankara is the capitol), is the largest city in Turkey, is very defendable, and used to be the capitol of the Eastern Roman, or Byzantine Empire (after the fall of Rome, the Roman Empire continued in the east for another thousand years).[20] When the Roman Emperor Constantine moved from Rome to Constantinople,[21] the satanic Prince of Rome moved from Rome to Constantinople with him,[22] where he remained in authority until the spirit behind the Ottoman Turks dethroned him (he could now be called the Prince of Constantinople).

Presuming that the Antichrist does not come from the Turkish division (he wouldn't have to attack it, he would already own it), the modern city of Istanbul is our most logical choice for an empire ruled by a satanic prince who used to rule in that city.

SUMMARY

The purpose of this vision is to narrow the search for the kingdom from which the Antichrist will initially launch his campaign of global domination, and to identify the "three horns" uprooted in the previous dream.

The ram represents the kingdom of Media-Persia, and the goat is the Grecian Empire. The four horns that rise out of the goat's head after the death of Alexander are the four divisions of the Grecian Empire ruled by his four former generals.

The Little horn rising out of one of the four is the Antichrist. He will charge out from one division of the Grecian Empire, and subdue the other three (the three uprooted horns on the four beasts in Daniel's previous dream), gaining control of the Mediterranean Confederacy of Ten Kingdoms in the process. Once the Antichrist finishes conquering the other three divisions, he will rule a "new and improved" version of

---

[20] "Byzantine" is a modern name for the Eastern Roman Empire derived from the name of the capital, Byzantium. It was never used by the people of this empire. They called themselves simply "Basileia Romaion," which means "Roman Kingdom," or "Roman Empire." The designation "Byzantine" was first coined in 1557 AD (about 100 years after the fall of the empire) in order to more readily distinguish between the Western and Eastern divisions of the Roman Empire.

[21] The original name of Constantinople was Byzantium. Today it is called Istanbul.

[22] We can assume the demonic prince moved with Constantine because the western portion collapsed shortly after Constantine moved, while the eastern half remained another thousand years. Since Daniel says that the demonic prince of a kingdom has to be defeated before the physical kingdom can fall, it is unlikely the demonic prince of the Old Roman Empire was defeated due to the continued existence of the same empire in the east, in the form of the Eastern Roman Empire, for another thousand years. The only logical explanation is that the spirit moved.

the Grecian Empire (including the area of the Old Grecian Empire, plus the other seven kingdoms of the Mediterranean Confederacy of Ten Kingdoms).

The little horn is AMONG the ten horns on the fourth beast in Daniel's previous dream to show that, while he is not one of the original ten kings (he is an eleventh king), he does have a close relationship to those kings. The little horn rises OUT OF a horn on the second beast in this vision to show the nature of the relationship between the little horn and the original ten horns. He rises to prominence in a kingdom already occupied by one of the original ten kings to become the real power in that kingdom, while keeping the other king as a figurehead (which we now know must be a division of the Grecian Empire). He then conquers three other kingdoms within the ten (the other three divisions, including what probably will be the capitol of the confederacy, which leads to the acquiescence of the rest of the kingdoms within the confederacy).

POINTS TO NOTE

Strictly speaking, the Antichrist is a "Grecian" king, not a "Roman" king, and the empire he reestablishes is NOT the Old Roman, but the Old Grecian. By calling him a "Grecian" king, however, we are NOT stating he rises from the "Grecian division" (that is, from modern day Greece) of the Old Grecian Empire. All we know so far is that he arises from ONE of the divisions of the Old Grecian Empire (at this point, we don't have enough information to determine whether his actual nationality will be Grecian, Turkish, Egyptian, Lebanese, Syrian, Palestinian, Iraqi, or Iranian, but we know it will be ONE of these). Note the Antichrist does NOT come from Rome or the Vatican, he is NOT a Roman emperor (neither a new one nor an old one resurrected), and he is not trying to reestablish Roman domination of the world.

QUESTIONS
FROM CHAPTER THREE

1) What kingdom does the ram represent?
2) What kingdom does the goat represent?
3) What happens on the goat's head, and what does it mean?
4) What does the little horn represent?
5) Why is the little horn "connected" to both the Grecian and Roman Empires?
6) Is the Antichrist a "Grecian" or "Roman" king, and how do we know?
7) What are some possible reasons that the Mediterranean Confederacy of Ten Kingdoms voluntarily submits to the little horn after he uproots only three of them?
8) Exactly how long will the little horn stop the morning and evening sacrifices in the temple?
9) What is the significance of the little horn coming up "among" the ten horns in the last vision, and it coming "out of" one of the four horns on the goat in this vision?
10) In the previous vision, the little horn uproots three horns; from this vision, who are the best candidates for the identities of those three?
11) When the little horn "uproots" three horns, what happens to those countries?

KINGS OF THE NORTH AND SOUTH:
Show me the Country!

Daniel receives two more messages from the Lord concerning the "distant future," and the "end of times." Gabriel delivers both messages (actually, the identity of the angel who delivers the second message is not given, but the most likely candidate is Gabriel), and both are completely different from any of the previous dreams and visions in two ways: they are not visions or dreams, but actual visits from an angel, and there is no symbolic language in these narrations. Instead of creating a representative illustration, the Lord describes each event as it will literally happen. Due to their close association with the events described here, we will also cover two corresponding prophecies in Ezekiel.

We will need very little actual "interpretation" in this section. Our primary goal will be to identify the people and events described here, and then find them in history until the message reaches the events relating to the end times. Tracing the events will provide more valuable information concerning the Antichrist, and most importantly, will allow us to identify the exact country (since there are no symbolic devices used in this section, the country is much easier to identify than is usually presumed) from which the Antichrist will spring.

SEVENTY WEEKS

In the second half of chapter nine in his book, Daniel relates Gabriel's message of Seventy Weeks. While it does not directly relate to discovering WHERE the Antichrist first seizes power, nor to pinpointing the identity of Babylon the Great, it does contain a few vital elements concerning WHEN the Antichrist shall arise.

"While I was seeking and praying, confessing my sin and the sin of my people Israel and making my request to

the Lord my God for his holy hill, while I was still in prayer,
Gabriel, the man I had seen in the earlier vision, came to
me in swift flight about the time of the evening sacrifice. He
instructed me and said to me. 'Daniel. I have now come to
give you insight and understanding. As soon as you began
to pray, an answer was given, which I have come to tell you,
for you are highly esteemed. Therefore, consider the
message and understand the vision:

   "'Seventy weeks are decreed for your people and your
holy city to finish transgression, to put an end to sin, to
atone for wickedness, to bring in everlasting righteousness,
to seal up vision and prophecy and to anoint the most
holy.'" (Daniel 9:20-24)

Daniel had discovered from reading the scrolls of Jeremiah (a contemporary of his) that Israel would remain in captivity seventy years (Jeremiah 25:11-12). This revelation toppled him into intense repentance for his people in a very moving petition for mercy. During this prayer Gabriel arrived to deliver the answer; this fervent prayer for mercy brought an answer so quickly that Gabriel INTERRUPTED Daniel's prayer to give him the answer! Talk about a man of faith!

Gabriel states that seventy weeks[23] are decreed for the Israeli people and for their holy city (Jerusalem). As we shall see, the seventy weeks are seventy groups of seven-year periods, or four hundred and ninety (490) years. Daniel's prayer causes God to enlighten Daniel concerning God's plans for the nation of Israel, and ultimately, for the world.

The answer to Daniel's prayer is that Israel shall not always rebel against God, for there are six things God will accomplish during this 490 year period through Israel and the Messiah who will come out of her. They are: to finish transgression; to put an end to sin; to atone for wickedness; to bring in everlasting righteousness; to seal up vision and prophecy; and to anoint the most holy.

TO FINISH TRANSGRESSION

The word translated "transgression" is *peshah*, which refers primarily to a rebellion or revolt of some sort. This actually says, "to finish REBELLION." Rebellion rears its ugly head in every generation of man, and will reach its peak in the last days with the rise of the

---

[23] The word translated 'week' does not imply "seven days," since it is simply the Hebrew word for the number 'seven.' Given that "seventy 'sevens'" or "seventy groups of seven" are kind of awkward, "week," if understood just to mean "seven," not "seven days," is an adequate substitute.

ultimate "man of sin" when it shall be crushed by the return of our Lord and God, Jesus. Rebellion is not yet finished, so this portion is not yet fulfilled.

TO PUT AN END TO SIN

One need only turn on a television to know the Lord has not yet put a complete end to sin. This does not refer to eliminating the sin in the hearts of God's people, but to the complete elimination of sin from the face of the Earth. This will also be accomplished at the Second Coming.

TO ATONE FOR WICKEDNESS

Jesus' death on the cross paid the penalty for our sins. This happened at the first coming, and now allows us to approach the throne without a barrier of sin between the Lord and us. Once atonement has been made for a debt, that debt is removed.

TO BRING IN EVERLASTING RIGHTEOUSNESS

At first glance this may seem like a mere rewording of "to put an end to sin," but it is not. The word translated "sin" in the first part refers to ACTIONS; it suggests actions that fall short of perfection and cause damage to the spirit and soul of the sinner, and potential emotional or physical harm to ourselves and others, putting an end to this simply means to eliminate all sinful actions.

To bring in everlasting righteousness is to cleanse the spirit and soul of mankind completely. It means to purify or cleanse us of all spiritual filth, impurity, contamination, uncleanness, and corruption. To make us completely clean on the inside. This is one way sin shall be put to an end (the other is through the judgment of those who never turned their hearts over to the Lord). The cleansing of corruption from the hearts and souls of mankind was started by the God who died on the cross, and raised Himself from the grave, and shall be completed by the God who charges out of the sky on a white horse to crush the forces of the Antichrist, both of whom just happen to be the same God.

TO SEAL UP VISION AND PROPHECY

This refers to the complete fulfillment all prophesies and visions God has given to His people through His prophets and His scriptures. After Jesus establishes the literal kingdom of God when He returns, it will mark the end of the "times of the Gentiles," and there shall come a time when every prophecy in scripture has been fulfilled. This has obviously not taken place yet.

TO ANOINT THE MOST HOLY

The word "messiah" simply means, "anointed one." God uses Most Holy of the Messiah, the inner portion of the temple that housed the Ark of the Covenant, and of the whole temple, depending on whether He meant the Most Holy ONE or the Most Holy PLACE. Here, as is made clear in verses 25 and following, He means the Most Holy One. This was fulfilled at the first arrival of the Messiah when He came as a prophet and sacrificial lamb.

FROM EZRA TO JESUS

"Know and understand this: From the issuing of the decree to restore and rebuild Jerusalem until the Anointed One, the ruler, comes, there will be seven weeks, and sixty-two weeks. It will be rebuilt with streets and a trench, but in times of trouble." (Daniel 9:25)

From the issuing of the decree to return to and rebuild the city (Narrated in Ezra and Nehemiah) until the anointed one comes will be seven weeks, and sixty-two weeks, or forty-nine years (49), and four hundred thirty-four years (434), a total of four hundred eighty-three years (483).

Artaxerxes I gave the authorization to rebuild Jerusalem to Ezra in about the year 458 BC.[24] The rebuilding of Jerusalem took place in the following years, in the face of much opposition, and is recounted in Ezra and Nehemiah. Four hundred eighty-three years after the issuing of the decree to rebuild Jerusalem, the Anointed One was to come. Four hundred eighty-three years later takes us to roughly the year 27 or 28 AD. If, as most scholars believe, Jesus was born somewhere between the years 5 and 2 BC, this lands us somewhere between the time he started His public ministry (at the age of 30) and his crucifixion (at 33).

FROM JESUS TO THE DESTRUCTION OF THE TEMPLE

"After the sixty-two weeks, the Anointed One will be cut off and will have no one. The people of the ruler who will come will destroy the city and the sanctuary." (Daniel 9:26a)

---

[24] This is NOT the same as the decree given by Cyrus to return and rebuild the temple (about 538 BC) nor is it the same as the re-authorization by Darius to continue building the temple (about 520 BC).

Three Years after His ministry started, the Romans crucified Jesus with no one standing by His side (the disciples were notably absent during his trial). Roughly forty years later the Romans plundered Jerusalem and the temple was destroyed to crush a Jewish rebellion. Fifty-five years after that, the Romans completely destroyed Jerusalem, and built another city in its place. Since we know that the Antichrist comes to power in a country within the boundaries of the Old Roman Empire, and ultimately controls the Mediterranean Confederacy of Ten Kingdoms, which is symbolic of the Old Roman Empire, these Romans can be considered the people of the ruler to come: the Antichrist.

THE SEVENTIETH WEEK

"The end will come like a flood: War will continue until the end, and desolations have been decreed. He will confirm a covenant with many for one week. In the middle of the week he will put an end to sacrifice and offering. And on a wing of the temple he will set up an abomination that causes desolation, until the end that is decreed is poured out on him." (Daniel 9:26b-27)

In the end times, everything will seem to go crazy all at once. Peace will seem to have fled from the earth. There will be wars, hostilities, and destruction everywhere. Jesus said we would hear of " . . .*wars and rumors of wars, but see to it that you are not alarmed. Such things must happen, but the end is still to come. Nation will rise against nation, and kingdom against kingdom. There will be famines and earthquakes in various places. These are but the beginning of the birth pains"* (Matthew 24:6-8). The end times will not come peacefully and quiet, but like a flood, as every nation in the world seems to be suddenly struck with insanity.

This section is a reference back to the previous verse (the Antichrist). He will make a peace pact with "many" for seven years, (which corresponds to the seven years of Tribulation in Revelation). Since this prophecy is to and about Israel, the "many" can only refer to the Jews.[25] Half way through the seven-year peace pact, he will invade Israel, gain control of the temple, and set up the abomination that

[25] It is possible that the "many" here actually means that many nations, including Israel, will be involved in a massive treaty for peace in the Middle East that is "brokered" or "authored" by the Antichrist. With the current world-wide (including USA, Russia, Europe, and many Arab nations) push for some kind of peace accord between Israel and the Palestinians, this is not a hard scenario to imagine. The bottom line is that whether it is JUST between the Antichrist and Israel, or involves many other countries, it will FOCUS on peace with Israel.

causes desolation. He will remain in control of the temple until he meets his end, as decreed by God, at the return of Jesus Christ.

After this final week, the Lord will return with a shout, crush the forces of the contemptible one, and will fulfill the four final purposes of this vision (finish transgression, put an end to sin, bring in everlasting righteousness, and seal up vision and prophecy).

GOG AND MAGOG

According to the message of the seventy weeks, the Antichrist will make a seven year covenant with Israel, but will break that covenant and invade after three and a half years. In Ezekiel, God describes the circumstances of that invasion.

> *"Son of man, set your face against Gog, the land of Magog, the chief prince of Rosh, Meshech, and Tubal, and prophecy against him and say: 'This is what the Sovereign Lord says: I am against you, O Gog, the chief prince of Rosh, Meshech, and Tubal. I will turn you around put hooks in your Jaws and bring you out with your whole army, your horses, your horsemen fully armed, and a great horde with large and small shields, all of them brandishing their swords. Persia, Ethiopia[26] and Libya[27] will be with them, all with shields and helmets. Gomer with all its troops and the house of Togarmah from the far north with all its troops, the many nations with you."* (Ezekiel 38:1b-6)

Ezekiel lived during the first half of the Babylonian Empire (he gave his last "datable" prophecy roughly thirty years before the fall of Babylon). Since none of these ancient cultures exist today, identification of the modern nations intended should stem from the locations of these old kingdoms at the time of the prophecy (sometime between 585 and 573 B.C.).

---

[26] Literally "Cush." Cush was located in what is now roughly the area of Ethiopia.
[27] Literally "Put." Put was located in what is now modern Libya.

Gog and Magog are prophetic names given to all the nations under Satan's control that stand against God in the last days (see Revelation 20:8), and in this case, Gog stands for the ultimate satanic empire: that of the Antichrist. As can be seen from the maps on the following page, all of the kingdoms mentioned here were within the area that will be controlled by the Antichrist. Magog, the land from which Gog originated, was at the intersection of northwestern Iraq, southeastern Turkey, northwestern Iran and northern Syria (roughly the area in which the Kurds of Iraq and Turkey live today).

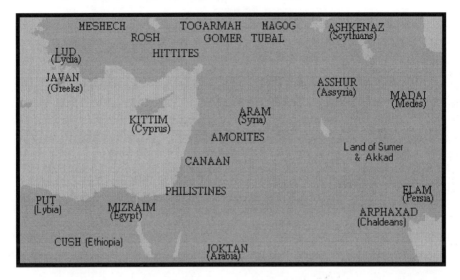

Rosh, Meshech and Tubal were located in what is now Turkey. Gomer, an offshoot of the ancient Cimmerians, had firmly established itself in modern Turkey by the time of this prophecy. Persia is modern Iran (at the time of this prophecy, the Persians occupied Iran exclusively; they would not begin the expansion of their empire into Turkey, Babylon, or Egypt for thirty to forty years). As best as scholars can tell, Togarmah[28] was located in the general area that is now either Armenia or Azerbaijan (the most northern of all these allies, thus the designation "from the far north").

The Antichrist will eventually control Libya, Sudan, and Ethiopia (as shown here and in Daniel 11:43 below), and as we shall show in chapter seven, Iran may also be under his control, or at the very least, will be in league with him. From the previous chapters of Daniel, we know he shall rule Turkey and Egypt as two of the four divisions of the Grecian Empire.

---

[28] Also called "Beth Togarmah," which means "the house of Togarmah."

"Get Ready: be prepared, you and all the hordes, gathered about you, and take command of them. After many days you will be called to arms. In future years you will invade a land that has recovered from war, whose people were gathered from many nations to the mountains of Israel, which had long been desolate. They had been brought out from the nations, and now all of them live in safety. You and all your troops and the many nations with you will go up, advancing like a storm: you will be like a cloud covering the land." (Ezekiel 38:7-9)

The Israel of this message has been recently gathered from many nations around the Earth. They came home to a desolate land, had rebuilt Israel, and were living in relative safety. This is the Israel of our day. After having made a seven-year peace-pact with the Antichrist, Israel will feel safe and secure, unaware that the Antichrist is planning an invasion.

"This is what the Sovereign Lord says: On that day thoughts will come into your mind and you will devise an evil scheme. You will say. 'I will invade a land of unwalled villages: I will attack a peaceful and unsuspecting people-- all of them living without walls and without grates and bars. I will plunder and loot and turn my hand against the resettled ruins and the people gathered from the nations, rich in livestock and goods. Living at the center of the land. Sheba, Dedan and the merchants of Tarshish and all the young lions will say to you, 'have you come to plunder? Have you gathered your hordes to loot. to carry off silver and gold, to take away livestock and goods and to seize much plunder?'

"Therefore, son of man, prophecy and say to Gog, 'This is what the Sovereign Lord says: In that day, when my people Israel are living in safety, will you not take notice of it? You will come from your place in the far north, you and many nations with you, all of them riding on horses, a great horde, a mighty army. You will advance against my people Israel like a cloud that covers the land. In days to come, 0 Gog, I will bring you against my land, so that the nations may know me when I show myself holy through you before their eyes." (Ezekiel 38:10-16)

Sheba was located in what is now Yemen, on the southern edge of modern Saudi Arabia. Dedan was in Edom, which is now Jordan. Scholars think that Tarshish may have been in southern Spain, and is considered Biblically to be the farthest nation away from Israel.[29] This passage seems to suggest that all of these nations are NOT under the control of the Antichrist, thus their apparent freedom to question his actions. This fits since from Daniel 11:41 below, we know Jordan will escape the Antichrist, and nowhere in scripture is there any evidence that the Antichrist will control Europe.[30]

> *"This is what the Sovereign Lord says: 'Are you not the one I spoke of in former days by my servants the prophets of Israel? At that time they prophesied for years that I would bring you against them. This is what will happen in that day: When Gog attacks the land of Israel, my hot anger will be aroused, declares the Sovereign Lord. In my zeal and fiery wrath I declare that at that time there shall be a great earthquake in the land of Israel. The fish of the sea, the birds of the air, the beasts of the field, every creature that moves along the ground, and all the people on the face of the earth will tremble at my presence. The mountains will be overturned, the cliffs will crumble and every wall will fall to the ground. I will summon a sword against Gog on all my mountains, declares the Sovereign Lord. Every man's sword will be against his brother. I will execute judgment upon him with plague and bloodshed; I will pour down torrents of rain, hailstones and burning sulfur on him and on his troops and on the many nations with him. And so I will show my greatness and my holiness, and I will make myself known in the sight of many nations. Then they will know that I am the Lord.'"* (Ezekiel 38:17-23)

---

[29] Jonah 1:3. This also shows that "nations afar off" are not necessarily those across the Atlantic or Pacific Oceans.

[30] We can deduce that the Mediterranean Confederacy of Ten Kingdoms will actually consist of countries in the Eastern Roman Empire, since we know that four of the ten countries in the confederacy will be New Syria, Turkey, Greece, and Egypt, and from Daniel 11 below that Lybia, Sudan, and possibly Ethiopia will be three others. This makes seven of the ten countries, all of which are in the Eastern portions of the Old Roman Empire. As we shall see in chapter eight, there is strong reason not to include any country west of Greece. After gaining control of the confederacy, in the eastern portion of the Old Roman Empire, the Antichrist is only mentioned attacking to the East and North (Daniel 11:44), NOT to the west.

There are scholars out there who have speculated that Ezekiel is about an invasion into Israel by Russia, and does not involve the Antichrist. The first verse in this section should put that theory to rest. In verse 17 God addresses ONE individual (not a group or nation), and comments that this is the one prophesied about by prophets from long ago. There is only ONE person that fits this description: the antichrist.[31] There is plenty of evidence that this section could only refer to the Antichrist, and verse 17 simply seals the issue.

When the Antichrist suddenly breaks his covenant with Israel and invades, the Lord responds with a mighty earthquake and with plagues from heaven. This corresponds to the events in Revelation 12, when the Dragon, identified in Revelation 12:9 as Satan,[32] brings the armies under his control against Israel, and Israel flees into the desert for the remaining three and a half years.[33]

This prophecy in Ezekiel suggests, with the supernatural plagues that follow in verse 22, that this earthquake is the beginning of the pouring out of the wrath of God upon the Antichrist's kingdom. If this is the official beginning of the wrath of God, the earthquake described here[34] and in Revelation 12:16 may also be the same as the earthquake that takes place at the opening of the sixth seal in Revelation 6:12-17.

Let us move now to the Book of Truth, and find out which division of the Grecian Empire will give birth to the Antichrist.

THE BOOK OF TRUTH

In what is most likely the same year that he received the message about the Seventy Weeks, Daniel sought the Lord and was host to another visit from Gabriel. This time Gabriel brought a small section of prophetic history from the Book of Truth concerning some kings that would come to power from Daniel's time right up to the Day of the

---

[31] In particular, there are "the Assyrian" prophesies of Isaiah and Micah, who were contemporaries, and both of whom prophesied well over 100 years before Ezekiel gave his first prophecy. These are very clear, very specific references to the Antichrist, as well as some of the earliest that name a specific individual as the ultimate enemy of Israel.

[32] "The great dragon was hurled down--that ancient serpent called the devil, or Satan, who leads the whole world astray."

[33] Revelation 12:13-17. The dragon pursues the woman (Israel), but she flees to the desert where she stays for "a time, times, and half a time" (three and a half years). The dragon spews a flood out of his mouth (the armies of the Antichrist), but the earth opens up and swallows the flood, so she escapes his wrath.

[34] The earthquake in Ezekiel is the same as the earth opening in Revelation 12:16. This is the scene when the Antichrist breaks the seven-year peace pact, invades Israel, and sets up the Abomination of Desolation in the Temple.

Lord. Gabriel does not reveal the exact nature of this "Book of Truth"; it may be a heavenly book in which the Lord has written the prophetic history of Israel, and possibly the whole Earth.

Daniel 10:21 contains the only reference in the Bible to this enigmatic book. . . oh that we could see this book today!

This passage in Daniel starts with an interesting bit of information about the spirit realm, and about how we interact with it. Daniel had been sorrowfully fasting and praying for understanding about the end times for three weeks. At the end of that time a terrifying angel appeared to him (very likely Gabriel, who had visited him earlier), and this is what happened.

> *I was left alone, looking at this great vision. No strength was left in me; my face grew deathly pale, and I was extremely weak. When I heard him speak I fell into a deep sleep, with my face to the ground. Suddenly, a hand touched me and I rose up as far as my hands and knees.*
>
> *He said to me, "Daniel, you are a man treasured by God. Understand the words that I'm saying to you. Stand on your feet, for I have now been sent to you."*
>
> *After he said this to me, I stood all the way up, still trembling.*
>
> *"Don't be afraid, Daniel," he said to me, "for from the first day that you purposed to understand and to humble yourself before your God, your prayers were heard. I have come because of your prayers. But the prince of the kingdom of Persia opposed me for 21 days. Then Michael, one of the chief princes, came to help me after I had been left there against the prince of the kings of Persia. Now I have come to help you understand what will happen to your people in the last days, for the vision refers to those days."*
> (Daniel 10:8-14)

Note that the angel had been sent from the very first day that Daniel started praying, but the delivery of that message had been delayed for a full three weeks due to the intervention of the satanic prince who was currently reigning supreme over this kingdom: the prince of Persia. He was only able to get past the prince of Persia when Michael showed up to help.

Next, the angel touches Daniel, who is so afraid that he will only look at the ground. At the angel's touch, Daniel feels strong again, and the angel continues his explanation.

*He said, "Do you know why I've come to you? I must
return very shortly to fight against the Prince of Persia, and
when I am done there, the Prince of Greece will come. No
one has the courage to support me against these princes
except Michael, your prince. However, I will tell you what is
recorded in the book of truth."* (Daniel 10:20-21)

Here we find out that this angel, possibly Gabriel, along with
Michael, are alone in their battle against this powerful satanic prince.
Further, they already know that after the Prince of Persia is defeated,
the Prince of Grecia will rise to power. So what is Daniel's response to
this bit of information?

*So in the first year of Darius the Mede, I took a stand to
strengthen and protect him.* (Daniel 11:1)

Daniel JOINED IN the battle against the satanic prince. WE can and
should assist the angels in their battles against the satanic princes and
powers of the spirit realm. Paul lays it out plainly in Ephesians.

*Put on the full armor of God, so that you may be able to
stand against the stratagems of the devil. For we wrestle not
against flesh and blood, but against principalities, against
powers, against the rulers of the darkness of this age,
against spiritual forces of evil in the heavenlies.* (Ephesians
6:11-12)

Some translations make it sound like Daniel 11:1 it is still the angel
speaking, and that the angel claims to have started strengthening and
protecting Michael during the first year of Darius the Mede. Aside from
the fact that Paul confirms that this is what we are supposed to be doing
(fighting with the spiritual forces of evil), there are two problems with
this interpretation.

The first is that the speaker dates the event using the reign of a
human king as the reference. No where in scripture does an angel ever
date his actions by the events of humanity. No angel is ever recorded
saying that he did something during one of the years of some earthly
king. However, Daniel uses this method of dating seven other times in
his book (Daniel 1:1, 21; 2:1; 7:1; 8:1; 9:1; 10:1). Since this is Daniel's
typical method of dating, the style and approach strongly indicated this
must be Daniel speaking.

The second problem is that it is said to have occurred in the first year of Darius,[35] yet we are told the angel's visit happens in the third year of Cyrus[36] which is incorrect timing if the angel is the speaker. The third year of Cyrus occurred 14 years PRIOR to the first year of Darius, so this cannot be the angel speaking. The angel would not be speaking in the past tense of a date that had not yet occurred, and since he and Michael were already resisting the Prince of Persia, this cannot be a reference to the angel starting his support of Michael in the future. The only thing this can be is an after the fact reference to when Daniel joined the battle to assist the angels in their fight against the Prince of Persia. Daniel did what Paul says we are supposed to do: he took a stand against the spiritual powers of evil, and in so doing, he strengthened the angels who were fighting those satanic princes.[37]

Now we come to the actual message the angel was sent to deliver: a section from the Book of Truth. The next seventeen verses, about the history of the Grecian Empire, may seem to have wandered far off the track, but stick with it; it ends by identifying the country from which the Antichrist will arise. We have carefully tracked this section point by point, specifically identifying each person and event from history, so that you can see with your own eyes that there is no symbolic language anywhere.

THE KINGS OF PERSIA

Before jumping into the meat of the message, Gabriel explains the events in Medio-Persia that lead to an invasion from Greece.

> *"Now then, I tell you the truth: Three more kings will appear in Persia, and then a fourth, who will be far richer than all the others. When he has gained power by his*

---

[35] This is Darius the Great, who reigned from 522 – 486 BC. The Darius who was 62 years old at the overthrow of Babylon is known in secular history as Cyxere II Astiages, who was the last king of the Median empire. His rule ended in 537 BC, during the second year of Cyrus' reign over Babylon.

[36] This would be the third year after he conquered Babylon, which would mean Daniel got this visit about 535 BC. Daniel started assisting the angels in their battles against the Prince of Persia roughly 14 years later, in about 521 BC (first year of Darius).

[37] Note that we are NOT saying Daniel prayed FOR the angels. The scripture does not specifically tell us how Daniel strengthened and supported the angels in their fight, but judging by what Paul says, the most likely conclusion is that he strengthened them by praying **against** the demonic Prince of Persia (a type of spiritual warfare frequently called "binding the strongman").

wealth, he will stir up everyone against the kingdom of Greece." (Daniel 11:2)

Daniel received this revelation during the third year of the reign of Cyrus over Babylon (roughly 536 BC). After Cyrus came Cambyses (roughly 530 to 522 BC), Gaumata (who ruled for less than a year in 522 BC), and Darius I (roughly 522 to 486 BC). After the death of Darius I, Xerxes I (also called Ahasuerus, the Persian king who was married to Esther, from 486 to 464 BC) came to power. About six years after ascending to the throne, Xerxes I attacked Greece (about 480 BC), but the fledgling republics defeated him.[38] Xerxes' hatred for Greece set the course for the Persian Empire for the next one hundred and fifty years; a period during which the Persian Empire tried repeatedly to annex the independent minded Grecian city-states.

Not mentioned in the section from the "Book of Truth," six kings arose in Persia after Xerxes: Artaxerxes I (approximately 464 to 424 BC), Xerxes II (reigned for about one year from 424 to 423 BC), Darius II (roughly 423 to 404 BC), Artaxerxes II (roughly 404 to 358 BC), Artaxerxes III (approximately 358 to 338 BC), and Darius III (338 to 330 BC). Darius III was the reigning Persian king during the fighting between the old Medio-Persian Empire and the rapidly developing Grecian Empire under Alexander the Great.

God left these kings out of the prophecy about Persia since the key issue was not how many kings would rise in Persia before its fall to Greece, but that the kings during the latter half of the Persian Empire constantly sought to overthrow Greece.

ALEXANDER THE GREAT

Gabriel jumps from the ascension of Xerxes I in Persia to the rise of Alexander in Greece.

> *"Then a mighty king will appear, who will rule with great power and do as he pleases. After he has appeared, his empire will be broken up and parceled out toward the four winds of heaven. It will not go to his descendants, nor*

---

[38] Darius had actually attacked Greece ten years prior to this, but was defeated in the famous battle of Marathon. After the battle, a messenger ran the 26 miles to Athens and then dropped dead after delivering his message that Greece was saved. Modern marathon races are 26 miles long to this day in honor of the run of that Greek messenger. Despite Darius' attempt to conquer Greece, it was Xerxes, that stirred up the Persian Empire against Greece.

*will it have the power he exercised, because his empire will
be uprooted and given to others."* (Daniel 11:3-4)

By the time Darius II came to the throne in Persia, Philip of
Macedon had united Greece. In 336 BC Philip's son, Alexander became
king and the war with Persia began in earnest. Alexander started with
about thirty five thousand soldiers and a tiny treasury, while Darius III
had, at various times, almost a million soldiers, including some fifty
thousand Greek soldiers hired before they could join Alexander, and a
treasury that brought in almost twenty times Alexander's treasury
EACH YEAR. Yet within thirteen years Alexander had conquered the
WHOLE Persian Empire from Egypt to India.

Shortly after conquering the Persians, Alexander died from a fever
at the young age of thirty-three. Alexander's five generals then agreed
to rule the various portions of Alexander's kingdom until Alexander's
son was old enough to take the throne. Each general really wanted to
rule the empire himself though, so in 311 BC, after the assassination of
the boy and his mother, they wasted no time mourning as war erupted
between the provinces of the empire.

Antigonus, arguably Alexander's best general, launched his attempt
to reconquer the empire first. The other four, nurturing a healthy
respect for Antigonus' abilities, banded together against him. The war
for control of Alexander's kingdom raged until about 280 BC.
Antigonus was eventually defeated, and the other generals established
themselves in four separate areas of Alexander's kingdom. Cassander
took Greece, Lysimachus took Turkey and Asia Minor,[39] Seleucus took
the eastern portion from Lebanon to the Indus river in modern Pakistan,
and Ptolemy took Egypt. None of these four kingdoms ever reunited
under one king again (although Antiochus IV came close), and none of
them ever had the military strength Alexander had exhibited.

The prophetic History of the Grecian empire Gabriel now embarks
upon the long, intertwined histories of two of the four kingdoms, whose
leaders he calls the "king of the North," and the "king of the South."
The identification of these two kingdoms depends on the detail and
accuracy of his narration. Since this is the Word of God, we know the
accuracy will be perfect, and as we shall see, the detail is amazing.

---

[39] Lysimachus never actually established the Turkish division, as his forces were
crushed by the Antigonids and Seleucids. The Turkish division did not actually exist
for another 17 years, when Peregmum gained independence from the Seleucids in 263
BC.

BROKEN COVENANT

"This king of the South will become strong, but one of his commanders will become even stronger than he and will rule his own kingdom with great power. After some years, they will become allies. The daughter of the king of the South will go to the king of the North to make an alliance, but she will not retain her power, and he and his power will not last, together with her royal escort and her father and the one who supported her." (Daniel 11:5-6)

The king of the South is Ptolemy II, who took the Egyptian portion of the Grecian Empire. The ruler of the Syrian division, called the king of the North in this prophecy, was a commander under Ptolemy during the battles with Antigonus. For almost fifty years, these two kings and their sons fought with one another, until the king in Egypt, Ptolemy II Philadelphus, and the king in Syria, Antiochus II Theos, reached an agreement for peace in 250 B.C. At the time of the treaty, Palestine and the Jews were under the control of the Syrian rulers.

The main article of the treaty called for Antiochus Theos to divorce his current wife, Laodice, and marry Berenice, the daughter of Ptolemy Philadelphus. For a few years, all was well on the Syrian throne; until Antiochus Theos tired of Berenice, left her in Antioch, and returned to his former wife, Laodice. Laodice knew that she would be exiled again when the fickle Antiochus Theos tired of her a second time, so she took matters into her own ruthless hands.

In the year 246 B.C. Laodice poisoned Antiochus II Theos, set her son on the throne, and had Berenice and her son assassinated ("the one who supported her" is most likely a reference to her infant son, whose life, while Antiochus Theos was alive, ensured her own, since he was legally the next in line to the throne). The women assigned to care for Berenice's needs tried to defend her, and many of them died in the process. No one knows whether the simultaneous death of Berenice's father in Egypt was coincidence or assassination.

REVENGE FROM THE SOUTH

"One from her family line will arise to take her place. He will attack the forces of the king of the North and enter his fortress: he will fight against them and be victorious.

He will also seize their gods, their metal images and their valuable articles of silver and gold and carry them off to Egypt. And he shall stand more years than the king of the

North. So the king of the South shall come into his kingdom, and then shall return into his own land." (Daniel 11:7-9)

Berenice's brother in Egypt, Ptolemy III Euergetes became king when Ptolemy II Philadelphus died. Consumed with grief over the assassination of his sister, he attacked the kingdom of Seleucus II Callinicus (Laodice's son), ravaged the whole kingdom all the way to India (Palestine now fell under Egyptian rule), did away with Laodice and her son, and took most of the riches back to Egypt with him. He probably would have annexed the entire Syrian division, but there arose a rebellion in his home province in Egypt, and Ptolemy Euergetes returned to Egypt to restore order. This sudden return to Egypt gave the sons of Seleucus II Callinicus, Seleucus III Ceraunus and Antiochus III the Great, time to recover and build an army of their own.

NORTH RISES AGAIN

"His sons will prepare for war and assemble a great army, which will sweep on like an irresistible flood and carry the battle as far as his fortress.

"Then the king of the South will march out in a rage and fight against the king of the North, who will raise a large army, but it will be defeated. When the army is carried off, the king of the South will be filled with pride and will slaughter many thousands. Yet he will not remain triumphant. For the king of the North will muster another army, larger than the first: and after several years, he will advance with a huge army fully equipped." (Daniel 11:10-13)

Seleucus III Ceraunus and Antiochus III the Great worked together building a large army to regain the Syrian division from the Ptolemys in Egypt. In 223 BC, before they could bring their plans to fruition, Seleucus Ceraunus died, so Antiochus the Great went to war against Egypt alone. Antiochus the Great got all the way to the boarder of Egypt before Ptolemy IV Philopator (Ptolemy Euergetes had died about two years after returning to Egypt) came charging out and defeated him near Gaza (217 BC). Antiochus the Great scampered back to Syria, and Ptolemy Philopator, feeling heady from his victory against a much larger army, went on a rampage, persecuting all those in the area under contention (Palestine); thousands of Jews were tortured and slain.

Over the next fourteen years, Antiochus the Great built another army, larger and better equipped than his first, and with help from

Philip of Macedonia, from the Grecian division, once again invaded the Egyptian held Palestine.

THE NORTH TRIUMPHANT

> *"In those times many will rise against the king of the South. The violent men among your own people will rebel in fulfillment of the vision, but without success. Then the king of the North will come and build up siege ramps and will capture a fortified city. The forces of the South will be powerless to resist: even their best troops will not have the strength to stand. The invader will do as he pleases: no one will be able to stand against him. He will establish himself in the Beautiful Land and will have the power to destroy it."*
> (Daniel 11:14-16)

With Antiochus the Great and Philip of Macedonia preparing to make war on Egypt, and still bitter from the persecution under Ptolemy Philopator, many Jews rebelled against their Egyptian rulers, figuring that helping Syria would encourage Antiochus to be kind to them after he beat Egypt. But the Egyptian General Scopas attacked the rebels in Palestine before Antiochus the Great could arrive, and defeating them, he took everything in sight back to Egypt as spoils (200 BC).

Shortly after this, Antiochus the Great did arrive, and he defeated the army of the new king of Egypt, Ptolemy V Epiphanes, lead by Scopas. No Egyptian troops could stand against Antiochus the Great, and no cities, even heavily fortified cities with tall walls, were able to withstand his sieges. He pushed the Egyptians completely out of Palestine, all the way back to the Nile River.

After pulling Palestine out from under the thumb of Egypt, Antiochus the Great was very kind to the Jews, allowing many of them to return from exile, and removing the tribute required of the priests to the ruling kingdom. Years of wars, crushed rebellions, and sieges against its cities had reduced Palestine to poverty stricken land filled with starvation and suffering; so it probably would have been unable to pay taxes to a ruling empire anyway.

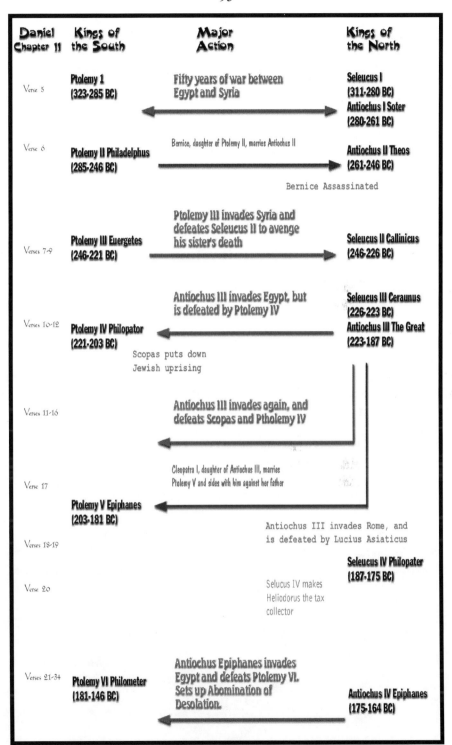

Daniel Chapter 11	Kings of the South	Major Action	Kings of the North
Verse 5	Ptolemy 1 (323-285 BC)	Fifty years of war between Egypt and Syria	Seleucus I (311-280 BC) Antiochus I Soter (280-261 BC)
Verse 6	Ptolemy II Philadelphus (285-246 BC)	Bernice, daughter of Ptolemy II, marries Antiochus II	Antiochus II Theos (261-246 BC)
		Bernice Assassinated	
Verses 7-9	Ptolemy III Euergetes (246-221 BC)	Ptolemy III invades Syria and defeates Seleucus II to avenge his sister's death	Seleucus II Callinicus (246-226 BC)
Verses 10-12	Ptolemy IV Philopator (221-203 BC)	Antiochus III invades Egypt, but is defeated by Ptolemy IV	Seleucus III Ceraunus (226-223 BC) Antiochus III The Great (223-187 BC)
		Scopas puts down Jewish uprising	
Verses 11-16		Antiochus III invades again, and defeats Scopas and Ptholemy IV	
Verse 17	Ptolemy V Epiphanes (203-181 BC)	Cleopatra I, daughter of Antiochus III, marries Ptolemy V and sides with him against her father	
Verses 18-19		Antiochus III invades Rome, and is defeated by Lucius Asiaticus	
Verse 20		Selucus IV makes Heliodorus the tax collector	Seleucus IV Philopater (187-175 BC)
Verses 21-34	Ptolemy VI Philometer (181-146 BC)	Antiochus Epiphanes invades Egypt and defeats Ptolemy VI. Sets up Abomination of Desolation.	Antiochus IV Epiphanes (175-164 BC)

While Antiochus the Great did not actually destroy Palestine, he did establish himself as the undisputed ruler in the "beautiful land," and he set the stage for following Syrian kings to wreak havoc among the Jews. The year is 197 BC; within thirty years the Jews would wish they were back under Egyptian control.

. . . THE WIFE SHALL CLEAVE TO HER HUSBAND

> *"He will determine to come with the might of his entire kingdom, and this he shall do, and he will make an alliance with the king of the South. And he will give him a daughter in marriage in order to overthrow the kingdom, but his plans will not succeed or help him."* (Daniel 11:17)

Antiochus the Great brought the full power of his kingdom to bear against Egypt, conquering most of it. By 194 BC he had control of Egypt, but Rome interceded on behalf of Ptolemy V Epiphanes, and ordered Antiochus out of Egypt. Antiochus was furious, but he pulled out as Rome demanded.

Antiochus the Great, however, did not give up on owning Egypt; he just attacked the problem from a different angle. Figuring if he couldn't get Egypt by force, he would get it by deception, Antiochus concocted a plan to get control of Egypt from the top down. His plan was simple: under the guise of making a treaty of peace, marry his daughter, Cleopatra I, to Ptolemy V Epiphanes. Using her as an inside accomplice, he would get rid of Ptolemy Epiphanes and set the stage for a lightning quick overthrow of Egypt's government. Ptolemy agreed to the peace treaty involving the marriage of Cleopatra I (an ancestor of the famous Cleopatra of the Nile with whom Marcus Antony fell in love), and took her as his bride in 194 BC

Cleopatra, however, loved her new husband, and warned him of her father's plans. Thwarted in his attempt to deceive his way into the Egyptian throne, and unwilling to attack the country now held in part by his daughter, Antiochus the Great turned his attention back to the country that had caused him to leave Egypt in the first place: Rome.

RATS! FOILED AGAIN!

> *"Then he will turn his attention to the coastlands and will take many of them, but a commander will put an end to his insolence and will turn his insolence back upon him. After this, he will turn back toward the fortresses of his own*

country but will stumble and fall, to be seen no more."
(Daniel 11:18-19)

Antiochus the Great turned toward the west and conquered the coastlands of the Mediterranean all the way to Greece, with Italy and Rome as his goal. In the year 190 BC the Romans met Antiochus in battle for the first time, with the results almost an omen of future events. The Roman consul Lucius Cornelius Scipio Asiaticus defeated Antiochus, driving him all the way back to the provinces of modern Syria.

As a war debt, the victorious Romans wanted fifteen thousand talents from Antiochus. His treasury did not contain enough gold, so he marched into his eastern most provinces to collect the extra taxes. Antiochus the Great died in 187 BC attempting to plunder a pagan temple in the province of Elymais to raise the needed money.

THE TAX COLLECTION MUST GO ON

"His successor will send out a tax collector to maintain the royal splendor. In a few years, however, he will be destroyed, yet not in anger or in battle." (Daniel 11:20)

After the death of Antiochus the Great, his son, Seleucus IV Philopator ascended to the throne. Rome still required Seleucus IV Philopator to pay the war debt, and he quickly decided that all of his father's conquering had accomplished little, except debt for the kingdom, so he remained at the palace and raised the taxes. He appointed Heliodorus to the office of minister of finance (the tax collector), who did his job very well, even plundering the Temple in Jerusalem.

In the year 175 BC, Heliodorus, desiring to be king, concocted a plot to get rid of the unpopular Seleucus IV Philopator (people have never liked higher taxes). He figured his plot would succeed since Rome said they would hold both the son and the brother of Seleucus Philopator as hostages until they received full payment on the war debt. Feeling secure in his plot, Heliodorus poisoned Seleucus, and prepared to ascend to the throne.

THE CONTEMPTIBLE KING

"He will be succeeded by a contemptible person who has not been given the honor of royalty. He will invade the kingdom when its people feel secure, and he will seize it through intrigue. Then an overwhelming army will be swept

away before him: both it and the prince of the covenant will be destroyed. After coming to an agreement with him, he will act deceitfully, and with only a few people he will rise to power. When the richest Provinces feel secure, he will invade them and will achieve what neither his fathers nor his forefathers did. He will distribute plunder, loot and wealth among his followers. He will plot the overthrow of fortresses, but only for a time.

"With a large army he will stir up his strength and courage against the king of the South. The king of the South will wage war with a large and very powerful army, but he will not be able to stand because of the plots devised against him. Those who eat from the king's provisions will try to destroy him: his army will be swept away, and many will fall in battle. The two kings, with their hearts bent on evil, will sit at the same table and lie to each other, but to no avail, because an end will still come at the appointed time. The king of the North will return to his own country with great wealth, but his heart will be set against the holy covenant. He will take action against it and then return to his own country.

"At the appointed time he will invade the South again, but this time the outcome will be different from what it was before. Ships of the western coastlands will oppose him, and he will lose heart. Then he will turn back and vent his fury against the holy covenant. He will return and show favor to those who forsake the holy covenant.

"His armed forces will rise up to desecrate the temple fortress and will abolish the daily sacrifice. Then they will set up the abomination that causes desolation, with flattery he will corrupt those who have violated the covenant, but the people who know their God will firmly resist him.

"Those who are wise will instruct many, though for a time they will fall by the sword or be burned or captured or plundered. When they fall, they will receive a little help, and many who are not sincere will join them." (Daniel 11:21-34)

After the death of Seleucus IV Philopator, Heliodorus and several others proclaimed themselves king. Since the true heir to the throne, Demetrius, the son of Seleucus Philopator, was still a captive in Rome, the kingdom became divided over who the real king should be. Of the many claimants to the throne, Heliodorus was the most obvious choice.

Unknown to him though, a monkey wrench, on its way home from Rome, was about to be thrown into the gears of his campaign for leadership.

No, it was not the true heir to the throne, Demetrius, who was just a young boy at this time; it was Antiochus, the brother of Seleucus IV Philopator. While Antiochus lacked a greater claim to the throne than Heliodorus, he had several things Heliodorus did not: a thorough understanding of the politics of persuasion (particularly in his home kingdom), friendly connections with several nearby rulers, the ability to charm a cobra, and the social dexterity of a chameleon.

He came home in peace, openly avowing allegiance to Heliodorus. He then charmed the nearby king of Pergamos, flattered the Romans through shrewd diplomacy (and much payment of back tribute owed them by the Syrian throne), and won the support of the Syrian people through a carefully orchestrated grass roots social strategy that painted him as "every man's friend." In short, he outflanked his opponents for the throne on every political front so effectively Heliodorus' control of the army could not even stand in Antiochus' path to the throne. Before the end of the same year that Seleucus IV Philopator had died, Antiochus IV Epiphanes had solidified his position and became the undisputed ruler of the Syrian division of the Grecian Empire. The contemptible king, not legally next in line to the throne, had seized the kingdom through intrigue.

Daniel 11:21-34 refers to events that we know from history have already occurred (most of which are recorded in I and II Maccabees, two books that, while not inspired scripture, contain accurate accounts of the historical events described), but at least some of them will occur again in the end times, with the Antichrist, instead of Antiochus Epiphanes as the main character. Jesus makes this abundantly clear when He says, in about 30 AD, to watch for something in the end times that already had occurred almost two hundred years before (the abomination that causes desolation). Since our main interest is in the Antichrist, we will try to describe how Antiochus Epiphanes fulfilled this prophecy as quickly and briefly as possible, so that we can jump to the Antichrist right away.

Shortly after coming to the throne in 175 BC, Antiochus Epiphanes claimed Palestine and several other provinces (which started a war with Egypt). There was very little actual fighting during the early part of the "war" with Egypt, but Antiochus Epiphanes was not just sitting around watching the royal gardeners mow the grass; he spent the first couple years of his reign plotting and replotting the invasion of Egypt, setting in motion a scheme to topple the king of Egypt, and beefing up his defenses in case Egypt attacked first. This went on just long enough for Ptolemy VI Philometor in Egypt to begin to feel secure that his uncle Antiochus Epiphanes would never invade.

Just as Ptolemy Philometor had quit worrying about an invasion, Antiochus attacked. Ptolemy met him with a huge army, but a plot among Ptolemy's advisors to disrupt his chain of command (which tactically immobilized his army) and destroy him, eliminated his advantage. Their plan was partially successful: a smaller army devastated Ptolemy's force, but Ptolemy escaped death.

After his victory, Antiochus Epiphanes had himself declared the king of Egypt (something none of his ancestors had been able to do), and took Ptolemy Philometor captive. Since Ptolemy Philometor was his nephew, Antiochus didn't cage him in a prison, but kept him under house arrest at his palace.

On his way back from conquering Egypt, Antiochus began to get involved in Jewish affairs. He had the high priest, assassinated. In his place, Antiochus set Jason up as high priest (Jason had bribed his way into the position), and negotiated a set amount that would be paid to Syria each year from the temple money. Shortly after agreeing to the amount proposed by Jason, Antiochus Epiphanes removed him from office and installed Menelaus in his place (Menelaus had offered to send more money to Syria than Jason). This kind of deceitfulness, private betrayal, and outright lying became a common occurrence during the reign of Antiochus Epiphanes.

Once Antiochus returned to Syria, trouble erupted in Egypt where the Alexandrians made Ptolemy Philometor's brother their king. In response to this crisis, Antiochus and the captive Egyptian king, Ptolemy Philometor, sat together in numerous conferences pledging their love and confidence in each other, and talked about how to work together to put down this interloper. They were privately plotting the destruction of each other's power and life; Antiochus plotting to use Ptolemy to get Egypt back, and then get rid of him, while Ptolemy planned to use Antiochus to regain his country, then have Antiochus assassinated and take control of Syria himself. Neither man's schemes and lies worked in his favor. With Ptolemy Philometor's apparent backing, Antiochus Epiphanes invaded Egypt again, pushing all the way to within seven miles of Alexandria, where the revolt originated. At that point, Rome intervened again; their chief naval commander confronted Antiochus in person, demanding that Antiochus return Egypt to its rightful owner, Ptolemy Philometor. Antiochus told the Roman Naval commander he would go consult with his advisors and allies, and then get back to him. But the Roman was fully aware of

Antiochus Epiphanes' reputation for deceit, and drew a circle around Antiochus in the sand, telling him he had to decide before he stepped out of the circle (no decision would be taken as a refusal of Rome's demand). Antiochus relented, but was furious to be so close to victory only to be denied, as his father had been, by the Italian busybodies.

While still in Egypt, Antiochus received word that Jason had garnered considerable backing in Palestine, and was besieging Jerusalem to take the high priesthood back from Menelaus. In a violent rage, Antiochus invaded Palestine, squashing Jason's army and slaughtering over forty thousand Jews. He raided the temple, stole the golden vessels used in worship, burst into the holy of holies, consecrated the altar to Zeus Olympus, and sacrificed a swine on the altar.

Jews were forbidden to sacrifice any animals on the altar, or to practice their religion in the temple in any way. As a last stab, he restored the evil Menelaus to the high priest's office.

This was too much for some Jews to tolerate, and a resistance developed, led by Matthias and Judas Maccabeus. During the intervening three-and-a-half-years of fighting between the Jewish rebels and the forces of Syria, Antiochus killed or persecuted thousands of Jews (traitors to the Lord abounded, and [40]were spared). After one thousand one hundred and fifty days, a victorious Judas Maccabeus rededicated the altar to the Lord God. Thus concludes the historical section of this prophecy.

THE SYRIAN DIVISION

Antiochus Epiphanes is symbolic of the Antichrist, the final "king of the North," in so much as he does some of the things the Antichrist will do. As the following verses will show, the Antichrist is the final "king of the North," and as such, will come to power in the Syrian Division[41] of the Grecian Empire.

The remainder of this prophecy continues as though it were still referring to Antiochus, but we know from history that Antiochus Epiphanes did not do any of the rest of the things described here. Just as earlier portions of this prophecy suddenly switched to the actions of

---

[40] It was in rededicating the temple to God that the miracle of the oil happened: one days worth of oil burned for seven days, giving the Jews time to acquire enough oil to refill the lamp without the flame burning out (which would have required ANOTHER rededication of the temple). This miracle is remembered today in the Jewish festival called Hanukah. The seven candles that are lit during Hanukah recall the number of days the oil miraculously kept burning.

[41] Also called the Persian division.

a new king without giving any indication that a new person was involved, so this now switches to the Antichrist exclusively without any warning. The final king of the North will do many of the same evil things Antiochus did, but he also will do much, much more.

As Antiochus Epiphanes did, the Antichrist will undoubtedly come to power through deceit and intrigue, will attack and conquer Egypt (recall from chapters two and three of this book that the Antichrist subdues the other three divisions of the Grecian Empire: Turkey, Egypt, and Greece), will invade Israel, will get control of the temple, and will set up an abomination that causes desolation. At this point, we leave the double reference portion of this prophecy, as the rest refers exclusively to the end times and the Antichrist, and not to Antiochus Epiphanes in any way.

This is the point at which many authors whose books and teachings we studied ran into trouble. Most of them recognize that up to now, every event described takes place in the Syrian and Egyptian divisions of the Grecian Empire, and that the "king of the north" referred to the Seleucid kings of the Syrian Division of the Grecian Empire. From here on, many of them arbitrarily decide this passage is no longer referencing Syria and Egypt, but represent another country. In other words, for no apparent reason, and without justification or warning, they suddenly decide that a detailed description of several hundred years of literal events is now symbolic. Why? The only reason we can think of is that the events simply have not happened yet.

Because most of them have so thoroughly convinced themselves that the Catholic Church is the ultimate enemy of "true" Christians that any scripture to the contrary MUST be symbolic. As a result, they interpret all scriptures from a foundation that the Vatican MUST be the center of all end times activity. So instead of taking this LITERAL section as a possible hole in their interpretation of SYMBOLIC sections, and thus, their theories, then reexamining other scriptures in light of the evidence presented here, they just assume this literal section suddenly turns symbolic because the Antichrist cannot possibly come from any other city but Rome.

The beauty of this excerpt from the "Book of Truth" is that it is NOT symbolic. It simply lists the events, exactly as they would happen, in sometimes startling detail. To decide that all unfulfilled portions are symbolic, when 100 percent of all fulfilled sections are literal, is the ultimate example of not remaining consistent.

Interpretation inconsistencies like these are unnecessary and only make scripture MORE difficult to understand, not less. If God is not consistent in His prophecies, particularly in relation to symbolic language, then it is truly impossible to be absolutely sure about what ANY symbol, parable, or allegory represents; we will not know for sure until the event actually happens.

However, God IS consistent. There is no reason for wildly ranging, subjective interpretations of most scriptures in Daniel and Revelation; if one stays consistent, it all fits together quite nicely.

This section clearly and undeniably lists the Antichrist as the last "king of the north." All previous "kings of the north" ruled in the Syrian division of the Grecian Empire. Not one came from some other area of the world. That means the Antichrist CANNOT come from Rome, America, Europe, Africa, the European Common Market, or any other place on the planet EXCEPT the Syrian division of the Grecian Empire. The only possible candidates are any modern countries that were within that division (Syria, Lebanon, Iraq, Iran, Afghanistan, and Pakistan).

A BRIEF REVIEW

Before we continue, what do we know about the Antichrist so far? We know from the previous chapters that he shall arise in one of the four divisions of the Grecian Empire, that his country will also be within the boundaries of the Old Roman Empire, that he shall start as a part of the Mediterranean Confederacy of Ten Kingdoms, shall attack the rest of the confederacy, forcibly subduing three countries (corresponding to the other three divisions of the Grecian Empire), and in the process, shall gain control of the whole confederacy. In line with this, we also know that, contrary to most popular theories, he shall NOT be a Roman Caesar, a Russian Premier, a Catholic Pope, an American President, or a false Jewish Messiah, but a "Grecian" king (not that he will be Grecian by nationality, only that he will arise in the area of the Old Grecian Empire).

From this chapter, we now know that he shall arise in the Syrian division of the Grecian Empire, which primarily covered the area included in modern Lebanon, Syria, Iraq, Iran, Pakistan, and a portion of Afghanistan. So which of these countries shall he rise from? Well, we can further narrow the search by remembering that the little horn that uprooted three horns rose up on the FOURTH beast in Daniel's vision of four beasts, and the fourth beast is primarily the Old Roman Empire.

He will rise from both the Old Roman Empire and the Syrian Division of the Grecian Empire, or more specifically, from the area that overlaps both empires: Lebanon and Syria. In addition to these two modern countries, the Antichrist's country will also need to control a portion of Iraq.

There are several very good reasons for including the western half of Iraq in the Antichrist's original domain. First, in Micah the Antichrist is called "the Assyrian," and in Isaiah he is called both "the king of Babylon," and "the Assyrian." (Isaiah 14:4-25; Micah 5:2-6). The Assyrians lived in the area currently occupied by modern Iraq along the Tigris River valley (roughly the area of the Babylonian Empire).

Second, the old Roman Empire actually controlled western Iraq up to the Persian Gulf for a short period in the second century (so it was briefly a part of BOTH empires).[42]

Third, the original capitol of the Syrian Division of the Grecian Empire, and thus the "home" province of the "kings of the north," was in the city of Babylon (before moving to Seleucia, and finally to Antioch in Syria). Finally, in Revelation we shall see that Babylon is not only his capitol city (before moving to Jerusalem), but is also the chief or "holy" city in the religion he develops to declare himself God, so he must have control of it from the start.

Since modern Syria occupies the majority of the area from which the Antichrist shall arise, and in the Syrian division of the Grecian Empire (during the reign of Antiochus Epiphanes, the primary symbol for the Antichrist) the seat of the government was in areas now within the boundaries of modern Syria, we shall refer to this future country from which the Antichrist shall spring as simply New Syria.

New Syria does not necessarily have to cover EXACTLY the same area as the Roman portion of the Syrian division and the Assyria Empire covered; it need only include ROUGHLY the area of each (approximately the area of modern Syria plus enough of Iraq to include the city of Babylon).[43] Since only a portion of modern Iraq is needed, while almost all of modern Syria should be included, New Syria will most likely annex the southern portion of Iraq (rather than Iraq annexing Syria). New Syria MAY include more than Syria and western Iraq, but it cannot control any less; this area, then, can be called the minimum dimensions of New Syria, the country from which the Antichrist will arise.

Let us now continue with the prophecy from the "Book of Truth."

---

[42] The Old Roman Empire controlled the western portion of modern Iraq all the way to the Persian Gulf from 114 to 118 AD, a mere four years. By itself, it would mean nothing, but coupled with the necessity of the city of Babylon being in the Antichrist's grasp, it lays the historic groundwork for his control of at least a portion of Iraq.

[43] The City of Babylon is located on the Euphrates River roughly straight across from the Jewish City of Tel Aviv.

REVIVAL IN ISRAEL

"Some of the wise will stumble, so that they may be refined purified and made spotless until the time of the end, for it will still come at the appointed time." (Daniel 11:35)

This is a reference to what the Lord will be doing in His church, except that Daniel had no knowledge of the church, only of saints from Israel. Since we know that the Lord is working in his body to create a church that is spotless and without wrinkle to meet the evil of the end times, this reference of those saints who are "refined, purified and made spotless until the time of the end," must be a reference to a revival within Israel during the last days, since the stumbling of the wise seems to be a direct reference to a basic tactic the Lord uses among intellectuals. Many from natural Israel shall join hands with those from spiritual Israel.

Jesus is called the stumbling block (I Peter 2:3-6; Matthew 21:44), and scripture says that "God chose the foolish things of the world to shame the wise." (I Corinthians 1:27). Since it is the "wise" who are stumbling so that they may be refined, purified and made spotless, this could very easily be a double reference to the arrival of Jesus in the first century and the stumbling blocks He brought to the Jewish Nation, as well as to a revival in Israel in the last day.

Some will balk at the suggestion of a revival in the end times, as the depictions of that period seem dark and nearly hopeless in Revelation, and the common teaching is that there will be a "great falling away" from the faith in the end times. When asked about the signs of the end times, Jesus said that false Christ's and false prophets would mislead **many**, and that **many** would fall away and betray one another.

> *As he sat on the Mount of Olives, the disciples came to him privately, saying, "Tell us, when will these things be, and what will be the sign of your coming and of the close of the age?"*
>
> *And Jesus answered them, "See that no one leads you astray. For many will come in my name, saying, 'I am the Christ,' and they will lead many astray. And you will hear of wars and rumors of wars. See that you are not alarmed, for this must take place, but the end is not yet. For nation will rise against nation, and kingdom against kingdom, and there will be famines and earthquakes in various places. All these are but the beginning of the birth pains.*

"Then they will deliver you up to tribulation and put you to death, and you will be hated by all nations for my name's sake. And then many will fall away and betray one another and hate one another. And many false prophets will arise and lead many astray. And because lawlessness will be increased, the love of many will grow cold. (Matthew 24:3-12)

Again, this sounds pretty bleak, and doesn't seem to leave much room for very many continuing to hold to the faith, much less there being a revival. While this does sound bad, and we do not wish to downplay the fact that this will truly be humanity's darkest hour, there are plenty of scriptures that give us reason to hope and trust in the continued power of the Gospel to change the hearts of men and women, even in the time of Satan's greatest strength.

First, let us continue this quote from Matthew for two more verses.

"But the one who endures to the end will be saved. And this gospel of the kingdom will be proclaimed throughout the whole world as a testimony to all nations, and then the end will come." (Matthew 24:13-14)

Jesus promised that despite the falling away, there are those who endure to the end, and that in the last days, the gospel will be preached throughout the whole world as a testimony to all nations. That simple fact, that the gospel will be preached to the whole world, speaks of a huge world-wide population of genuine believers who are getting out in their communities and proclaiming the gospel.

Jesus did not say that everyone would fall away. In fact, He did not even say that MOST would fall away. He said "many" would fall away. Note this reference to the same time period in First Timothy.

Now the Spirit expressly says that in later times some will depart from the faith by devoting themselves to deceitful spirits and teachings of demons, through the insincerity of liars whose consciences are seared, who forbid marriage and require abstinence from foods that God created to be received with thanksgiving by those who believe and know the truth. (1 Timothy 4:1-3)

Note here that it says SOME will depart from the faith. While "some" would be difficult to reconcile with "most," saying that "some" will fall away can be a reference to the exact same number as when we say that "many" will fall away. The difference is simply your perspective.

When we say that "many" will fall away, we are just counting the number that fall away. We are making no comment on how many do not fall away. For example, if the actual number that fall away turns out to be two hundred million, that is certainly MANY. This is important to note however: that does NOT tell us how many believers REMAIN in the faith.

When we say "some" will fall away, we are starting from a consideration of the whole, and commenting on the amount that fall away *compared* to the amount that do not. By using the word "some," we are actually saying that the number of those who fall away is SMALLER than the number of those who do not. If the number of those who fall away were MORE than those who did not, we would say MOST will fall away. If sixty percent fall away, that is *most*, but if twenty-five percent fall away, that is *some*.

If the total world wide estimates of the number of Christians alive today (about eight hundred million) are even roughly accurate, two hundred million and twenty-five percent happen to be the same amount, which would make BOTH of these scriptures completely accurate; that is very MANY people, but only SOME of the total number of believers on the planet. That would LEAVE six hundred million believers, which is more than enough to preach the gospel throughout the entire world, and more than enough to bring about an end times revival.[44]

So you can see that this reference to a revival in Israel is NOT out of line with the rest of scripture. No matter what the actual numbers are, the "many" from Matthew and the "some" from Timothy are the same number, and not only will there be MORE believers who STAY IN the faith than who fall away, those left will be very serious about their faith, and will be boldly out in their communities preaching the gospel.

THE BLASPHEMOUS KING

"The king will do as he pleases. He will exalt and magnify himself above every god and will say unheard-of things against the God of gods. He will be successful until

---

[44] Please note that the numbers we use here are examples only. We are NOT claiming that there really are 800 million Christians in the world (we do not know if, in reality, this statistic is too high or too low), or that exactly twenty-five percent will fall away. Our point is that based on the wording used in these two scriptures, there will be more Christians who remain true to their faith than those who do not.

the time of wrath is completed, for what has been determined must take place." (Daniel 11:36)

Just as the little horn on the fourth beast spoke boastfully against the Ancient of Days, so this king speaks "unheard-of things against the God of gods." This king will be successful until the time of wrath is completed, just as the little horn was successful until the Ancient of Days ruled against him in the Heavenly Court. The obvious reason is this blasphemous king and the little horn are the same man: the Antichrist.

Notice God has mentioned three times that, in spite of all these things, the end will still come at the proper time (verses 27, 35, and 36). The implication is that the demonic spirits involved are somewhat aware of the plans of God and are constantly trying to alter those plans, to the point of attempting to delay or speed up the arrival of the Antichrist, thus enabling them to defeat God by throwing His plans into disarray. Despite their scheming and maneuvering, the end shall still come at the appointed time; all Satan's power, coupled with that of his chief demons' cannot even DELAY their demise, much less prevent it.

A MAN WHO THINKS HIMSELF A GOD OF WAR

"He will show no regard for the gods of his fathers or for the one desired by women,[45] nor will he regard any god, but will exalt himself above them all. Instead of them, he will honor a god of fortresses: a god unknown to his fathers he will honor with gold and silver, with precious stones and costly gifts. He will attack the mightiest fortresses with the help of a foreign god and will greatly honor those who acknowledge him. He will make them rulers over many people and will distribute the land at a price." (Daniel 11:37-39)

Some have speculated that because the Antichrist disregards the "gods of his fathers,"[46] that he must be a renegade Jew, and by

---

[45] The Hebrew is somewhat vague here, it could also be translated "or for the desire of women," implying that he will not be swayed by sexual lusts for women. The context of the sentence, however, which is of gods the Antichrist will disregard, seems to suggest the intention is of a type of god. This god is either desired by women, or somehow related to or involved in the desire of women.

[46] That the word translated "gods" ("elohim") is plural is irrelevant to either side of this issue, since God the Father is frequently identified with the plural "elohim" throughout the Old Testament. It is correct to translate this plural word in the singular when

extension, a "false messiah." Their reasoning is that because the true God is identified by His connection to the fathers of Israel ("the God of Abraham, Isaac, and Jacob"), the Antichrist must be a Jew. The problem with that view is that it does not say "our fathers," or even "the fathers"; it clearly says "his fathers." If, for example, a man's family had always been Hindu, and he became a Christian, he would be disregarding the "gods of his fathers." There is no reference to Judaism here.[47]

The full implications of the Antichrist's lack of regard for the gods of his fathers, and his action of exalting himself above all gods will be explored in Revelation. Notice it says he does not regard any god, and then, in the next sentence it talks about a god of fortresses he honors. He will exalt himself above all known gods, but there is one he will honor, although not as most people honor gods; the Antichrist, by exalting himself above all others, will be honoring a god of war and destruction, a god foreign to his people, a god of death and hate: Satan. It is unique to Satan that when a person exalts and honors themselves above all gods, they are actually exalting Satan above all others. Why? Because he originated the idea of exalting oneself above God, and a key element in his plan for world domination is to make man so self-centered, selfish, and self-deifying that he will reject the true God under any circumstances. As difficult as it may be to believe, when Jesus splits the skies, His sudden appearance will not cause mass repentance. Even though they will have definitive proof that Jesus is God, the years of bitterness, hatred, and violent animosity for any god other than themselves (and Satan) will be too much for many people to put aside. Instead of repenting, they will scream their hatred toward God at the top of their lungs.

The Antichrist will attack and subdue many powerful countries (the Mediterranean Confederacy of Ten Kingdoms and some kingdoms to the north and east). He will apparently distribute the conquered lands to those who can afford to purchase them from him, thus raising more capital to continue financing his wars with other countries. Those who can afford it will be made governors, mayors, etc. This program of rule

---

referring to the True God; the plural nature of the word does not directly indicate that there is more than one God (in many languages, such as Hebrew or German, the proper polite or "royal" usages of many words are actually in the plural tense at all times, but should still be translated in the singular), but it does hint at the mystery of the Trinity within Godhead.

[47] In addition, according to Daniel's vision of seventy weeks, Israel will make a seven year peace pact with the Antichrist. It is inconceivable that Israel would bother with a peace pact with someone they accept as their messiah! Instead of making a seven-year covenant with him, they would open their country to him and make him king!

by the rich will, of course, promote corruption, incompetence, and economic instability. The Antichrist, though, will not care in the least, so long as this program continues to shuttle money into his war machine.

THE WORLD AT WAR

> *"At the time of the end the king of the South will engage him in battle, and the king of the North will storm out against him with chariots and cavalry and a great fleet of ships. He will invade many countries and sweep through them like a flood. He will also invade the Beautiful Land. Many countries will fall, but Edom, Moab and the leaders of the Ammon will be delivered from his hand. He will extend his power over many countries: Egypt will not escape. He will gain control of the treasures of gold and silver and all the riches of Egypt, with the Libyans and Nubians in submission. But reports from the east and the north will alarm him, and he will set out in a great rage to destroy and annihilate many. He will pitch his royal tents between the seas at the beautiful holy mountain. Yet he will come to his end, and no one will help him."* (Daniel 11:40-45)

From the moment he comes to power, the Antichrist is a man of war, however, notice that in this first engagement, it is Egypt that invades. Egypt attacks the Antichrist first ("*the king of the south will engage him in battle.*" Literally, "*will push at him*" showing that the king of the South initiates the conflict), and the Antichrist responds with an all out counter-invasion. His first war is against the king of the South, Egypt, and grows to include the other two countries that make up the Grecian Empire. When he finally wins this conflict, he gains control of the Mediterranean Confederacy of Ten Kingdoms.

This scripture also says he will gain control of Libya and Nubia (Ethiopia and Sudan),[48] which seems to suggest that these will be among the remaining countries in the Mediterranean Confederacy of Ten Kingdoms that voluntarily submit to him after his military conquest of Egypt, Turkey, and Greece.

---

[48] It is possible that the Antichrist will not actually control Sudan and Ethiopia, but they will simply border the southern edge of his empire. The verse actually says that the "Nubians are at his feet," which could be a reference to their location (meaning he does not go south of them), instead of a reference to their submission.

Edom, Moab, and the leaders of Ammon will not be ruled by the Antichrist. The area of the ancient kingdoms of Edom, Moab, and Ammon are now roughly the area of modern Jordan. Though the Antichrist will be conquering countries on all sides of Jordan, he will feel it unnecessary to take the Jordanian area (probably because Jordan would add nothing to the Antichrist's domain defensively, economically, politically, militarily or any other way, and he will be busy conquering many more important regions).

This scripture also points out that in the midst of conquering "many countries," the Antichrist shall invade the Beautiful Land (Israel). He will also pitch his royal tent between the seas at the Beautiful Holy Mountain. The Beautiful Holy Mountain is the temple mount; the Antichrist shall move his base of operations to Jerusalem, probably at or in the Temple, located between the Mediterranean Ocean and the Dead Sea. Jerusalem will then become his new capitol city.

At one point the Antichrist receives some reports from the North and the East. This section does not reveal what the reports contain (we address that later), but the contents of those reports alarm him, and he then sets out to destroy many. These are reports from or about kingdoms to the North and East of his empire, and the Antichrist then attacks and conquers those kingdoms. Biblically, the most likely candidates to the north and east are the Moslem republics in the southern portion of the Soviet Union (Azerbaijan, Uzbekistan, Tajikistan, and Turkmenistan) and the Moslem countries of Afghanistan and Pakistan.

What makes these kingdoms more likely than Russia, Eastern Europe, India, or China? These countries were part of the Grecian Empire, Medio-Persian Empire, or both. No other countries in this region appear in scripture (the "biblical world," that is, the only sections of the earth ever mentioned in scripture, extends from the western edge of India in the east, to the southern republics of the soviet union and southern Europe in the north and west to the northern portion of Africa, including Sudan and Ethiopia in the south). When we get to chapter 17 in Revelation, additional evidence will be presented to seal this view.

THE SECOND COMING

"At that time, Michael, the great prince who protects your people, will arise. There will be a time of distress such as has not happened from the beginning of nations until then. But at that time your people - everyone whose name is found written in the book - will be delivered. Multitudes who

sleep in the dust of the earth will awake: some to everlasting life, others to shame and everlasting contempt. Those who are wise will shine like the brightness of the heavens, and those who lead many to righteousness, like the stars for ever and ever." (Daniel 12:1-3)

Verse one of Daniel chapter twelve says "at that time" twice. At what time? The sentence just prior to this one says, "yet he will come to his end, and no one will help him." (Daniel 11:46). So it is at the time of the very end, when the Antichrist comes to his end. Or more accurately, "after" the Antichrist has accomplished all of the things attributed to him in chapter eleven, verses thirty-six to forty-six, and "during" the time period when he meets his end.

This section indicates that there are several key things that will be happening "at that time": first, it will be a time of distress unparalleled in human history. Second, Michael will once again arise to protect Israel. Third, the living saints will be delivered. Fourth, the righteous dead will arise to everlasting life, and the wicked dead to eternal punishment.[49] Fifth, the Antichrist will be defeated and killed. Notice that the deliverance of the saints and the resurrection of the dead happen at the "end" of the reign of the Antichrist, not at the beginning. The resurrection of the dead and the deliverance of the saints are not mentioned in verse thirty-six, at the beginning of the Antichrist's reign, but in chapter twelve, at the end of his reign. While Daniel is referring to the deliverance of the Jewish saints, we know from the New Testament that the resurrection of the righteous dead happens simultaneous to the deliverance of the Church, so this will include ALL saints.

This is the very first blatant reference in scripture to what is commonly called "the rapture" in Christianity. Notice that throughout the book of Daniel, he continuously suggests the saints of God will be on EARTH during the reign of the Antichrist (it would be extremely difficult for the Antichrist to make war on saints who were already in heaven).

ARMAGEDDON

The previous verses describe the events surrounding the return of the Lord. During the time of the very end, among the many things that shall happen, the Antichrist shall finally meet his end. In chapter 38 of Ezekiel, as we have already seen, God describes the Antichrist's

---

[49] This last judgement, of the wicked dead, happens after the millenium, which is not referenced prophetically in Daniel.

invasion half way through the seven-year peace pact. In chapter 39 of Ezekiel, God describes the Antichrist's second invasion into Israel, at the battle of Armageddon, when the Antichrist finally meets his end, as stated above in Daniel.

> *"Son of man, prophecy against Gog and say: 'This is what the Sovereign Lord says: I am against you, O Gog, chief prince of Meshech and Tubal. I will turn you around and drag you along. I will bring you from the far north and send you against the mountains of Israel. Then I will strike your bow from your left hand and make your arrows drop from your right hand. On the mountains of Israel you will fall, you and all your troops and the nations with you. I will give you as food to all kinds of carrion birds and to the wild animals. You will fall in the open field, for I have spoken, declares the Sovereign Lord. I will send fire on Magog and on those who live in safety in the coastlands, and they will know that I am the Lord.*
> *"'I will make known my holy name among the people Israel. I will no longer let my holy name be profaned, and the nations will know that I the Lord am the Holy One in Israel. It is coming! It will surely take place, declares the Sovereign Lord. This is the day I have spoken of."* (Ezekiel 39:1-8)

The Lord brings the Antichrist and his hordes down into Israel, where He destroys them. In verse three God says he strikes the bow and arrows from the Antichrist's hands, which corresponds to the description in Revelation, at the first seal, of the rise of the Antichrist: He is not holding a sword, but a bow (Revelation 6:2).

The Lord says he will destroy the Antichrist and his allies with fire from heaven on the terrible Day of the Lord, and that they shall be food for the wild birds and animals. From that point on, God says He will no longer allow His holy name to be profaned, Israel will finally know their God again, and the nations of the whole earth will know that God is in Israel. This corresponds perfectly with the description of the Second Coming in Revelation 19:11 - 20:6.

THE AFTERMATH

> *"Then those who live in the towns of Israel will go out and use the weapons for fuel and burn them up--the small and large shields, the bows and arrows, the war clubs and*

spears. *For seven years they will use them for fuel. They will not need to gather wood from the fields or cut it from the forests, because they will plunder those who plundered them and loot those who looted them, declares the sovereign Lord.*

"On that day I will give Gog a burial place in Israel, in the valley of those who travel east toward the Sea. It will block the way of travelers, because Gog and all his hordes will be buried here. So it will be called the Valley of Hamon Gog.[50]

"For seven months the house of Israel will be burying them in order to cleanse the land. All the people of the land will bury them, and the day I am Glorified will be a memorable day for them, declares the sovereign Lord.

"Men will be regularly employed to cleanse the land. Some will go throughout the land, and in addition to them, others will bury those that remain on the ground. At the end of the seven months they will begin their search. As they go through the land and one of them sees a human bone, he will set up a marker beside it until the grave diggers have buried it in the Valley of Hamon Gog. (Also a town called Hamonah will be there.) And so they will cleanse the land.

"Son of man, this is what the Sovereign Lord says: Call out to every kind of bird and all the wild animals: 'Assemble and come together from all around to the sacrifice I am preparing for you, the great sacrifice on the mountains of Israel. There you will eat flesh and drink blood. You will eat the flesh of mighty men and drink the blood of the princes of the earth as if they were rams and lambs, goats and bulls-- all of them fattened animals from Bashan. At the sacrifice I am preparing for you, you will eat fat till you are glutted and drink blood till you are drunk. At my table you will eat your fill of horses and riders, mighty men and soldiers of every kind, declares the Sovereign Lord.

"I will display my glory among the nations, and all the nations will see the punishment I inflict and the hand I lay upon them. From that day forward the house of Israel will know that I am the Lord their God. And the nations will know that the people of Israel went into exile for their sin, because they were unfaithful to me. So I hid my face from

---

[50] Hamon Gog means "the hordes of Gog."

*them and handed them over to their enemies, and they all
fell by the sword. I dealt with them according to their
uncleanness and their offenses, and I hid my face from
them.*

*"Therefore this is what the Sovereign Lord says: I will
now bring Jacob back from captivity and will have
compassion on all the people of Israel, and I will be zealous
for my holy name. They will forget their shame and all the
unfaithfulness they showed toward me when they lived in
safety in their land with no one to make them afraid. When I
have brought them back from the nations and have gathered
them from the countries of their enemies. I will show myself
holy through them in the sight of many nations."* (Ezekiel
39:9-27)

This section describes the fate of the Antichrist and his hordes:
dinner for the vultures. There are so many dead in the valley of Hamon
Gog that it will take the whole nation of Israel seven months to bury
them all. At the end of the seven months, men will be employed to go
throughout the land searching for human bones. From this we may
postulate that not only are the millions of soldiers in the valley of
Hamon Gog wiped out, but God also kills any of the Antichrist's
soldiers patrolling other parts of Israel.

How many soldiers are in the valley? Their weapons will provide
Israelis with fuel for seven years. This is poetic justice. For seven years
these weapons fueled the Antichrist's inner hatred, and kept his
destruction raging through the villages and towns of the Mediterranean.
Then after his death, for seven years those same weapons will provide
the fuel for comfort, rebirth, and warmth to those the Antichrist hated
most.

Some have raised the objection that modern weapons could not be
burned as fuel because metal will not burn. This is true. Most modern
weapons, such as AK-47 machine guns, T-70 tanks, armored personnel
carriers, and ammunition cannot be burned as fuel. From this
information, some have concluded that this part must be symbolic.
However, there is a lot more to a modern army than metal. The cloth,
rubber, and wood could be stripped from most military and supply
vehicles (tires, seats, wire insulation, packing crates and boxes, cloth,
etc). There could be huge stockpiles of diesel fuel and gasoline needed
to power all those vehicles. There are the tents the soldiers live in, the
clothing the people were wearing, the straps on their weapons, the oil
used to lubricate their guns, and the explosive powders and chemicals,

if treated properly, could possibly be used for fuel. There is plenty of material to burn.

This section in Ezekiel wraps up with a description of how God will be merciful to Israel, and of how they will finally repent and believe forever after.

Some have postulated that Ezekiel chapters 38 and 39 do not refer to Armageddon, but to an earlier invasion by armies from another country (the most popular choice is Russia). There is, however, considerable evidence within this section that this is the LAST battle in the end times to be fought in Israel or anywhere else.

First, God destroys the armies supernaturally, which does not happen in Revelation anywhere except at Armageddon. Second, the call to all the scavengers of the earth to gather for a feast matches the same call at the return of Jesus in Revelation 19:17-19. Third, God says that after this battle, He will not allow His holy name to be profaned; if the Antichrist were not killed in this battle, then at least one individual would still be blaspheming God. Fourth, verse eight suggests that this is THE ultimate day of retribution for the enemies of God. Finally, the end result is that the whole world will know that God is in Israel.

This final event does not happen until the return of Jesus.

SUMMARY

The first part is Gabriel's message about the "Seventy Weeks." This message gives the exact length of time from the first order by a Persian king that the Jews may return to Jerusalem to the beginning of Christ's ministry. After that, it tells us about the final seven years of this present age.

At the beginning of the final seven years, the contemptible king (the Antichrist) makes a seven-year peace pact. Half way through the covenant, he breaks his word and invades Israel, succeeding in capturing the temple and setting up the abomination of desolation. In Ezekiel and Revelation, we are informed that after Gog (the Antichrist) invades the unsuspecting Israel, the Lord causes a huge earthquake to stop his forces so most people in Israel can flee into the desert to escape him. At this point, God begins to pour devastating supernatural plagues upon the Antichrist and his empire.

The second part in this chapter traces the history of the Grecian Empire, focusing on the Syrian (kings of the North) and Egyptian (kings of the South) divisions. The history consists primarily of a series of wars over the disputed area of Palestine, and culminates in the rise a contemptible king in the Syrian Division. Antiochus Epiphanes performed a few of the acts attributed to the contemptible king, but from verse thirty-six on, they apply only to the Antichrist.

This prophecy identifies that the final king of the North will be the Antichrist, and since the king of the North uniformly represents the ruler in the Syrian division of the Grecian Empire, the Antichrist must arise in the modern equivalent of the Syrian or Persian portion of Alexander's kingdom. In the previous chapter we discovered that the Antichrist also rises out of the area occupied by the Old Roman Empire, so we can conclude that the Antichrist's kingdom, which we shall call New Syria, will consist of modern Syria with enough of Iraq to include the city of Babylon.

Among the many evil actions the Antichrist will take, several stand out. He will exalt himself above all gods. He will gain control of Jerusalem and pitch his royal tent there. He will set up an abomination that causes desolation in the temple. He will attack and conquer Egypt (and many other countries). He will not conquer Jordan. Reports from the North and East will anger him, and he will go out and annihilate the subject or source of those reports.

At the time of the destruction of the Antichrist, depicted in Ezekiel 39, Michael will once again rise to protect Israel, the saints of God will be delivered, and the dead will rise.

END TIMES PREDICTIONS BASED ON SECTION ONE

1) In the Middle East, in the area of the old Eastern Roman Empire, an Arab "league," or "confederacy" shall arise consisting of ten members, of which Egypt, Turkey, Greece, New Syria, and possibly Libya, Sudan, and Ethiopia will be members.

2) In the coming years Turkey will begin to take more of a leadership role in Middle Eastern affairs. Starting from within Turkey, a movement pushing for an Arab confederacy will arise (very likely to ensure that Arabs can solve their own problems without "western" influence), and the capitol of the confederacy will most likely be in the modern city of Istanbul.

3) Iraq will cease to exist as an independent country, and will partially (at least up to the city of Babylon) be absorbed by Syria, with the other half most likely absorbed by Iran.

4) Almost all future peace negotiations will center on getting a treaty between Israel and Syria. After the formation of the confederacy, New Syria, the most powerful member of the confederacy, will make a seven-year peace treaty with Israel, which will be hailed as a sign of a new age of peace in the Middle East and around the globe.

5) Someone will come to power in Syria who is not directly in line for the throne.

6) The cry in the Middle East to get westerners out of "Arab" affairs will increase, the United States will get its hand bit a few times, and will eventually pullout (or be thrown out) of the region almost completely.

7) Some type of league or confederacy will form in the Middle East (what we call the Mediterranean Confederacy of Ten Kingdoms), for the purpose of bringing economic, political, and military stability to the region. It will do exactly the opposite, as the member countries squabble among themselves.

8) After signing a peace agreement with Israel, to ensure that they will stay out of the fight, New Syria will launch its bid to overthrow the confederacy, and war will once again erupt in the Middle East.

9) The war will rage for roughly three and a half years, after which, because most of the confederacy surrenders voluntarily, the leader of New Syria will allow the confederacy to continue, with one major change: they are no longer ten kings over ten independent countries, but ten regional governors over ten "states" in New Syria's empire.

10) The King in Jordan will probably continue much as he is today: never for sale, but always for lease. For the first three and a half years he will verbally throw in with New Syria, and thus the contemptible king will have no reason to attack him.

11) Upon having established the first true empire in the region since the fall of the ottoman Turks, the new and improved Grecian Empire will suddenly invade Israel, catching them completely off guard.

12) The king in Jordan will become sickened by the slaughter of the Jews at the Antichrist's hands, and

having his heart softened by God, will open his borders to the fleeing Israelites.

13) Before the Antichrist can seriously contemplate invading Jordan to get the Jews and punish that turncoat on the Jordanian throne (the Antichrist's lease ran out), a major revolution in some northern and eastern independent Muslim republics (no longer a part of the USSR) will catch his attention. This rebellion by the "stans" (Turkmenistan, Uzbekistan, Afghanistan, Pakistan, Tajikistan) will primarily be against the religious rule of the Antichrist, sparked by the regional destruction of Islam within his empire (this will be discussed in detail later).

14) The revolution will spread enough to begin to threaten the political and military stability of the brand new "Grecian Empire." Having "just" finished stabilizing his kingdom, the Antichrist is not about to let anyone waver now, and will charge forth in a fury to stomp this new threat to his rule.

15) After beating the revolutionaries, the Antichrist will return to Israel where he will be destroyed.

16) At the time of the destruction of the Antichrist, when the Lord splits the skies, the dead shall be raised, which Paul says must happen BEFORE the living saints are raptured: so the rapture shall take place at the time of Christ's Second Coming.

QUESTIONS FROM CHAPTER FOUR

1) What is the purpose of the seventy weeks?
2) How many of the seventy weeks have already transpired?
3) What natural catastrophe does God cause at the first invasion of the Antichrist midway through the tribulation?
4) What country does the "king of the north" rule?
5) What country does the "king of the south" rule?
6) Who is the last "king of the north?"
7) From what country shall the Antichrist originate?
8) How do we know the section about the kings of the north and south is not symbolic?
9) Are the saints delivered and the dead raised before, at the time of, or after the destruction of the Antichrist?
10) How do we know that at least ONE of the things attributed to Antiochus IV Epiphanes will also be accomplished by the Antichrist?
11) When are the saints delivered, and the dead raised from the grave?
12) What means does God use to destroy the Antichrist's troops at Armageddon?
13) How do we know that the invasions described in Ezekiel 38 and 39 are the first and second invasions of the Antichrist into Israel during the middle and at the end of his seven year peace pact with Israel, rather than unrelated invasions by some other country (like Russia)?

THE SEVEN HEADED LEOPARD WITH TEN HORNS, AND THE TWO-HORNED LAMB BEAST
Introduction to the Players

THE PLOT THICKENS

Now that we have identified the country from which the Antichrist will arise (New Syria), it is time to move to our main goal: identify Babylon the Great, the Mother of Harlots in Revelation, chapter seventeen. The trail that will lead us to the identity of this mysterious woman started in Daniel, with the pinpointing of New Syria. From Daniel it jumps to Revelation, chapter thirteen, where it continues with three new beasts, a dragon, a lamb, and a leopard-like beast. Let us start with the dragon and the leopard.

SEVEN HEADED BEAST

"And I saw a beast coming out of the sea. He had ten horns and seven heads, with ten crowns on his horns, and on each head a blasphemous name. The beast I saw resembled a leopard, but had feet like a bear and a mouth like that of a lion. The dragon gave the beast his power and his throne and great authority. One of the heads of the beast seemed to have a fatal wound, but the fatal wound was healed. The whole world was astonished and followed the beast. Men worshipped the dragon because he had given authority to the beast, and they also worshipped the beast and asked, 'Who is like the beast? Who can make war against him?

"The beast was given a mouth to utter proud words and blasphemies and to exercise his authority for forty-two months. He opened his mouth to blaspheme God, and to slander his name and his dwelling place and those who live

in heaven. He was given power to make war against the saints and to conquer them. And he was given authority over every tribe, people, language and nation. All inhabitants of the earth will worship the beast--all whose names have not been written in the book of life belonging to the lamb that was slain from the creation of the world.

"He who has an ear, let him hear.

"If anyone leads into captivity, into captivity he will go. If anyone kills with the sword, with the sword he will be killed.

"This calls for patient endurance and faithfulness on the part of the saints." (Revelation 13:2-10)

RECAP

John sees a beast rise out of the sea. The beast has ten horns, each with a crown, and seven heads, each with a blasphemous name written on it. He says the beast resembles a leopard with bear's feet and lion's mouths. Another beast, called the dragon, gives the beast his power, throne, and great authority. One head seems to have a fatal wound, but the wound heals, which amazes the whole world. Many men then worship both the dragon and the beast. People exclaim that no one is like the beast because they say that no one can make war against him.

The beast speaks blaspheme, and exercises his authority for forty-two months (three and a half years). He wages a successful war against the saints, and receives authority over the world. Everyone in the world not a believer in Christ worships the beast.

There is a warning based on reaping what you sow, and the final sentence tells us that this calls for patience and faith by the saints.

THE LEOPARD BEAST

The first beast in this section has ten horns, each with a crown, seven heads, each with a blasphemous name, and it primarily resembles a leopard, although its feet are those of a bear and its mouth is that of a lion. Unfortunately God does not interpret any of this at this point, but there are some things we can glean based on what we already know.

We know from Daniel that beasts represent earthly empires, and there are several similarities between the beasts in Daniel's visions and this beast. In Daniel's dream of four beasts, he saw the beasts rise out of a sea; this beast rises out of a sea. The first beast Daniel saw was a lion; this beast has a lion's mouth. The second beast was a bear; this beast has a bear's feet. The third beast was a leopard; this beast primarily resembles a leopard. The fourth beast had ten horns; this beast has ten horns. (Daniel 7:2-7).

There are also some important differences: this leopard beast has seven heads (the leopard in Daniel has four heads), each of these heads has a blasphemous name, one head somehow recovers from a fatal wound, each horn on this beast has a crown, and in Daniel it was the little horn who spoke blasphemes while here is the beast itself who does the speaking.

In Daniel the ten horns represented ten kings who would all rule simultaneously in the Mediterranean Confederacy of Ten Kingdoms. The most logical conclusion would be that the ten horns represent the same thing here, since the crowns upon each horn signify that each is a king. If the ten horns are the Mediterranean Confederacy of Ten Kingdoms, it would only seem logical that this beast must ultimately represent the same thing as the ten horned beast in Daniel: the Old Roman Empire, the Mediterranean Confederacy of Ten Kingdoms, and the Antichrist's Kingdom.

A key element is missing here though: where is the little horn that rose up among the ten and spoke blasphemes against the Ancient of Days? While there is no little horn in this vision, there are some similarities between this WHOLE beast and the little horn in Daniel: this beast speaks blasphemes against God, makes war on the saints, and rules for three and a half years, just as the little horn did in Daniel. (Daniel 7:24-25). However, this beast also has body parts that point to the first three beasts just as much as the fourth.

This beast has the mouth of a lion, and we know from Daniel that the lion is Babylon. It also has the feet of a bear, Medio-Persia, and John says it resembled a leopard, which was the Grecian Empire. So which is it? Does this beast represent Babylon, Medio-Persia, Grecia, Old Rome, the Mediterranean Confederacy of Ten Kingdoms, or the Antichrist's Kingdom? There is another possibility: It could represent ALL SIX (like the multi-metallic statue from Nebuchadnezzar's dream). Clearly, if this beast somehow represents ALL six empires, it is NOT the same as the fourth beast in Daniel (which represented only three of six).

Before we can be sure though, we must find out what the SEVEN heads represent. There is no parallel in Daniel for the seven heads on this beast. In Daniel, multiple heads represented divisions within an empire (the four-headed leopard), but none of the empires had seven divisions, and there have been no indications that the Mediterranean Confederacy of Ten Kingdoms or the Antichrist's Kingdom would have an additional seven divisions. Until we receive more information, we can only guess that the symbols on this beast represent the same things they did in Daniel, and the seven heads must remain a mystery.

One head on the beast had a fatal wound. It is not mentioned which head had the wound, nor does the Lord tell us who wounded the head. What the Lord does mention is that someone or something heals the wound, which seems to astonish the whole world, causing them to follow the beast. What is the nature of the wound? We don't know yet.

THE DRAGON

The other beast mentioned in this section, a dragon, lacks a parallel in Daniel. Fortunately God explains the dragon in the previous chapter.

> "*Then another sign appeared in heaven: an enormous red dragon with seven heads and ten horns and seven crowns on his heads . . . the dragon was hurled down--that ancient serpent called the devil, or Satan, who leads the whole world astray.*" (Revelation 12:3,9).

The dragon represents Satan, and since the beast gets his power, authority, and throne from the dragon, the empire or empires represented by the leopard beast are clearly NOT godly kingdoms. In Daniel, we discovered that satanic or angelic princes control earthly kingdoms, so this implies that Satan himself controls the kingdom or kingdoms represented by the leopard beast.

Notice that the dragon, like the leopard beast, has seven heads and ten horns. We know the dragon represents Satan while the leopard beast is an earthly empire (or some combination of earthly empires), so what is the significance of the similarities between the two? Since the answer rests on the true meaning of all the symbols on the leopard beast, we don't have enough information for a sure evaluation yet.

THE WHOLE EARTH

John states that every inhabitant of the earth whose name has not been written in the lamb's book of life will worship the dragon and the leopard beast. As mentioned earlier, this does not mean every person on the planet, it means every person within the area controlled by the Antichrist; otherwise called the whole "biblical" earth (from the western edge of the Mediterranean to India, and from central Europe to the Sahara in Africa).

Whatever this beast represents, all people within the biblical earth recognize and worship the beast as some sort of god, and because of the beast, everyone worships Satan. In line with this satanic worship, the beast blasphemes God, and slanders His name, Heaven, and the inhabitants of Heaven.

The beast is given the authority, for three and a half years, to conquer every kingdom of the biblical earth, including the saints of God. This beast attacks everything that is a part of or has a connection to God. He verbally attacks God and those in Heaven, and he physically attacks the saints on the Earth.

In spite of this assault against God and the saints, the Lord admonishes us to patience and faith because, "*if anyone leads into captivity, into captivity he will go. If anyone kills with the sword, with the sword he will be killed.*" (Revelation 13:9). In other words, you reap what you sow, and this beast will get his in the end.

Even if we don't know the exact interpretation of the seven heads, the actions of this beast are starting to sound very familiar. There is only one person described in any book in scripture who dares to do the things attributed to this beast: the Antichrist. This would fit with the beast primarily resembling a leopard (in Daniel the leopard stands for the Grecian Empire, which we discovered the spirit behind the Antichrist will desire to bring back to life). In much the same way that the whole multi-metallic statue in Daniel represented the Antichrist while the individual parts symbolized the other kingdoms, the parts on this beast seem to represent previous kingdoms while the whole beast is the Antichrist himself. The information in the seventeenth chapter of Revelation will clarify all of this.

SYNOPSIS

The leopard beast seems to represent at least the Antichrist's kingdom, and possibly all the empires before him (this uncertainty clears up in chapter seventeen of Revelation). The dragon symbolizes Satan, who gives the beast his throne, including all the power and authority that comes with it. The beast receives authority over the whole biblical world, including the saints, for three and a half years, and all the people under his control worship him and the dragon.

THE TWO HORNED LAMB

John saw another beast after this one:

> "*Then I saw another beast, coming out of the earth. He had two horns like a lamb, but he spoke like a dragon. He exercised all the authority of the first beast on his behalf, and made the earth and its inhabitants worship the first beast, whose fatal wound had been healed. And he*

performed great and miraculous signs, even causing fire to come down from heaven to earth in full view of men. Because of the signs he was given power to do on behalf of the first beast, he deceived the inhabitants of the earth. He ordered them to set up an image in honor of the beast who was wounded with the sword and yet lived. He was given power to give breath to the image of the first beast, so that it could speak and cause all who refused to worship the image to be killed. He also forced everyone, small and great, rich and poor, free and slave, to receive a mark on his right hand or his forehead, so that no one could buy or sell unless he had the mark, which is the name of the beast or the number of his name.

"This calls for wisdom. If anyone has insight, let him calculate the number of the beast, for it is a man's number. His number is 666." (Revelation 13:11-18).

RECAP

A two-horned lamb beast, which speaks like a dragon, rises out of the earth. This beast exercises the authority of the leopard beast on his behalf, with the ultimate goal of causing the whole earth to worship the leopard beast. The lamb does miracles to validate the claims of the leopard beast, including causing an image of the leopard beast to speak. He makes everyone take the name or number of the beast on his right hand or forehead. The number is 666.

OUT OF THE EARTH

We know when a beast rises out of the sea, it means the empire symbolized by the beast rises out of the violent interactions of mankind. So what does it mean when a beast rises out of the earth? It means roughly the same thing as the sea (both symbolize mankind), where the sea symbol places more emphasis on the strife and violence of mankind, and the earth symbol, places more emphasis on mankind as opposed to God (in other words, if it rises out of the earth, it is NOT of divine origin). In Daniel, for example, he sees the four beasts rising out of the sea, yet later Gabriel says the four beasts are four kingdoms that will come out of the Earth (to emphasize that they are not from God, Daniel 7:17). So both symbols focus on mankind, with "the sea" emphasizing strife and violence while "the earth" stresses separation from God.

The reason for the earth symbol with this beast and the sea symbol with the first beast is to emphasize that the first beast arises from the violent interactions between the nations, while second, although still rising up from mankind, does not arise from conquering another kingdom. Rising from the earth emphasizes that, despite an appearance as a lamb, this new kingdom is NOT from God; it is from mankind.

SHEEP'S CLOTHING

This beast looks like a lamb with two horns (many types of sheep actually do have horns). Unlike a bear, lion, or leopard, a lamb is a common symbol in the Bible. It symbolizes holiness, innocence, and purity, and it is the most widespread symbol of Jesus (particularly in Revelation) in the Scriptures. The representation of this empire looks like a lamb. It is an empire of holiness, purity, and cleanliness. At least, on the outside.

Although the beast looked like a lamb, it spoke like a dragon. An empire with the outward appearance of holiness and purity, but with the words and actions of Satan. To the entire world this beast appears to be holy and righteous, but underneath the veneer of godliness lies a heart sold out to Satan.

We know from Daniel that the Antichrist will subdue the Mediterranean Confederacy of Ten Kingdoms, but will allow it to continue after he takes control. Since the Antichrist allows the leaders of the ten confederate kingdoms to continue ruling their individual countries after he becomes the supreme ruler, both empires can be said to exist simultaneously. Though one controls the other, there are still TWO empires at the return of our Lord.

Two, not three.

In Nebuchadnezzar's dream both empires stand together in the forms of the feet (where the Rock strikes) and the whole statue. In Daniel's dream of four beasts we see the two simultaneous empires as the ten horns and the little horn on the fourth beast. If the whole leopard beast in chapter thirteen of Revelation represents the Antichrist, as seems evident from his actions, the Lord again illustrates both kingdoms with the ten horns on the beast's head, and the whole beast. So why is there another beast in this vision? We have already accounted for both empires, and no other vision depicts THREE simultaneous empires in the end times. What third empire could the lamb beast represent that will rule concurrently with the Antichrist and the Mediterranean Confederacy of Ten Kingdoms, while slipping past earlier visions without leaving the slightest hint of its existence?

That a third empire in the end times could completely side step the book of Daniel seems extremely unlikely. Another explanation comes to mind: the lamb beast represents the same thing as the leopard beast, just from a slightly different perspective. Unfortunately, this explanation does not stand up either, since the lamb beast does his evil miracles for the leopard beast, NOT for himself (showing the two must be separate). So as unlikely as it may initially seem, the evidence that the lamb beast is a third empire, or more specifically, the leader of a third empire, which somehow slipped past all previous visions, is mounting.

Our struggle to uncover the meaning of the lamb beast starts with several very large obstacles. God does not interpret this section. This beast does not appear anywhere else in the Bible. No other vision depicts three concurrent empires in the last days. The empire represented by the lamb does not arise from conquering another empire, it seems to spring from nowhere. The Antichrist does not forcibly subdue this empire (as he does with the Mediterranean Confederacy of Ten Kingdoms), but it voluntarily submits itself to the leopard beast, and actively seeks to promote the Antichrist. Unfortunately, it seems we must interpret this lamb beast strictly from the information in this section.

WHO IS THE LAMB BEAST?

Let us review the basics, so we have a place to start.

A beast represents an empire, or more specifically, it represents the leader of that empire. The primary attributes and actions of a beast frequently trace back to one or two kings within the empire (the lion in Daniel primarily depicted Nebuchadnezzar, not Nabonidus or Belshazzar, and the conquests of the Medio-Persian Empire, depicted by the three ribs in the mouth of the bear, illustrate the actions of only two of the eleven kings).

Horns on the head represent divisions within the empire, and any changes on the head depict structural changes within the empire. In the vision of the ram and goat, the single large horn on the goat represented Alexander the Great, and when it broke off, and was replaced by four horns, it represented the dividing of the empire into four divisions. In the vision of the four beasts, when the little horn uprooted three of the original ten horns on the fourth creature, it represented one new leader conquering three countries, and gaining control of the entire empire.

Finally, a beast can depict MORE than one empire. The fourth beast in Daniel represents three (the entire beast is the Old Roman Empire, the ten horns are the Mediterranean Confederacy of Ten Kingdoms, and the little horn depicts the rise of the Antichrist as he conquers the Confederacy and establishes his own empire). As we have discussed above, the leopard beast here may include them all.

Now what do we know about the lamb beast?

This beast looks like a lamb, but does not talk or act like one. It talks and acts like Satan. As previously mentioned, a lamb is a very common symbol with a very specific meaning in Scripture, which makes it a very peculiar symbol to use for an empire. The Lord uses it exclusively as a spiritual or religious symbol, which has nothing to do with the governmental, military, economic, or political state of a kingdom. The lamb symbol (with the dragon's voice) means that the kingdom, and thus the leader, has the appearance of RELIGIOUS purity or holiness, but by God's standards is spiritually evil and corrupt.

A religious symbol for an empire? What kind of strange empire would be represented by a religious symbol? The use of a religious symbol seems to imply that this is not a normal empire, but a "religious empire," or more specifically, a religion (with a front of holiness, but really filled with evil) that is also an empire.

So based on the symbols, our first few deductions about the lamb beast are:

It is a lamb – *it is a religion, it presents itself as holy and pure, and that means it has a set of moral codes; definite ideas as to right and wrong.*

It is a beast – *although it is a religion, it is also an empire.*

It speaks like a dragon – *despite the holy appearance, it is Satanic in nature, and thus, although it recognizes the existence of right and wrong, it is evil and corrupt by God's standards.*

This "religious empire" has two primary divisions, shown by the two horns, and those divisions have existed almost from the very beginning with no significant changes. A lamb, representing a religion that is an empire, with two major divisions, controlled by Satan. This sounds like a perfect mirror of Christianity (Jesus is our Lamb, there are two major groups within Christianity: the Catholics and the Protestants, and the Lord teaches us that Christianity is the KINGDOM of God inside us). The problem, of course, is that the two primary divisions within Christianity are not stable, and have not existed since the beginning. Catholicism arose starting in about the sixth century. Protestantism arose almost a thousand years later, [51] and steadily grew

---

[51] Although the argument can be made that the protestant movement is a return to the original beliefs and doctrines of Christianity, the fact still remains that the position it represents declined in influence, then increased again, which would not be illustrated by two stable and unchanging divisions.

in influence and numbers for several hundred years. That does not fit a religious empire that has not experienced any significant changes within its two divisions. So now we add the following to our deductions:

Two unchanging horns – *it has two relatively stable and unchanging divisions within it.*

Despite the division issue, it does sound like the leader depicted by this lamb beast is trying to portray himself as a type of imitation Christ and that his religion is at least somewhat a mimicry of Christianity. Just as Christ and the prophets point us to the Father, this beast points everyone to the Antichrist. Jesus voluntarily submitted Himself under the Father, and this lamb beast voluntarily submits to the Antichrist. Jesus said He received His power and authority from the Father, while this beast receives his from the Antichrist. The miracles of Jesus demonstrated the power of God, and this beast performs miracles to prove the power of the Antichrist. The ultimate miracle was when Jesus, having been dead for three days, raised Himself from the dead, and this beast SEEMS to give the power of life to a "dead" statue. To gain eternal life, we must repent, submit to Jesus our Lord, and let Him cleanse our spirits with His (Paul calls this "circumcision of the heart," which is a type of "spiritual mark"). This beast requires everyone to receive a physical mark to buy or sell, which is vital to physical life in today's world. The parallels between Christ and this beast are phenomenal, but it is important to note that they point in opposite directions. This lamb beast points to Satan, while Christ points to God.

Just as with this beast, everything about the Antichrist is the opposite of Christ. Christ came from above (John 6:38), while the beast who represents the spirit behind the Antichrist ascends from the pit (Revelation 11:7). Christ came in His Father's name (John 5:43), while the Antichrist comes in his own name (John 5:43). Christ humbled Himself (Philippians 2:8), while the Antichrist exalts himself (2 Thessalonians 2:4). Christ came to do His Father's will (John 6:38), while the Antichrist came to do his own will (Daniel 11:36). Christ came to save (Luke 19:10), while the Antichrist came to destroy (Daniel 8:24). Christ is the True Vine (John 15:1), while the Antichrist is the Vine of the Earth (Revelation 14:18). Christ is the Truth (John 14:6), while the Antichrist is the lie (2 Thessalonians 2:11). Christ is the Holy One (Mark 1:24), while the Antichrist is the lawless one (2

Thessalonians 2:8). Christ is the Son of God (Luke 1:35), while the Antichrist is the son of destruction (2 Thessalonians 2:3).[52]

Based on this information, we now know the following:

Glorifies the Leopard Beast – *this religion is a satanic imitation, as a complete negative or polar opposite, of Christianity*

THE IMAGE OF THE BEAST

The lamb beast orders his followers to build a statue of the leopard beast, and later we find that the followers are forced to worship this statue (he caused "*...all who refused to worship the image to be killed.*" Revelation 13:15). The stipulation that all people must "worship or die" leads to another deduction:

Worship the Statue or Die – *this religion is exclusive (presents itself as the only truth), and is extremely intolerant of other religions, and of those who wish to practice other faiths.*

At first glance this would appear to be typical, run of the mill idolatry (by definition, worshipping a statue is idolatry) much like that constantly encountered and condemned in the Bible. This is, in fact, reminiscent of what happened with Shadrach, Meshach and Abednego when they refused to worship a statue of Nebuchadnezzar and were thrown in a fiery furnace. Then later, during the Medio-Persian Empire, Daniel refused to worship the king and ended up thrown into the lions' den. But the lamb beast, through his miracles, tries to convince his followers that this is not idolatry because they are worshipping a true god (and worship of a true god is not idolatry).

There are three very significant miraculous events that will allow the lamb beast to fool his followers into believing this is not really idolatry: this statue appears to have **BREATH**, it **SPEAKS** and finally, it also **PASSES JUDGEMENT** (which will cause people to fear it) on those who refuse to worship it. These are three fundamental points that are mentioned in the Old Testament showing why we should NOT follow idols.

---

[52] This list is taken from a longer list compiled by Clarence Larkin in his book, "Dispensational Truth," page 116.

Everyone is stupid and ignorant. Every goldsmith is put to shame by his carved image, for his cast images are a lie; **there is no breath in them**. (Jeremiah 10:14)

"What profit is the idol when its maker has carved it, or an image, a teacher of falsehood? For its maker trusts in his own handiwork **when he fashions speechless idols**. *Woe to him who says to a piece of wood, 'Awake!' To a* **mute stone**, *'Arise!' And that is your teacher? Behold, it is overlaid with gold and silver, and* **there is no breath at all inside it**. (Habakuk 2:18-19)

For the customs of the people are foolishness; the idol is wood cut from the forest that is worked by the hands of a craftsman with a cutting tool. They cover it with silver and gold. They fasten it up with hammer and nails so that it will not fall over. It is like a scarecrow in a field, for **it cannot speak**! *It must be carried, because it cannot walk!* **Do not fear it, for it can do neither harm nor good to you**. (Jeremiah 10:3-5)[53]

There are several key things happening here. First, because the statue "appears" to have breath, can speak, and can even pass judgment on those who disobey it, the lamb beast can deceive his followers into believing this is NOT a true idol. Idols don't speak, they don't breathe and you certainly don't have to fear them. These particular miracles are so specifically designed to "fix" the "shortcomings" of idols that it is very likely this religion actually HAS a "no idol" command, and the Lamb Beast is thwarting or modifying it with these "supernatural signs."

Second, giving the statue life adds a key element of the "god mythos" to the claims of the lamb beast, and a considerable degree of authority to his demands that people worship the leopard beast, and his image, as though they are gods. Only GOD can "create life" from non-living matter. As far as anyone can tell, this statue, made of metal and stone, will come to life.

---

[53] Some have claimed this passage is a reference to Christmas trees (wood cut from a forest, and decorated with silver and gold). The bottom line is that this is a condemnation of idols, so if you worship your Christmas tree as an idol, believing that it can do you good or harm, then this does apply to you. If you do not worship it, then this passage does not apply to you.

Make no mistake, this is an illusion. It will probably rank as one of the all time most amazing deceptions in human history, but a deception it will be. The statue does not literally come alive, nor does it actually breathe. The lamb beast sends a demonic spirit into the statue to manipulate it and produce the voice.

There have been a number of leaders down through the years that have made claims to divinity without needing to resort to miracles and supernatural signs to prove those claims. From Nebuchadnezzar to the Roman Caesars, and as recently as the Japanese Emperor, divinity claims by tyrants have gone largely unchallenged (with the sole exception of Jews and Christians, who were usually killed due to their objections). The reason this happens so easily and so often is that some religions are tailor made for this kind of doctrine, meaning those leaders who make that claim don't have to do much to "prove" their divinity beyond threatening to kill anyone who disagrees. The very fact that the Lamb Beast goes to such extreme measures by performing these very specific "divine" miracles (statue breathes and talks, fire is called down from heaven) seems to indicate that this particular religion is NOT necessarily constructed so that divinity claims are readily or easily accepted. It appears that the divinity claims might actually need to be PROVEN in order for the followers to accept that the Leopard Beast is a god. And even then, there will apparently STILL be those who refuse to accept, and will need to be eliminated.

That leads us to the possibility that the religion of the people within the area of the Leopard Beast might **not** be constructed so that divinity claims are easily accepted. The initial doctrines of the religion might need to be modified, or it is possible the religion contains specific criteria that need to be met in order for the claims to be accepted. Either way, no one will have a means of refuting the kinds of miracles the Lamb Beast uses to prove his claims, and once the most vocal holdouts are killed, there won't be much reason or motivation for the vast majority of the populace to reject the idea that the Leopard Beast is a god. All of this leads to two crucial deductions about the lamb beast religion:

Performs Miracles – *this religion accepts the existence of miracles.*

Lamb Beast "Proves" Divinity of First Beast – *the theology of this religion is structured so that claims of divinity need to be proven and are not easily accepted by many followers.*

At first glance, it might seem unlikely that modern audiences would be very impressed with such a deception. After all, a few well placed speakers would accomplish the same thing. Most of us have probably seen this exact scenario in movies where slick westerners fool those gullible natives by using amplifiers and speakers to make their idols talk (and say what the westerners want them to say). We are used to special effects, to voices seemingly coming from out of thin air, and to amazing scientific accomplishments that at times seem to border on magic. A modern audience would never be fooled by such a charade, right?

Possibly, but consider the following. First, the lamb beast doesn't make the statue; he compels the people to make it, then he appears to bring their craftsmanship to life. They will KNOW that there was nothing special about that statue because they built it.

Second, it not only has a voice, it has BREATH! It is not just talking, it genuinely appears to be alive. There is no reason that the demonic spirits cannot actually cause the face to move as it speaks, and its chest to move as it breathes. Since this is a "miracle" generated by spiritual beings, there will be no scientific way to discredit it. It will truly appear that the lamb beast made the statue come alive.

The final straw will be when the statue orders the death of each and every person who is NOT fooled or who refuses to bow down. The terror generated by this type of tactic is very well known and understood by those who would crave supreme, absolute power, which can only be maintained through tyranny. Those who use power to oppress know that for many of the people under their thumbs, there is no more convincing argument than abject fear. You couple that fear with unexplainable miracles, and you have an "argument" that even modern audiences would find compelling.

In the end this "one-two" punch will be more than the average follower can resist, and the scriptures say that the Lamb Beast is successful in its plan, as it deceives the inhabitants of the earth. That means that this religion has a very large following throughout the "Biblical Earth," and is the dominant religion in the area where the antichrist will come to power. So this deduction is:

Deceives the Inhabitants of the Earth – *has a large following, and is the dominant religion where the antichrist comes to power.*

Finally, this lamb beast is not content to just force people to worship the beast, he also compels everyone, rich or poor, to receive a special mark on his left arm or forehead. The taking of the mark is enforced with a law that precludes someone from buying or selling if they do not have the mark. This mark is both public (economic control) and private (psychological control), and makes allegiance to the first beast a very easily identifiable thing, as well as extending the control of the beast into almost every aspect of the follower's life. Literally, if they do not have the mark, they cannot work at a job or buy food. Their very existence and survival now depend on their willingness to submit to the lamb beast. This is a legalism that is far beyond anything yet experienced by modern people. It is extreme, and all controlling, going well beyond mere "afterlife salvation," to dictating the criteria for physical survival. That leads us to our last two deductions:

Lamb Beast is Making all the Rules – *this religion must be structured so that one person could rule it as a type of "chief prophet" or "top religious leader."*

Forced Worship, Death Sentences, and the Mark – *this religion is extreme and legalistic in its control of every aspect, public and private, of a follower's life.*

EXAMINING THE DETAILS

In order to pinpoint the exact identity of the religion that is also an empire (which is what this lamb beast seems to represent), we must find one that fits the facts shown in this section. To summarize what we have deduced about the lamb beast religion, the passage describing the lamb beast shows us the following:

(1)   It is a type of religion.
(2)   It is also a type of empire.
(3)   It must have a definitive set of moral codes (it must recognize the existence of "right" and "wrong").
(4)   It must be exclusive (present itself as the ONLY truth).
(5)   It must be extremely intolerant of other religions, and of those who wish to practice other faiths.[54]
(6)   It must portray itself as very righteous and holy.

---

[54] The followers of religions that do not present themselves as the ONLY TRUTH and do not recognize the existence of an absolute RIGHT and WRONG, such as Buddhism, have no interest in threatening death on those who will not convert to their religion and worship their god. Buddhism, for instance, teaches that all religions have some measure of truth, and as such are compatible. It teaches that the existence of right and wrong is an illusion, and that ultimately, there is no god to worship (once you reach enlightenment, you realize that the existence of ANYTHING, including yourself and a god, is an illusion).

(7)   The fundamental teachings and primary behaviors (both as encouraged now and as exhibited by the founder) of this religion must reflect evil and corruption by God's standards (its idea of "good and bad" must be skewed from God's).

(8)   It must be so organized that one man could control the religion as a type of prophet.

(9)   The religion must have two stable divisions within it.

(10)   It should recognize and accept the existence of miracles.

(11)   It must have a very strong "Anti-Christ" teaching at its core.

(12)   It most likely will have a very large following (it deceives the inhabitants of the earth).

(13)   It must be the dominate religion in the area where the Antichrist will rule.

(14)   It is extreme and legalistic in its control of both the public and private behavior of a follower's life

(15)   Its theology is structured so that claims of divinity would need to be proven, and would not be easily accepted by many followers.

There is one major problem with identifying a religion by such criteria as "the evil done in its name." Do we judge a religion from the actions of the average follower, or from the "ideals" professed in whatever stands as its ultimate source of truth (the teachings of a holy book or founding prophet)? Anyone who has ever tried to explain that Christianity is not what "I" can do, but what Jesus has already done, and the teachings of Christianity are not what "I" exhibit, but what Scripture says, will know that a true presentation of any religion must be of the teachings at its source. Just as we would not want Christianity judged by our failings, weaknesses or sins, the actions of the followers of any religion are only relevant to a clear evaluation of that religion in areas where they are obviously in line with the teachings of that religion. Our guideline will be to look to the actions and teachings of the founder, including the fundamental teachings found within the "holy book" of the religion, and to only include the actions of the followers where they clearly line up with the teachings of the "supreme authority" within the religion (the teachings of the founder, the chief prophet, and/or the "holy book" of the religion).

THE ONES EVANGELICALS LOVE TO BLAME

As evangelicals ourselves, if there is finger-pointing here, it is back at our own (as a group). Some of us have jumped to the first and most obvious conclusion that this lamb beast must be Catholicism because, in comparing it to the criteria above, we get the following results:

(1) Catholicism is, in many ways, a separate religion from Protestants (their Bible is even different from ours).

(2) Catholicism seems like an empire (until recently, they had their own armies, and Vatican City is even a separate country from Italy).

(3) Catholicism has no lack of rules dictating what is right and wrong.

(4) Catholics believe they have the only Truth, and the official position is that you cannot have salvation if you are not a Catholic.

(5) As the Crusades and the Inquisition proved, Catholics have been extremely, even violently intolerant at various times in their history.

(6) The Catholic Church puts on a front of complete holiness, most of which is completely grounded in legalism and ritual.

(7) History has shown that corruption has frequently run rampant in the Vatican, and many of their central views are seriously skewed from God's (Paul condemns those who "forbid to marry," as Catholic Priests are; Jesus condemned those who made tradition equal with scripture, as the Catholics did in 1453 AD; etc.).

(8) Catholics believe that the Pope has the final word on ALL matters (the perfect pedestal for the Antichrist).

(9) There are two major divisions within the Catholic Church: Roman Catholics and Greek Orthodox Catholics. Those divisions have been relatively stable and unchanged for many centuries.

(10) It recognizes miracles (and uses them as a primary means of designating "saints").

(11) It has a long history of actions that are not even remotely Christ-like, and it has a strong "Anti-Protestant" tendency.

(12) It has a huge following (hundreds of millions).

(13) It seems to be everywhere in the whole world.

(14) Holiness in the Catholic Church is almost exclusively dictated by legalism: from the rituals performed each Sunday to which foods should be eaten on certain days of the week to such intimate dictates as forbidding

contraception, none of which have anything to do with true holiness.

(15) The office of the Pope is a perfect platform from which someone could be declared a god.

This seems like a formidable stack of evidence, but there are several HUGE problems with this theory.

The first is that we now know the area from which the Antichrist will come (New-Syria). How will the Antichrist use Catholicism to rise to power when there are virtually no Catholics in the entire middle-eastern region? In terms of population percentages, there are less than one tenth of one percent (0.1%) of the population in the region the Antichrist will arise that are Catholics. While it is theoretically possible that over the next fifty years or so, Catholicism will completely drive all Muslims out of Syria, Lebanon, and Iraq, it is incredibly unlikely. Islam moved in and conquered the region about thirteen hundred years ago. From that time on, it has not even come close to being pushed out.

There is a second problem. While it is true that the Catholics have been fairly intolerant in the past, that is highly unlikely to reappear in the future. They are extremely sensitive to criticism of their past excesses (even recently issuing an apology for the inquisition), and with international news like it is today, there is no way they could get away with returning to those old ways without the news of it getting out. It is so unlikely that they will suddenly start killing people who don't agree with them in the modern era of nearly instantaneous news that it is hardly worth considering.

The most important problem is that, no matter how many errors we can find in their theology, and no matter how often they have failed to exhibit Christ to the world, THEY ARE NOT ANTI-CHRIST (point number eleven: "the religion must have a very strong 'Anti-Christ' teaching at its core"). The most basic, fundamental belief of the Catholic Church is that Jesus is GOD! While they may have fought with the Protestants in the past over the role and identity of Mary (and many other issues), they have NEVER disputed the identity of Jesus Christ, and the Catholic Church will not dispute the fundamental doctrine that salvation is by grace through faith (although as Martin Luther discovered when he read Romans for the first time, and as the ingrained Catholic doctrine of penance proves, they do not understand nor practice the full depth and breadth of grace beyond a person's initial salvation).

Clearly the Catholic Church has many problems with their theology and doctrine. As Protestants, while we firmly disagree with many of their theological stands and regret that there are numerous fundamental scriptural truths they do not accept or understand, we also acknowledge that the identity of Jesus Christ is NOT one of them. They WORSHIP Jesus as Lord and God and THAT is the ultimate measure against which God judges all of Christianity! Jesus made His identity the fundamental core of His ministry and of Christianity when He said, "If you do not believe that I Am, you will die in your sins."[55]

No where in Scripture is a proper understanding of church authority (such as whether or not there is a biblical foundation for a lone human leader, the Pope, who speaks inerrantly for God to the church), the identity of Mary, clergy marriage, or any other doctrine where we clearly disagree with the Catholics, presented as a fundamental doctrine necessary for salvation. Paul handled the disputes between divisions within the Corinthian church by pointing each division back to looking at Jesus, not at the man preaching about Him (even tossing out such closely related doctrines as Baptism). He repeatedly came back to one central issue:

> *"For I resolved to know nothing while I was with you except Jesus Christ, and Him crucified."* (I Corinthians 2:2)

From a Protestant perspective, we feel like the Catholic Church has so completely clouded the salvation issue as to make it as difficult as possible for a sincere seeker within their church to become a true follower of Jesus Christ, but it is NOT impossible. And that is a vital and important point. Despite the claims of some of our Protestant brothers, just as it is possible to be a Baptist, or Lutheran, or Methodist, or be a member of any other Protestant church and NOT be a Christian, it is also possible to be a Catholic and STILL be a Christian.

The second problem is that Catholicism is not the primary religion in the area that will be ruled by the Antichrist (point number 13: "it must be the dominate religion in the area where the Antichrist will rule"). From the eastern edge of Greece across the Middle East to Pakistan, and south into Africa (including the entire Mediterranean coast of Africa) there are almost no Catholics (or Christians of any denomination). Except for southern Europe, there are almost no

---

[55] John 8:24. Some translation read "I am he," or "I am who I say I am," but the Greek says simply "ego eimi," without additional modifiers, which means "I am." This is one of three times in chapter eight of John that Jesus uses the title "I Am" as a direct reference to Exodus 3:14, and as such, is claiming to be God (verses 24, 28, and 58). But even without recognizing the reference back to Genesis, it is clear that Jesus is making His IDENTITY the central issue of gaining forgiveness of sins.

Christians (Catholics or Protestants) within the area occupied by the Old Roman and Old Grecian Empires.

So what religion fits ALL the criteria for the lamb beast? Rather than jumping to any conclusions at this point, let us wait until we get to the seventeenth chapter of Revelation, where the evidence will become overwhelming. At this point, we know the lamb beast represents a religious empire that will champion the Antichrist, and more specifically, a leader or king within that religious empire.

SATANIC MIRACLES

The lamb beast is given the power to exercise ALL the authority of the leopard beast on his behalf. The leopard beast originally received his authority from Satan, but he allows the lamb beast to put it to use. Why not just use the power himself, perform his own miracles, and proclaim himself a God from his own actions.

If one is claiming to be a god, what could possibly be more convincing than performing supernatural miracles? How about having another man who steps in as your "prophet," exhibits the same awesome powers, and testifies that he received those powers from you? Not only can you do mighty supernatural works yourself, but you also have the ability to give that power to another. Now THAT is a god!

John says the lamb beast "*performed great and miraculous signs, even causing fire to come down from heaven in full view of men.*" The "even" indicates the lamb did many other miraculous signs, among which was the one mentioned here. John specifically mentions "even fire from heaven" because, since the time of Elijah, people have viewed fire from the sky as the ultimate sign that the prophet in control received his power from God (Elijah and the priests of Baal, I Kings 18:18-40). When in competition directly against the TRUE God, Satan could never call fire down from heaven. In the end times, however, God will stand back and Satan will be allowed to use whatever supernatural power he has to the fullest.

As mentioned earlier, the lamb beast also has a statue constructed in honor of the leopard beast, and uses his power to make the statue breathe and talk. Anyone who refuses to worship the statue is executed. This miracle will make it APPEAR that the Antichrist has the power to give life to inanimate stone. [56] The power to create life is another great and miraculous sign that is possible only to the TRUE God.

---

[56] The NIV says, "*He was given power to give **breath** to the image of the first beast.*" Actually the Greek says he gives "a spirit" (pneuma) to the statue. Although usually translated "spirit," the root meaning of pneuma is "to breathe," and given the context, that is the most likely intention in this passage, but the statue does not actually come to

Although the statue will not actually come to life, there will need to be far more to this "miracle" than just a voice coming from a carved mouth. If that were all there was to this miracle, modern audiences would simply assume audio speakers had been placed inside the mouth. In addition to employing demons to speak out audibly from the mouth of the image, Satan will physically manipulate the stone so that the lips move and it's chest heaves (as though it were breathing). It may even blink, move its eyes, turn its head, and look around. In other words, the statue will need to seem like it has suddenly come "alive," not just produce sound. This supernatural show, as with everything else Satan ever undertakes, ultimately boils down to a high powered trick to deceive the nations. As shown in verse fourteen, these tricks are successful, and he deceives the inhabitants of the earth.

The final action undertaken by the lamb beast is to control and track the people under the leopard beast's authority through physically branding them (like cattle). The lamb beast requires each person, no matter their rank, to receive a mark on his right hand or (if he does not have a right hand) forehead. To enforce compliance, anyone who refuses branding cannot buy or sell goods.

This branding is as much a psychological tactic as an administrative one. By allowing oneself to be permanently marked with the Antichrist's symbol, there must be a mental acceptance of ownership. Each person must accept that they are now "owned" by the leopard beast. This tactic not only breaks the final flicker of rebellion (physical or psychological) against the Antichrist's rule, it provides a universal symbol (and reminder), worn upon each person's body, proclaiming who is in control. In middle-eastern cultures, if you take the mark of a leader upon your body, you have pledged your loyalty and allegiance to that person for life. To break that pledge meant instant death.

There are two forms of the mark: the name of the beast and the number of his name. John says that the calculation of the number of the beast requires wisdom and insight. Since true wisdom and insight can only come from the Holy Spirit, no amount of natural reasoning will solve the mystery of the number.

The name of the beast can only have a number attached to it in a language in which the alphabet also serves as the number system (such as Greek, Hebrew, or Arabic). In Greek, for example, each name can have only one number attached to it (in Greek, Jesus is Iesous. iota = 9, eta = 7, sigma = 90, omicron = 60, upsilon = 200, so the number of

---

life, nor does it literally breathe: while it may "appear" to be breathing, it is actually being manipulated by an evil spirit sent from Satan at the request of the lamb beast in order to deceive people into believing the statue has come to life.

Jesus is 9+7+90+60+200+90 which equals 456). In English our alphabet and numbers are separate, so attaching a number to a person's name is completely arbitrary.

John does NOT present this number as the key to identifying the Antichrist, especially since thousands, maybe millions of people's names could be made to calculate out to 666 through one method or another. Trying to identify the beast through a number derived from his name is futile. Fully understanding the meaning and implications behind the mark of the beast is a long, involved study, and would be a distraction from the purpose of this book. Since it will not add anything to our search for the identity of the lamb beast here, nor the identity of Mystery Babylon later, we will resist the temptation to explore it more fully, and move on.

In chapter nineteen, at Armageddon, John describes the fate of the leopard beast.

> *"And the beast was captured, and with him the false prophet who performed the miraculous signs on his behalf. With these signs he had deluded those who had received the mark of the beast and worshipped his image. The two of them were thrown alive into the fiery lake of burning sulfur."* (Revelation 19:20).

Notice that in chapter nineteen, John says it is the false prophet, who performs miracles on behalf of the leopard beast for the purpose of deceiving the nations, yet in chapter thirteen, John says it is the lamb beast who does this.

In the first appearance of the Dragon and the leopard beast, in Revelation chapter thirteen, their partner is the lamb beast. In the second description of the two (Revelation 16:13), the third companion is the false prophet. In chapter thirteen, the lamb beast performs miracles on behalf of the leopard beast to deceive the nations, yet in chapter nineteen, John says it is the false prophet who did those things. Since the lamb beast does not appear outside of chapter thirteen, while his actions do, and are attributed to the false prophet, there is only one conclusion possible: the lamb beast is the false prophet.

The title "False Prophet" fits the behavior of the lamb beast. The lamb beast represents a deceitful religious empire, who puts on a front of holiness, but whose heart is sold out to Satan. It does many miracles on behalf of the leopard beast. The lamb beast's purpose in life is to get the nations to worship and serve the leopard beast and the dragon by whatever means: deception if possible, economic pressure if that doesn't work, and even threat of death if necessary. This lamb beast is not "A false prophet," he is "THE False Prophet."

SUMMARY

There are three beasts in this section: a dragon, a leopard beast, and a lamb beast. God identifies the dragon in the previous chapter as Satan. There is not enough information in this chapter for a complete identification of the leopard beast (we must wait until we get to chapter seventeen of Revelation for that), but the leopard beast seems to represent at least the Antichrist's empire, and possibly all the previous empires as well.

The lamb beast, while not explicitly interpreted by John in this chapter, seems to represent the leader of a "religion that is also an empire." This interpretation is strongly supported by the description in Chapters sixteen and nineteen of the "false prophet," whose actions show that he is the leader symbolized by this lamb beast. The common theory that he is the leader of the Catholic Church is severely flawed, since the Catholic Church accepts Jesus as God. We will wait until chapter seventeen of Revelation to identify the religion.

The actions of both the leopard and the lamb beast will be reexamined from the new information provided in chapter seventeen of Revelation.

KEY POINTS TO REMEMBER

Keep in mind that one of the leopard's heads receives a fatal wound, only to recover; that the lamb beast represents a religion that is also an empire, or more accurately, it represents the leader of that religious empire; that the lamb beast has two horns; and that every action taken by the lamb beast (mostly supernatural actions) is for the glorification of the leopard beast.

QUESTIONS FROM CHAPTER FIVE

1) What does the dragon with seven heads and ten horns symbolize?

2) Although there is not enough information in this chapter for a complete evaluation, what does the leopard beast with seven heads and ten horns SEEM to symbolize?

3) What evidence do we have that the lamb beast with two horns represents a man who is a "leader" of a "religious empire?"

4) What twelve things must be true of the religion symbolized by the lamb beast?

5) Some have claimed the lamb beast must represent the Catholic Church. How do we know this cannot be true?

6) What "person" in Revelation is depicted doing what the lamb beast does?

7) Does the lamb beast "literally" give life to the image of the beast? What does the Bible literally say he does? What does this mean?

8) What is the meaning of the "sea" and the "earth" from which these beasts arose?

THE SEVEN HEADED LEOPARD WITH TEN HORNS:
Final Depiction of the Antichrist

The primary problem encountered in chapter thirteen of Revelation was that God did not interpret the leopard beast, which severely limited our investigation of the empire or empires it represents. Fortunately, this beast appears again in chapter seventeen of Revelation, and here, the Lord does interpret them for us. This time his companions are not a dragon and a lamb, but a woman with the *title "Mystery, Babylon the Great, the Mother of Harlots and of the Abominations of the Earth."* (Revelation 17:3-5).

God deals with the leopard beast and the woman simultaneously in chapter seventeen, but in order to understand them thoroughly, we will have to deal with each separately.

We will start with the leopard beast.

THE LEOPARD BEAST

> *"One of the seven angels who had the seven bowls came and said to me. 'Come, I will show you the punishment of the great harlot, who sits on many waters, with her the kings of the earth committed adultery and the inhabitants of the earth were intoxicated with the wine of her adulteries.*
>
> *"Then the angel carried me away in the Spirit into a desert. There I saw a woman sitting on a scarlet beast that was covered with blasphemous names and had seven heads and ten horns."* (Revelation 17:1-3).

This is the seven-headed, ten-horned leopard beast that received his power from the dragon. Notice that we now have a little more information, most notably, a harlot sits astride the beast. After describing the woman's appearance, John tells us that the angel interpreted the beast.

"I will explain to you the mystery of the woman and of the beast she rides, which has the seven heads and ten horns. The beast, which you saw, once was, now is not, and will come up out of the Abyss and go to his destruction. The inhabitants of the earth whose names have not been written in the book of life from the creation of the world will be astonished when they see the beast, because he once was, now is not, and yet will come.

"This calls for a mind with wisdom. The seven heads are seven mountains on which the woman sits. They are also seven kings. Five have fallen, one is, the other has not yet come; but when he does come, he must remain for a little while. The beast who once was, and now is not, is an eighth king. He is out of the seven and is going to his destruction.

"The ten horns you saw are ten kings who have not yet received a kingdom, but who for one hour will receive authority as kings along with the beast. They have one purpose and will give their power and authority to the beast. They will make war against the Lamb, but the Lamb will overcome them because He is the Lord of lords and the King of kings - and with Him will be His called, chosen, and faithful followers.

"Then the angel said to me, "The waters you saw, where the harlot sits, are peoples, multitudes, nations and languages." (Revelation 17: 7b-15)

RECAP

The beast "once was, is not, and yet will come." (Revelation 17:8b). The seven heads are seven mountains[57] and seven kings. Five have fallen, one is, and one is yet to come. The whole beast is the eighth king. The ten horns are ten kings who have not yet received a kingdom, but will with the beast for a short time. The waters upon which the woman sits are all the people of the biblical earth.

---

[57] For the Greek word sometimes translated "hills" in verse nine ("oros"), most scholars prefer "mountains." While it can occasionally be translated "hill," the primary meaning is of a "tower of earth," or what we usually call a mountain. Since there is a separate word for hill ("bounos"), but "oros" is the only Greek word that means "mountain," verse nine should be properly translated, as most translations do, "the seven heads are seven mountains."

THE WATERS

Just as in Daniel, waters or seas represent humanity. In chapter thirteen John said that the leopard came out of the sea, and here he says the woman who is sitting on the beast is ALSO sitting on many waters (verse 1). This suggests the empire or empires represented by the leopard beast consists of "*peoples, multitudes, nations, and languages*" (Revelation 17:15); they are not "spiritual" kingdoms, but literal earthly kingdoms made up of people from a variety of nationalities, ethnic backgrounds, regional cultures, and countries, with different languages and dialects. Not just a country with one culture, but empires ruling over many differing nationalities.

The big question that we could not answer in our last chapter is: do the symbols on the leopard beast represent one empire, as most of the beasts in Daniel did, or do they represent many empires, as the multi-metallic statue did?

SEVEN HEADS

In Daniel, multiple heads on a beast represented the multiple kings within an empire when it split into smaller divisions. John says the seven heads are seven kings. So we now know that "heads" in Revelation represent the same basic thing as "heads" in Daniel: kings, and through them, kingdoms. But do the seven heads on the leopard beast also represent divisions within one original empire, as they did in Daniel, or do they now represent separate, independent empires, akin to the sections on the multi-metallic image? Are the "kings" symbolized by the seven heads ruling "full empires," or divisions of an empire?

John also says that the seven heads are seven mountains. From Daniel we know that mountains represent kingdoms or empires,[58] not divisions within an empire, but whole empires. Because the heads are kings, we know they are kingdoms, and because they are mountains, we know they are full kingdoms, not several divisions of what was once a larger empire. So the seven heads are seven separate empires, and the leopard beast is similar to the multi-metallic image in that it represents, not one or two, but at least seven different empires.

THE "CATHOLICS ARE THE ENEMY" THEORY

There is a very common theory that the heads are not figurative mountains, but literal hills. Since we know that the woman sits upon those seven hills, and verse 18 says the woman is the great city that rules over the kings of the earth, this theory states that the heads on the

---

[58] Daniel 2:44-45, where the rock becomes a mountain and Daniel says the mountain represents the Kingdom of God.

leopard beast are not seven kingdoms, but the seven hills of the city of Rome.

The theory states that the leopard beast represents the Antichrist, and since Rome sets on seven literal hills, he shall arise in Rome. The woman is the Roman Catholic Church (the vatican is also in Rome). This theory is founded almost exclusively upon the interpretation of the seven mountains: are the mountains symbolic of empires, or literal hills in Italy? As we shall see, a literal interpretation causes far more problems than a symbolic interpretation.

The first problem: even if the mountains are literal hills, it does not help us identify the intended country or city. Rome is not the only city built upon seven hills; one notable city also built on seven hills is Jerusalem (four large hills and three small hills). Just because Rome is more famous for its hills does not mean God intends Rome. Just because WE think of Rome when we hear of seven hills does not exclude all other cities from God's consideration, nor does it mean that is what GOD was thinking of when he mentioned seven hills.

The second problem is one of mixing symbols. The scripture says the "woman you saw is the great city that rules over the kings of the earth." (Revelation 17:18). It does not say the leopard beast is that great city; it says the seven heads on the leopard beast are seven hills and the WOMAN is the city. Why does the beast have seven hills, and not the woman? If the woman represents Rome, then what does the leopard beast represent? The same thing? The city sits on itself? Even if the leopard beast represents the leader (with the idea that the city rests upon his shoulders), and not the city or country, why does the leader of the city have seven hills, rather than the city.

Some would say that the woman represents both the city and the religion in the city, which eliminates this problem. We will grant that the woman is a double reference to a city AND a religious system, but this does not solve the problem of the exact interpretation of the woman and the leopard beast. Even if the woman also represents the religion that is dominant in the Antichrist's home city, she STILL represents the city also; so what does the leopard beast represent?

The third problem is that John says one head receives a deadly wound, only to recover. (Revelation 13:3). If the heads are seven hills, as verse nine states, how is a hill wounded to death? And how can you tell when a hill recovers from a fatal wound? We suppose this could explain why the whole world is astonished at the beast because of the deadly wound that heals. We too would be pretty astonished to see a hill fatally wounded, then recover from the wound.

The fourth problem is one of continuity. In every other vision, each part of the beast or statue represented something about the nature of the empire's government, military, leadership, political structure, and so on. Why would God suddenly destroy this continuity by including symbols for the DIRT upon which the Capitol City rests? The Lord said nothing about the geography of any other capitol city,[59] so why would he suddenly start here?

The fifth problem is that John says each head on the leopard beast has a blasphemous name (Revelation 13:1). Since each head is a hill, what does it mean that each hill has a blasphemous name? A true blasphemous[60] name shows the blasphemous intentions and actions of whoever has the name, and hills are fairly incapable of intentions and actions, blasphemous or otherwise. What is it that would make EACH hill in the city of Rome inherently blasphemous?

The sixth problem is that if the leopard beast represents the city of Rome, then the Antichrist will come to power in Rome, yet Daniel eliminates any country outside the Syrian Division of the Grecian Empire. When Daniel pinpoints New Syria, he does it in a section containing no symbolic language (just a point by point narration of actual events in Egypt and Syria, Daniel 11:2 - 12:4), where this section in Revelation contains a considerable amount of symbolic language. It is very unsafe to use a personal interpretation of the symbols in a section containing mostly symbolic language to refute the evidence in a non-symbolic section. According to Daniel, the Antichrist CANNOT arise in the city of Rome.

The text in the eleventh chapter of Daniel is so clear that we cannot simply disregard it because we want the seven heads to represent literal hills. We should not disregard a literal interpretation of Daniel eleven until it is OBVIOUS that the symbols in Revelation, including the angelic interpretation of those symbols, do not support a literal

---

[59] The ancient city of Babylon, for instance, set directly over the Euphrates River, yet was a completely walled city. This is much more unique, interesting, and distinctive than the number of hills in another city.

[60] Strictly speaking, true blaspheme involves claiming to be equal with God (or that God is no better than anyone else, or even that God is no better than Satan) or trying to overthrow Him, and can only apply to people. As with most sin, blaspheme is a reflection of the condition of the heart. Objects created by God cannot be blasphemous; they can be unholy, sacrilegious, or unclean, and they can be put to blasphemous USE, but since blaspheme is primarily an action, a natural object cannot be blasphemous. The exception would be something that a man creates for the purpose of attacking God (such as a blasphemous painting, art object, movie, etc.), but this is still an expression of the heart of the one who created it. Since man did not create hills, trees, rocks, rivers, mountains, animals, and so on, they cannot be inherently blasphemous.

interpretation. As we shall see, the symbols in Revelation correspond perfectly with the events in Daniel's eleventh chapter.

We have found that very few scholars who believe the seven heads are seven literal hills will change their views from the evidence provided in this book, because this interpretation allows them to brand Catholicism as the ultimate tool of Satan. The force behind their adherence to the "literal hills" theory is an intense distrust of the Catholics, and a refusal to believe that any person in a denomination so thoroughly grounded in works could still find salvation through Grace. It is not an unshakable trust in their interpretation of the symbols that drives them, but a fervent distrust of the Catholic Church.

When one accepts that these mountains are symbolic of empires, not of mounds of dirt, the whole theory in which the Catholics cause the rise of the Antichrist falls to the ground. Without this interpretation, there is NO evidence to support it ANYWHERE in Daniel, Revelation, Ezekiel, or in any other Apocalyptic section in scripture. For the record, as evangelical Protestants, we state the following whole-heartedly.

THE CATHOLICS ARE NOT THE ENEMY. THEY WILL NOT BE INVOLVED IN THE RISE OF THE ANTICHRIST. ROME WILL NOT BE HIS CAPITOL NOR WILL IT EVEN BE A PART OF THE CONFEDERACY. Most importantly, **THE SEVEN HEADS ARE NOT SEVEN LITERAL HILLS UPON WHICH ROME OR ANY OTHER CITY STANDS.**

As we previously mentioned, the seven mountains and seven kings represent seven empires. John says that five kings have fallen, one is, and the other has not yet come. Since we know these kings are empires, we can pinpoint the empires from this information.

Five have fallen and one is still here. When John wrote Revelation, the Old Roman Empire ruled the biblical world. Before the Old Roman Empire, John says that five empires ruled the world. By John's day, all five had perished. History shows that those five fallen empires are (1) the Egyptian Empire, (2) the Assyrian Empire, (3) the Babylonian Empire, (4) the Medio-Persian Empire, and (5) the Grecian Empire. The sixth head, the one that was still here (when John was writing), is (6) the Old Roman Empire.

John says that the seventh head is yet to come, and when it does come, it will only exist for a short while. From Daniel we know the next empire, immediately after the Old Roman Empire, will be (7) the Mediterranean Confederacy of Ten Kingdoms, symbolized in Daniel by ten toes and ten horns. This beast also has ten horns, which the angel tells John are symbolic of ten kings who have not yet received a kingdom. This fits the Mediterranean Confederacy of Ten Kingdoms, since it has not yet arrived, and when it does, ten kings will rule it.

THE EIGHTH KINGDOM

From Daniel we also know that another kingdom will arise after the seventh kingdom on this list, the Mediterranean Confederacy of Ten Kingdoms, and shall dominate the confederacy while allowing it to continue to exist. So to line up with the prophecies in Daniel, there must be another kingdom in this vision; an eighth kingdom by John's reckoning. We have a problem though, since this beast only has seven heads, and we have already accounted for each head. It seems that we

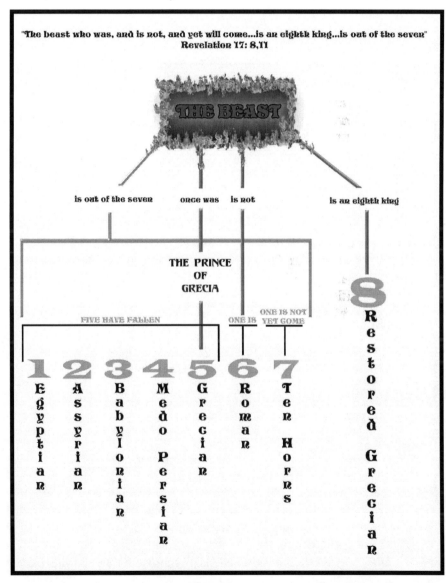

"The beast who was, and is not, and yet will come...is an eighth king...is out of the seven"
Revelation 17: 8,11

need an eighth head to symbolize the next empire, the Antichrist's empire.

John does mention an eighth kingdom, in verse eleven, but not an

The Seven Heads are Seven Kingdoms

"The seven heads are seven mountains upon which the woman sits. And they are seven kings. Five have fallen, one is, and the other is not yet come; but when he does come, he must remain for a little while."

Revelation 17: 9-10

1) Egyptian
2) Assyrian
3) Babylonian —————————— **Five have FALLEN**
4) Medio Persian
5) Grecian
6) Roman —————————————— **One IS**
7) Mediterranean Confederacy (Ten Horns)————**One is NOT YET COME**

The Beast is the Eighth Kingdom

"The Beast who once was, and now is not, is an eighth king. He is out of the seven, and goes into destruction."

Revelation 17: 11

1) Egyptian   **The beast is**
2) Assyrian ——— **OUT OF THE SEVEN**
3) Babylonian
4) Medio Persian
5) Grecian ——————————————— **The beast ONCE WAS**
6) Roman ————————————————— **The beast NOW IS NOT**
7) Mediterranean Confederacy (Ten Horns)   **The beast**
8) Antichrist's Kingdom (Restored Grecian)——— **IS AN EIGHTH KING**

The Satanic Prince of Grecia

"The beast, which you saw, once was, now is not, and will come up out of the abyss and go to his destruction. The inhabitants of the earth whose names have not been written in the book of life from the creation of the world will be astonished when they see the beast, because he once was, now is not, and yet will come."

Revelation 17: 8

1) Egyptian
2) Assyrian
3) Babylonian
4) Medio Persian
5) Grecian ———————————————— **The beast ONCE WAS**
6) Roman ————————————————— **The beast NOW IS NOT**
7) Mediterranean Confederacy (Ten Horns)
8) Antichrist's Kingdom (Restored Grecian)——— **The beast**
                                              WILL COME UP
                                              OUT OF THE ABYSS

eighth head. In verse eight the angel tells John that the leopard beast once was, now is not, and will come up out of the Abyss. In verse eleven the angel says the *"beast who once was, and now is not, is an eighth king."* In other words, each head represents an empire (seven heads stand for seven empires), and the whole beast, heads and all, represents an eighth empire. Just as each body section on the Multi-Metallic Statue represented an empire, while the entire statue represented the last empire.

So we see that the parallels between this beast and the lion, bear, leopard, and fourth beast are real. The mouth of a lion, feet of a bear, body of a leopard, and ten horns really are intentional references back to Daniel's vision of four beasts. But the kingdoms represented by those four beasts are already symbolized with the seven heads on the leopard beast, so why duplicate the symbols with allusions to the lion, bear, leopard, and ten-horned beast?

The purpose is to connect this beast into all three "empire" visions in Daniel (the multi-metallic statue, the four beasts, and the ram and goat). This connection drives home the simple fact that you must start with Daniel if you hope to understand the symbols in Revelation. The connection to the multi-metallic statue is, as previously stated, that both the statue and this leopard beast represent ALL the kingdoms on one image, and the final kingdom (the Antichrist's kingdom) is a summation of all the others. God makes the connection between Daniel's vision of four beasts, and this leopard beast with the lion's mouth, bear's feet, leopard's body, and ten horns. What is the connection to Daniel's vision of the ram and goat? We must explore the leopard beast a little more first. Read on.

In the interest of avoiding confusion, an item of clarification must be made at this point. If you recall from Daniel, there were six Gentile empires that oppressed Israel, yet here we list eight empires. You may have noticed in our list above that we have added two empires before Babylon; the Egyptian Empire and the Assyrian Empire. These empires are crucial to understanding the end times because it makes the list of oppressive Gentile empires complete (Egypt was the very first empire to oppress Israel and Assyria the second).

Daniel does not mention these two kingdoms because both he and Nebuchadnezzar desired only to know what events were going to take place after Babylon; they already knew what had happened in the past. God left the full revelation concerning gentile kingdoms to the church, and ultimately reveals it here in the book of Revelation. Because Revelation goes back to Egypt, it refers to seven kingdoms, not five (so here in Revelation Babylon is the third, Medio-Persia is the fourth, and so on), and the mysterious sixth kingdom in Daniel is the eighth kingdom here in Revelation.

So we know the whole leopard beast represents the Antichrist, and through him, his whole kingdom. John says this beast "*once was, and now is not, and yet will come."* (Revelation 17:8b). What does this mean? How could the Antichrist exist before, cease to exist in John's day, and then come into existence again in the last days? John further explains that when the beast comes into existence in the future, he will come *"up out of the Abyss and go into destruction."* (Revelation 17:11). What does this mean?

Some have speculated that this means the Antichrist is a king who lived long ago, had died before John's day, and will somehow be resurrected by Satan to rule as the Antichrist in the end times. This, they say, is the explanation of coming up out of the Abyss, and of the head (remember, John says the seven heads are seven kings) that received the fatal wound, and recovered.

There are several problems with this theory, the most glaring of which is that Satan, does NOT have the power to resurrect anyone from the dead. Resurrection from the dead is the definitive sign that Jesus is God, and is a power reserved exclusively for God. In addition, Jesus, not Satan, holds the keys of death and Hell, so Satan does not have the power to release anyone from Hell (Revelation 1:18).

The second problem is that this beast comes up out of the ABYSS. God depicts the Abyss, throughout the Old and New Testament, as the holding place of satanic angels. No where in scripture is it ever said that God condemns people to the Abyss. So a man resurrected from the dead could not come out of the Abyss, he would have to come out of Hell.

Scripture indicates there are four areas in the region under the Earth.

(1) The lake of fire, which is the final place of punishment for all evil beings (Revelation 19:20; 20:10-15; 21:8).

(2) The Abyss ("abussos" or "tartaros"), which is the deepest pit of the underworld and the prison for chained satanic angels (Luke 8:27-31; II Peter 2:4; Revelation 9:1-11; 11:7; 17:8; 20:1-3).

(3) Hell ("hades" or "geenna"), which is the prison for the wicked dead (Luke 16:19-31; Revelation 20:13-14).

(4) Paradise ("paradeisos"), which is the former holding place for the righteous dead, now empty (Luke 23:43; 16:19-31; Ephesians 4:8-10).

Occasionally the Greek "hades" is used to refer to ALL the regions under the earth simultaneously.

The symbols on the leopard beast can be completely reconciled without attributing to Satan power he does not have. It is true that the beast represents the Antichrist, and that the beast used to be on earth, then was not any longer, and will be again in the last days. It is also true that this beast has spent the last two thousand or more years in the Abyss, and will come up out of the Abyss when he returns in the end times. In spite of what it sounds like though, this does not mean a man will be resurrected to be the Antichrist.

If you recall from chapter one, the beasts, body sections, and etc. have three levels of representation. The first level is of satanic princes who rule those empires (from the beginning to the end of an empire, the same demonic prince rules). The second level is of the kings of that empire (who come and go throughout the existence of the empire). The third level in the symbolism is of the whole kingdom.

Since we know the Abyss is a holding cell for satanic angels, and since this leopard beast comes up out of the Abyss, John must be describing the return of a satanic prince; not of the Antichrist himself. This satanic prince used to rule over an empire, but when John came along, he and his empire had disappeared ("*he once was, and now is not*," Revelation 17:8). He used to rule some other empire, spent thousands of years locked up, and will rule the Antichrist's kingdom ("*The beast who once was, and now is not, is an eighth king. He belongs to the seven, and is going into destruction*." Revelation 17:11).

So if he used to rule an empire before the Old Roman Empire, which empire was it? From the evidence in Revelation alone, we would have no way of knowing, but fortunately, Daniel provides the necessary clues for us to determine which satanic prince is trying to revive his empire.

Our first problem is that ALL the previous empires seem to get re-established. In Daniel's vision of the four beasts, we discovered that the Antichrist will militarily conquer three of the countries in the Mediterranean Confederacy of Ten Kingdoms en route to gaining control of the confederacy. From Daniel's vision of the ram and goat and from the history out of the Book of Truth, we know that the Antichrist will launch this campaign from New Syria, and the three countries he overthrows must be modern countries corresponding roughly to Greece, Turkey, and Egypt. Once he has done this, he will have REESTABLISHED a new and improved version of the Old Grecian Empire.

The reestablishment of the Old Grecian Empire will encompass all the previous empires. When the Antichrist conquers Egypt, he will gain control of what used to be the Egyptian Empire. His original country, New Syria, will encompass a large portion of what used to be the Assyrian, Babylonian, and Medio-Persian empires. After gaining control of the Mediterranean Confederacy of Ten Kingdoms, he will rule the approximate area of the Old Roman Empire. He will have them all, and as the Multi-Metallic statue in Daniel suggests, he will be a conglomeration of ALL their area, power and authority, both physically and spiritually.

From this perspective, we could almost say that he reestablishes ALL the previous empires, so how can we be sure the leopard beast represents the satanic prince of the Old Grecian Empire? We can quickly eliminate the Old Roman Empire because John says, during the days of the Old Roman Empire, that the beast once was, but now is not. So the empire he seeks to reestablish could not be the Roman.

The rest can be eliminated simply by noticing that Daniel does not present the Antichrist as the final king of Egypt, Assyria, Babylon, or Medio-Persia. In Daniel's vision of the ram and goat and in the section from the Book of Truth the Antichrist is clearly the final GRECIAN king, from the Syrian Division of that Empire. It is undeniably the demonic prince of GRECIA that comes up out of the Abyss to rule again for a short while, and to meet his ultimate destruction at the coming of our Lord, Jesus Christ.

In Revelation chapter thirteen, John said one head of the beast received a deadly wound, but the fatal wound healed. Since the heads refer to empires, this deathblow symbolizes the previous death of an empire, and the recovery symbolizes the return of that empire. Since we know the returning empire is the Old Grecian Empire, we can deduce that it was the fifth head that received the fatal wound, only to recover.

If the wounding of a head symbolizes the destruction of a previous empire, why is only ONE head wounded? Since all of the first five heads had passed away by John's day, why did the Lord not say that FIVE heads received deathblows and ONE of them recovered from the wound?

There are three reasons for this apparent "oversight." First, the Lord is not emphasizing the death of an empire, but the resurrection of one. His main focus is not on the passing of the previous empires, but on the return of one, and it would be very difficult to depict the resurrection of an empire if the death is not first illustrated.

The second reason, and even more important than the first, is that "spiritually" the previous kingdoms ADD their power to the Antichrist's kingdom. The Antichrist's kingdom contains all the satanic evil, power, influence, authority, and deceitfulness, both physically and spiritually, of all the previous kingdoms combined. As we saw with the Multi-Metallic statue, it is important that these elements from the previous kingdoms be depicted "alive" in the last days, not dead.

We can now show the connection between this leopard beast and Daniel's vision of the ram and goat. The primary purpose of the vision of the ram and goat is to reveal that the Grecian Empire will be in existence in the last days; that it will reemerge through the power of the satanic prince of Grecia, to function as the base of operations for the Antichrist. Here in the seventeenth chapter of Revelation, God constantly precedes the leopard beast with the words, *"the beast who once WAS, and now IS NOT, and yet WILL COME."* These words, as we have shown, allude to the resurrection of the Grecian Empire.

The third reason for mentioning the death and revival of only one head stems from the double reference nature of the symbols. As we mentioned previously, each symbol actually represents three things: the kingdom, the king or kings who rule the kingdom, and the spiritual prince behind the kingdom. The simple fact that the resurrection of one of the heads is mentioned over and over again, and that the world is said to marvel because of the resurrection of the head,[61] shows that something more than just the revival of an old empire is going on. The wording here seems to strongly indicate that the king of this last empire, the one that is resurrected, will himself receive a wound that appears to kill him, and he will completely recover from the wound. The death and resurrection symbolism here is a double reference to both the empire, and to the "apparent" resurrection of the final king, the Antichrist, after he appears to be killed.

Some have thought that maybe the leopard beast here in Revelation is the same as the FOURTH beast in Daniel's vision of four beasts. Strictly speaking, the leopard beast is not EXACTLY the same as ANY symbol in Daniel, since none of them depicted the Egyptian and Assyrian Empires. If we do need to connect directly to any of the symbols in Daniel, instead of fixating on the existence of ten horns on this beast and on the fourth beast in Daniel, let's look at the whole leopard beast.

When considering the whole leopard beast, there is really only one choice in Daniel: the multi-metallic statue. Both the leopard beast and the statue represent ALL the empires under consideration in their

---

[61] 13:3: "And I saw one of its heads, as having been slain to death, and its deadly wound was healed. And all the earth marveled after the beast." 13:12 "…and it causes the earth and those dwelling in it to worship the first beast, of which was healed its deadly wound." 13:14 "…saying to those dwelling on the earth to make an image to the beast who has the wound of the sword, and lived."

respective books (from Babylon to the Antichrist in Daniel, and from Egypt to the Antichrist in Revelation). Both contain a depiction of the ten kings of the Mediterranean Confederacy of Ten Kingdoms (ten toes on the statue and ten horns on the leopard beast), and in both illustrations, it is the summation of all the previous kingdoms that make up the final kingdom.

THE DRAGON

The Antichrist's kingdom is not the last gentile nation to oppress Israel, it is the culmination of thousands of years of satanic hatred, violence, evil, rage, and power, all rolled into one final assault against God and His people. Satan has used all of the previous empires to build his power, influence, authority, and control to a peak, and with the Antichrist, he unleashes it all at once.

So all the heads must be there in the last days. This is clear from the dragon, which symbolizes Satan, and also has seven heads and ten horns. The seven heads and ten horns on the dragon correspond to the seven heads and ten horns on the leopard beast. They are on the dragon to show that the empires symbolized on the leopard beast were and will be satanic. Satan formed and empowered them, not God.

Additionally these symbols on the dragon are the ultimate definition of Satan, and show the fundamental plan that fuels Satan's existence. These eight kingdoms are not just empires that have arisen during the natural course of human events, they are key steps in Satan's ultimate plan to rule forever. If a being can be defined by its actions and plans, then these kingdoms are the definitive "definition" of Satan: all that Satan has ever done and will ever do can be summed up in these eight empires. THAT is why God depicts Satan as a dragon with seven heads and ten horns.

THE TEN HORNS

In our chapters on Daniel we stated that after the little horn uproots three of the ten horns, the others voluntarily submit to the little horn without any further battle, and after their submission, the little horn "replants" the three he previously uprooted.

Here in Revelation we see the justification for those assumptions. The angel says,

> *"The ten horns you saw are ten kings who have not yet received a kingdom, but who for one hour will receive authority as kings along with the beast. They have one purpose and will give their power and authority to the beast."* (Revelation 17:12-13).

From this we know these ten horns are the same as the ten horns in Daniel: ten kings from the Mediterranean Confederacy of Ten Kingdoms who will rule simultaneously with the Antichrist. From Daniel we know that the Antichrist uproots three of the ten kings, yet here, ALL TEN kings voluntarily give their power and authority to the Antichrist. Thus we know the Antichrist replants the three horns, and that these replaced kings, with the other six, voluntarily submit to his authority.

The ten kings and the Antichrist rule for a very short time (called "one hour" here) in comparison with the length of time each previous kingdom survived. The Babylonian Empire lasted about eighty-seven years. The Medio-Persian lasted a little over two hundred years. The Grecian lasted about two hundred and seventy years. The Roman Empire lasted over fifteen hundred years (about five hundred with Rome as the capitol, one hundred with dual capitols, and nearly a thousand with the capitol in Constantinople). The Antichrist's Empire, in stark contrast, will last exactly three and a half years in its full, completely restored form.[62]

The ten kings will form the Mediterranean Confederacy of Ten Kingdoms just prior to the rise of the Antichrist. We have no way of knowing how long the confederacy exists before the Antichrist sets out

---

[62] From the time the Antichrist arrives on the scene and makes a seven year peace pact with Israel (and possibly other nations), it takes him three and a half years to completely subdue the Mediterranean Confederacy of Ten Kingdoms, so he really only has complete control of the empire for the last three and a half years.

to control it. It could be anywhere from a couple months to one or more years, but the depiction of the ten horns is so closely connected to the rise of the Antichrist in every vision that it is unlikely they will be in power for very long prior to being conquered.

Shortly after the formation of the Mediterranean Confederacy of Ten Kingdoms, the Antichrist rises to power. He reigns for seven years, but he only has full power and authority for the last three and a half years of that reign. During the first half of his seven-year reign the Antichrist is consolidating his power, "convincing" the Mediterranean Confederacy of Ten Kingdoms that he is emperor, and setting himself up as a god. It is during 'the last three and a half years that the ten kings reign with the Antichrist for "one hour," and give their power and authority to him.

SUMMARY

There are eight gentile empires that have persecuted, and will yet persecute Israel. God includes a representation for each of the eight upon the leopard beast. The seven heads on the leopard beast represent seven mountains and seven kings. The kings show that each head stands for a kingdom, while the mountains show that each kingdom is a whole empire, rather than a division within an empire. Five of the empires had fallen by John's day, one was in existence, and one was yet to come. The fallen five are 1) Egypt, 2) Assyria, 3) Babylon, 4) Medio-Persia, and 5) Grecia. During John's day, (6) Rome ruled the world, and the one to come is (7) the Mediterranean Confederacy of Ten Kingdoms.

The whole beast is the final kingdom, (8) the Antichrist's kingdom.[63] The rejuvenated wound represents the reestablishment of the Grecian Empire under the Antichrist.

Using one beast to represent all the empires, with the last empire consisting of all the previous kingdoms combined ties this beast into the multi-metallic statue in Daniel. The lion's mouth, bear's feet, leopard's body, and ten horns tie this beast into Daniel's vision of four beasts. The depiction of the resurrection of the Grecian Empire ties the

---

[63] From Daniel 9:27 we know his reign will be seven years, but from Daniel 7:25; 8:14; 12:11-12 and from Revelation 13:5 we know he will only have his full authority for the last three and a half years. As will be shown in chapter seven, the consolidation of his power in the first three and a half years primarily entails subjugating the Mediterranean Confederacy of Ten Kingdoms, destroying the previous religion of the region, and establishing a new religion with himself as god. It is not until after he firmly establishes himself as the absolute ruler of nearly the whole Middle East that he breaks his seven year peace covenant, invades Israel, captures the Temple, and establishes the abomination of desolation.

leopard beast into Daniel's vision of the ram and goat. The leopard beast's assent from the Abyss illustrates the return of the satanic Prince of Grecia, who, after bringing about the reestablishment of the Grecian Empire, shall rule over the Antichrist's kingdom in the spiritual realm. The equivalent symbols on the dragon show the satanic nature of these kingdoms, and that these empires are the major steps in Satan's plan to rule forever. These empires can serve as a "definition" of Satan.

QUESTIONS FROM CHAPTER SIX

(1)   John tells us the seven heads on the beast represent two things. What are they?

(2)   What do mountains represent in scripture?

(3)   Are the seven kingdoms symbolized on the leopard beast simultaneous divisions in one empire, or seven separate, consecutive empires? How do we know?

(4)   What are the problems with the theory that states the seven mountains are the seven literal hills upon which the city of Rome is built?

(5)   What is the ultimate reason (from something in Daniel), that the seven mountains cannot be a reference to Rome?

(6)   The seven heads are seven kingdoms: five have fallen, one is, and one is yet to come. What are they?

(7)   What symbolizes the eighth kingdom? How do we know this?

(8)   In what way does the leopard beast connect to the three visions in Daniel (the Multi-Metallic Statue, the four beasts, and the ram and goat)?

(9)   Why are there six empires listed in Daniel, but eight in Revelation?

(10) What are the four areas under the earth?

(11) What are the two things that the wounding and recovery of one head of the leopard beast represent?

(12) Why does the dragon have seven heads and ten horns, like the leopard beast?

(13) How do we know the ten kings of the Confederacy will remain in power, although subordinate to the Antichrist, when he gains control of their empire?

BABYLON THE GREAT, THE MOTHER OF PROSTITUTES
Satan's Ultimate Religion

If you turned straight to this section, please go back and read the rest of the book first. Without a thorough understanding of the key elements established in the first half of this book, some of our conclusions in this chapter, and the next, will seem to spring from nothing. Most importantly, our thesis in this book can only be true if our verdict about the origin of the Antichrist is true.[64] Since our conclusions are contrary to most of the currently popular theories about the Antichrist, most people will need to study our proofs on that topic before these next two chapters will make any sense. Additionally, those who initially assume that our declaration about the Mother of Prostitutes arises from the frequency with which the Middle East and Islam are in the news lately, or due to an over-reaction to the 9/11 terrorism, will be greatly relieved to discover the solid biblical foundations for our assertion.

This is where everything has been leading: what is the meaning of the woman sitting on the leopard beast, with the title, "Mystery, Babylon the Great, the Mother of Prostitutes and of the Abominations of the Earth?"

THE MOTHER OF PROSTITUTES

"'Come, I will show you the punishment of the great Prostitute, who sits on many waters, with her the kings of the earth committed adultery and the inhabitants of the earth were intoxicated with the wine of her adulteries.'

"Then the angel carried me away in the Spirit into a desert. There I saw a woman sitting on a scarlet beast that was covered with blasphemous names and had seven heads and ten horns. The woman was dressed in purple and scarlet, and was glittering with gold, precious stones and

---

[64] Most importantly, that the Antichrist will come to power in New Syria, NOT Rome.

pearls. She held a golden cup in her hand, filled with abominable things and the filth of her adulteries. This title was written on her forehead: Mystery, Babylon the Great, the Mother of Prostitutes and of the Abominations of the Earth.[65]

"I saw that the woman was drunk with the blood of the saints, the blood of those who bore the testimony to Jesus.

"When I saw her, I was greatly astonished. Then the angel said to me: "Why are you astonished? I will explain to you the mystery of the woman and of the beast she rides, which has the seven heads and ten horns. This calls for a mind with wisdom. The seven heads are seven hills on which the woman sits.

"Then the angel said to me. 'The waters you saw, where the prostitute sits, are peoples, multitudes, nations and languages. The beast and the ten horns you saw will hate the prostitute. They will bring her to ruin and leave her naked; they will eat her flesh and burn her with fire. For God has put it into their hearts to accomplish his purpose by agreeing to give the beast their power to rule, until God's words are fulfilled. The woman you saw is the great city that rules over the kings of the earth.'" (Revelation 17:1b-7, 9, 15-18)

RECAP

The angel calls the woman on the leopard beast "the great prostitute." The title written on her forehead says she is "Babylon the Great," "the Mother of Prostitutes of the earth," and "the Mother of Abominations of the earth,"[66] and that she is a mystery, or more

---

[65] Some scholars have recently postulated that this verse could also be translated, "this mysterious title was written on her forehead: Babylon the Great . . .." They feel this is possible since both the Greek words for "title" (onoma) and "mystery" (musterion) are in the nominative case in this sentence, and therefore, "musterion" could serve as an adjective. However, since in the Greek "musterion" would also have to be nominative to appear as the first word in the title, it is separated from "onoma" by the verb, and is delineated with commas, there is really very little reason to believe it could be translated adjectivally. This is further supported by the evidence that in no major translation, in any language, from any era, did the scholars involved translate "musterion" adjectivally in this sentence.

[66] While the English is vague, the Greek clearly states that she is "the Mother" of both the "prostitutes of the earth" and of the "abominations of the earth."

accurately, a secret.[67] He also states she is the great city that rules over all the kings of the earth, and that the wine of her adulteries intoxicates those kings.

She is dressed in royal garb of purple and scarlet, with many precious gems and metals adorning her costume. She is holding a golden cup filled with the abominable things she has done in her adulteries. She had apparently been drinking the blood of the saints, and was drunk because of it.

She is seated on the beast, on the seven heads (which are mountains and kings upon which she also sits), and upon many waters. From the previous chapters, we know the beast is the Antichrist's kingdom, the seven heads are the seven empires that have ruled and will rule the biblical earth before the Antichrist, and the waters represent the many different peoples, nationalities and languages under her authority.

Finally, we are told the ten horns and the beast will come to hate her, and will ruin her, stripping her of her wealthy clothes to leave her naked, eating and burning her, en route to destroying her.

THE PROSTITUTE

In all of the visions we have examined in this book, this is the first one that includes a woman in the symbolism. Nowhere in scripture does God use a woman symbol for empires in the same way that he uses beasts or men. Wild beasts and men, when depicted symbolically have military, political, or economic significance, and God frequently displays them conquering or being conquered.[68] Women, on the other hand, denote a moral or religious rendering in symbolic visions and dreams, and are depicted courting adultery or fleeing evil.[69] From this we can predict that the woman on the leopard beast will likely represent

---

[67] Musterion is usually translated "mystery," but is probably better translated "secret." It is used of information that may be known by only a few, such as the ancient Greek "musterion" cults, and could be discovered with enough research, time, and effort. One of the definitions of the English word "mystery" is that it is "inexplicable" or "cannot be explained." This is NOT what musterion means. The answer to a musterion frequently can be discovered, figured out, and even explained.

[68] Daniel 2:1-45; 7:1-27; 8:1-26. The exceptions are "dragons," mythical beasts that are generic symbols of all the enemies of God, both religious and military (Psalms 74:14; Isaiah 27:1; Ezekiel 29:3), and especially of Satan, the ultimate enemy of God. Another seeming exception is the "lamb beast" in Revelation chapter thirteen. A "lamb" is a religious symbol, and a "beast" is a kingdom symbol, so the "lamb beast" is both: an empire and a religious system.

[69] Zechariah 5:5-11; Ezekiel 23:1-49; Song of Solomon; Revelation 12:1-17. Women can represent whole countries, since Israel is frequently depicted as a prostitute, but when used symbolically of kingdoms or empires, the "woman" symbol still emphasizes the moral or religious actions of the kingdom.

the moral, spiritual, or religious purity or wickedness of the empires upon which she sits.

The angel calls her the "great prostitute," and the title on her forehead says she is the "Mother of Prostitutes." Prostitutes and prostitution are symbolic in scripture of wickedness and corruption in

THE BEAST	Empire	John's Identifier	Image (Daniel 2)	2 Beasts (Daniel 7)	4 Beasts (Daniel 8)	Ruling Satanic Spirit	State Religion
First Head	Egyptian	Fallen				Prince of Egypt	Egyptian
Second Head	Assyrian	Fallen				Prince of Assyria	Mesopotamian
Third Head	Babylonian	Fallen	Head of Gold	lion with 2 Wings		Prince of Babylon	Mesopotamian
Fourth Head	Medio-Persian	Fallen	Arms of Silver	Bear w/ribs in Mouth	Ram with Uneven Horns	Prince of Persia	Zoastrianism
Fifth Head	Grecian	Fallen	Belly of Brass	Leopard w/4 Wings	Goat with 1 Horn, then 4 Horns	Prince of Grecia	Ancient Grecian
Sixth Head	Roman	One Is	Legs of Iron	Beast with Iron teeth Brass claws		Prince of Rome	Ancient Roman
Seventh Head	10 Kingdoms	One is yet to Come	Feet and Toes of Iron/Clay	Ten Horns		Prince of Rome	Islam
Whole Beast	Antichrist's Kingdom	Is an Eighth King	Whole Image	Little Horn w/Eyes & Mouth	Little Horn	Prince of Grecia	Neo-Islam

general (Isaiah 1:21; 23:17; 57:3-13), but more specifically of spiritual fornication and idolatry.[70] The false religion could range from some

---

[70] Judges 2:10-19; Jeremiah 2:20-30; 3:1-14; Ezekiel 16:1-63; the whole book of Hosea. There probably is not enough room to list all the scriptures illustrating that prostitution is symbolic of serving false gods, but these should serve to make the point.

form veneration of a false god, such as Baal worship, to witchcraft and demonology, but it was all considered idolatry, and therefore, spiritual prostitution.

Thanks to Sadaam Hussein, and the war in the Persian Gulf, most Westerners now understand the middle-eastern designation, "mother of." When Hussein said, "the mother of all battles has begun," he meant the biggest, bloodiest, most devastating war in history had just begun. He predicted hundreds of thousands of casualties on both sides, and months, maybe years of fighting. His proclamation turned upon him when the war turned into the "mother of all victories" for America and the allies, as his army, the fourth largest in the world, was crushed in about forty-two days. The only thing that kept him from being conquered outright was the single-minded goal of the coalition to merely liberate Kuwait, and nothing more.

Likewise, the "Mother of Prostitutes" designation means this woman represents the ultimate in spiritual and religious deception. She is the most destructive, evil, corrupt, and dangerous religion Satan has ever devised. More specifically, she symbolizes the culmination of all of Satan's demonic attempts at a murderous, yet seductive alternative to worshipping the True God: Jesus.

She is the culmination of thousands of years of work by Satan to construct a religious system. She is fleshly enough to look very good to mankind, and attract lots of followers. She is militant enough to be used to actively make war on the True Faith (physically, spiritually, and morally). She is broad ranging enough in her precepts to allow religious control of the governments of man. She is so constructed that she can be used in Satan's efforts to bring one man to power for a final thrust at the destruction of the saints and Heaven's throne.

The religion that she represents is so bad that it is not only "the mother of prostitutes," it is also "the mother of abominations." An abomination refers to a thing that is the most foul and detestable in God's eyes, and is frequently used of the practices of idolatrous and pagan worshipers (Deuteronomy 18:9-12; 29:17-18; II Kings 16:3-4).

Any form of spiritual prostitution is an abomination to God, and since this woman represents the ultimate in spiritual prostitution, she also represents the ultimate in abominations. That she is destructive and murderous is clear from her drunkenness, a state obtained through shedding the blood of countless saints. Her main pastime is persecuting and martyring those who bear the testimony of Jesus. She will not tolerate the preaching of the Gospel of Christ, and so strong will be the concentration of demonic powers in her domain that the religion will even persecute and kill any of her own people that repent and accept the cross of Jesus.

That she is seductive is also clear. The kings of the Earth have voluntarily committed adultery with her, and all the inhabitants of the biblical world are intoxicated from the constant consumption of the wine of her adulteries. She is decked in fine linen, pearls, gold, and precious stones. She is rich and beautiful to behold. Due largely to the promise of this wealth, she is a religion whose bondage is so appealing that it is beyond the ability of most people to resist.

The kings and merchants of the world have prostituted themselves to her, and follow whatever legalism, perversion, or blasphemy she decrees, because she helps them gain wealth and prestige. As chapter 18 indicates, she is not beloved of the world because of her enlightening philosophies, but because she brought everyone riches and wealth beyond measure. She has used her seductiveness to dominate the kings of the world, and thus rule the biblical world, and the kings and merchants of the world have used her many carnal charms to become rich and powerful.

This is a religion spread through the dual edged sword of terror and prosperity. Kill those who refuse to deny the Almighty God, and offer wealth and prosperity to those who convert to her prostitution. She is the ultimate dream of mankind: a religion that has the outward appearance of holiness, yet actually feeds the flesh, nourishes the carnal lusts of man, excuses the filthy, darkened soul, and gets rid of those pesky fanatics whose troubling words take the fun out of everything. She has mankind in a rank bondage, but in their darkened, spiritually blinded state, her followers think their slavery is sweet, unaware that her hollow riches and momentary pleasures lead them to certain death.

In verse seven, the angel says he will explain the mystery of the woman and the beast, and then proceeds to explain the beast and its actions in detail, ending with one short sentence about the woman. "*The woman you saw is the great city that rules over the kings of the earth.*" (Revelation 17:18)

This suggests that a clear understanding of the woman cannot be obtained without a thorough understanding of the beast. In other words, to discover the secret of the woman, first figure out the beast. Since the information from verses eight through seventeen focuses on the IDENTITY of each of the kingdoms involved, knowing the identity of the beast, and of the symbols upon the beast, must be key elements in figuring the identity, and thus the secret, of the woman. When we know where each of the empires on the beast have ruled or will rule, and where the empire represented by the whole beast shall arise and rule, we will know where to look for the identity of the woman. In the first six chapters of this book, we solved these puzzles: the empires are in the Middle East, centering on the region surrounding the modern country of Syria. How then, does this information help us identify the woman? First a little more on the prostitute herself.

Before we get to the prostitute, we need to address a small point, and this is a good time. There is a common belief that the phrase "that great city that rules over the kings of the earth" (Revelation 17:18) MUST be a reference to Rome (since Rome ruled over the kings of the earth at the time that John wrote this revelation). In context, however, this interpretation does not hold up. The phrase "great city" occurs ten times in Revelation. In two references, one early in Revelation, and one at the end, it clearly refers to Jerusalem (old Jerusalem: 11:8, New Jerusalem: 21:10). In two references just before 17:18 (14:8, 16:19), and in five references directly after 17:18 (18:10,16,18,19, and 21), the "great city" is specifically identified as Babylon. The section in chapter 18 that specifically identifies "the great city" as Babylon five times begins with the very NEXT verse after John says, "the woman you saw is that great city that rules over the kings of the earth." It simply is not reasonable to read this section in context and conclude that "the great city that rules over the kings of the earth" is anything other than the same "great city" repeatedly mentioned just a few verses later, and specifically identified as Babylon. The great city of Babylon, reborn and rebuilt in the end times, will be a city that rules over the kings of the earth. Politically and religiously over some, economically and psychologically over others. It is THE city on the earth during the end times. John makes this very clear in this section.

CHURCH AND STATE

She is wearing scarlet, and the beast is colored scarlet. God uses the bloody scarlet color throughout the bible to depict the sinfulness of man that will eventually lead him to death. There is only one way to rid oneself of sin: blood must flow, and the only permanent cure for man's terminal case of scarlet sin is the cross.

> *"Though your sins are like scarlet, they shall be as white as snow; though they are red as crimson, they shall be like wool. If you are willing and obedient, you will eat the best from the land; but if you resist and rebel, you will be devoured by the sword."* (Isaiah 1:18-19)

The leopard beast and the prostitute share the same color, showing the intimate relationship between the two. They partake of the same sin and deception, and it has stained them both the same. This, along with her adulteries with the kings of the world, and her position on top of the leopard beast, strongly reflect the tight "church and state" relationship between this woman's religion and the leopard beast's empires. The prostitute is not just some religion that happens to be in the empire, she is an official religion that takes part in the governing process.

As an official "state" religion, it will be the government that persecutes and kills any believers within its realm, guided and encouraged, of course, by the priests or religious leaders. Remember that these are demonic empires; upon the seven heads of the leopard beast were BLASPHEMOUS names, and the beast itself was COVERED with blasphemous names (Revelation 13:1 and 17:3). This prostitute not only enjoys the official recognition of the government, but the religion she represents CONTROLS the government to the degree that it can make policy, force the passage of beneficial laws, and dictate the use of government funds for religious "crusades." She has made the kings of the earth rich, and they, drunk from their adultery with her, will do anything she desires in return.

WICKEDNESS, ABOMINATION, AND INSANITY

She is holding a golden cup in her hand. The people of this religious system believe they are drinking a pure religion from her golden cup. In God's eyes, however, it is a witches cauldron of spiritual wickedness and corruption. Rather than spiritual truth, the cup is full of the abominations she has committed, and the filth of her adulteries. Remember, just as she is the mother of prostitutes, she is also the "Mother of Abominations."

The golden cup in her hand is a fitting symbol of a woman who is also called Babylon the Great. "*Babylon was a golden cup in the Lord's hand: she made the whole earth drunk. The nations drank her wine: therefore they have now gone mad.*" (Jeremiah 51:7)

The nations are inebriated from the wine of the abominations that flow from the cup in her hand. They are not only drunk from the wine, but the corruption, sin, and deception of this religion is so strong that they have gone mad. The demonic forces behind this false religion will corrupt the minds of the inhabitants of the Middle East until they are not able to function rationally. The actions of the rulers of the biblical world will reflect the gross demonic darkness that has descended upon their spirits and souls, and they shall act in violence, madness, and rage. People will think, hear, and do nothing but evil all day. Demon possession will be commonplace, and with the increased demonic activity will come an outpouring of religious deception and persecution. Satan's control will become so strong that a believer's worst enemies will be those of his own household. From the individual level the evil will spread and violence will fill the earth as the nations rise in war against each other all over the world.

News of continual wars, and of new wars brewing, will be commonplace. Jesus said the following:

> *"Watch out that no one deceives you. Many will come in my name, claiming, 'I Am,' and will deceive many. When you hear of wars and rumors of wars, do not be alarmed. Such things must happen, but the end is still to come. Nation will rise against nation, and kingdom against kingdom . . . You must be on your guard. You will be handed over to the local councils and flogged in the synagogues. On account of me you will stand before governors and kings as witnesses to them.*
>
> *Brother will betray brother to death, and a father his child. Children will rebel against their parents and have them put to death. All men will hate you because of me, but he who stands firm to the end will be saved.*
>
> *"When you see 'the abomination that causes desolation' standing where it does not belong--let the reader understand--then let those who are in Judea flee to the mountains . . . pray that this will not take place in winter, because those will be days of distress unequaled from the beginning, when God created the world, until now and never to be equaled again. If the Lord had not cut short those days, no one would survive. But for the sake of the elect, whom he has chosen, he has shortened them. At that time if anyone says to you, 'Look, here is the Christ!' or, 'Look, there he is!' do not believe it. For false Christs and false prophets will appear and perform signs and miracles to deceive the elect -- if that were possible."* (Mark 13:5-9,12-14,18-22)

God's judgments and plagues will clearly indicate that THE end is near, but Satan will have corrupted the minds of mankind so much that all not covered by the blood of Jesus will be blinded by the darkness and rebellion in which they live. Jesus promised that if we kept our eyes on him, we would be able to determine when the end was near:

"Now learn this lesson from the fig tree: As soon as its twigs get tender and its leaves come out, you know that summer is near. Even so, when you see all these things happening, you know that it is near, right at the door." (Mark 13:28-29 and Matthew 24:32-33)

The minds of unbelievers will be so darkened that another of Jesus' prophesies concerning the end times will be fulfilled in them.

"As it was in the days of Noah, so it will be at the coming of the Son of Man. For in the days before the flood, they were eating and drinking and giving in marriage, up to the day Noah entered the ark; and they knew nothing about what would happen until the flood came and took them all away." (Matthew 24:37-39)

God describes what the world was like in the days of Noah.

"Now the earth was corrupt in God's sight and was full of violence. God saw how corrupt the earth had become, for all the people on earth had corrupted their ways. So God said to Noah, 'I will put an end to all people, for the earth is filled with violence because of them. I am surely going to destroy both them and the earth.'" (Genesis 6:11-13).

Just as with Noah's world, our world will be filled with corruption and violence, spurred on by the demonic hordes from the woman and her abominations.

THE CITY OF BABYLON

In Revelation 17:16-17, we find out that the ten kings, under the influence of the beast, come to hate, and then destroy the prostitute. What does it mean that they "destroy" the prostitute? When they burn her with fire, is that the same as the destruction of the literal city of Babylon that is depicted in chapter 18?

So far, we have been focusing on the woman as a symbol of a religion, yet verse eighteen clearly says she is a city, and chapter eighteen goes on to describe the destruction of this woman in the form of a city. So which is it? Does the woman represent a city or a religion? As is frequently the case in scriptural symbolism, she represents BOTH. She is the City of the Antichrist, AND the religion centered in that city.

First, let us look at Revelation eighteen.

"After this I saw another angel coming down from heaven. He had great authority, and the earth was illuminated by his splendor, with a mighty voice he shouted: 'Fallen! Fallen is Babylon the Great! She has become a home for demons and a haunt for every evil spirit, a haunt for every unclean and detestable bird. For all the nations have drunk the maddening wine of her adulteries. The kings of the earth committed adultery with her, and the merchants of the earth grew rich from her excessive luxuries.'

"The I heard another voice from heaven say: 'Come out of her, my people, so that you will not share in her sins, so that you will not receive any of her plagues; for her sins are piled up to heaven, and God has remembered her crimes. Give back to her as she has given; pay her back double portion from her own cup. Give her as much torture and grief as the glory and luxury she gave herself. In her heart she boasts, 'I sit as queen; I am not a widow, and I will never mourn.' Therefore in one day her plagues will overtake her: death, mourning and famine. She will be consumed by fire, for mighty is the Lord God who judges her.

"'When the kings of the earth who committed adultery with her and shared her luxury see the smoke of her burning, they will weep and mourn over her. Terrified at her torment, they will stand far off and cry, 'Woe! Woe, 0 great city, 0 Babylon, city of power! In one hour your doom has come!'

"'The merchants of the earth will weep and mourn over her because no one buys her cargoes anymore -- cargoes of gold, silver, precious stones and pearls; fine linen, purple, silk and scarlet cloth; every sort of citron wood, and articles of every kind made of ivory, costly wood, bronze, iron and marble; cargoes of cinnamon and spice, of incense, myrrh and frankincense, of wine and olive oil, of fine flour and wheat: cattle and sheep: horses and carriages: and bodies and souls of men.

"'They will say. 'The fruit you longed for is gone from you. All your riches and splendor have vanished, never to be recovered.' The merchants who sold these things and gained their wealth from her will stand far off, terrified at

her torment. They will weep and mourn and cry out: 'Woe! Woe, O Great City, dressed in fine linen, purple and scarlet, and glittering with gold, precious stones and pearls! In one hour such great wealth has been brought to ruin!'

"'Every sea captain, and all who travel by ship, the sailors, and all who earn their living from the sea, will stand far off. When they see the smoke of her burning, they will exclaim, 'Was there ever a city like this great city?' They will throw dust on their heads, and with weeping and mourning cry out: 'Woe! Woe, O great city, where all who had ships on the sea became rich through her wealth! In one hour she has been brought to ruin!'

"'Rejoice over her, O heaven! Rejoice, saints and apostles and prophets! God has repaid her for the way she treated you.'

Then a mighty angel picked up a boulder the size of a large millstone and threw it into the sea, and said: 'with such violence the great city of Babylon will be thrown down, never to be found again. The music of harpists and musicians, flute players and trumpeters, will never be heard in you again. No workman of any trade will ever be found in you again. The sound of a millstone will never be heard in you again. The light of a lamp will never shine in you again. The voice of the bridegroom and bride will never be heard in you again. Your merchants were the world's great men. By your magic spell all the nations were led astray. In her was found the blood of prophets and of the saints, and of all who have been killed on the earth.'" (Revelation 18:1-24)

RECAP

In the angel's declaration about the fall of Babylon, he mentions five facts about the city. First, that it had become the dwelling place of demons. Second, that it had become the dwelling place of unclean birds. Third, that all the nations have partaken of the maddening wine of her adulteries. Fourth, that the kings of the earth have committed adultery with her. Fifth, that the merchants of the world have grown rich from her excessive luxuries.

Then another voice from Heaven cried out, commanding the people of God to leave Babylon. The voice went on to describe how God decided to punish Babylon because of her sins, describes her boasts, and spends twelve verses describing the mourning and lament of the kings and merchants of the earth, and ends by calling on the saints to rejoice at her destruction.

This section ends with another angel who demonstrates how violent the destruction of Babylon will be by casting a stone into the water. He goes on to make five prophetic statements about Babylon. No music shall be played in her again. No merchants shall trade in her again. The millstone will not be heard in her again. Lamplights shall not shine in her again. The bride and bridegroom will not be heard in her again. These five predictions cover the five fundamental things that are necessary to almost any city, and certainly to a prosperous one: recreation (music), industry and trade (merchants), agriculture (milling houses), a residential population (lamps in the houses), and residential growth (bride and bridegroom). Without these five elements, you don't have a city.

The angel ends with a note that Babylon controlled the merchants through sorcery, and that she is responsible for the murders of the saints throughout the biblical world.

THE DESTRUCTION OF THE CITY OF BABYLON

This is the destruction of the city that houses the wickedness in the basket (Zechariah 5:5-11; see page 143 below), and become the central city of the Antichrist's religion. The destruction of this city is not caused by the ten kings or the Antichrist, because verses nine through twenty clearly say that ALL the kings and merchants mourned her, not all except the ten. This is the destruction that takes place when God pours out his wrath upon the city of Babylon with the seventh bowl.

> "*The seventh angel poured out his bowl into the air, and out of the temple came a loud voice from the throne, saying. 'It is done!' Then there came flashes of lightning, rumblings, peals of thunder and a severe earthquake. No earthquake like it has ever occurred since man has been on earth, so tremendous was the quake. The great city split into three parts, and the cities of the nations collapsed. God remembered Babylon the Great and gave her the cup filled with the wine of the fury of His wrath. Every island fled away and the mountains could not be found. From the sky huge hailstones of about a hundred pounds each fell upon men. And they cursed God on account of the plague of hail, because the plague was so terrible.*" (Revelation 16:17-21)

In chapter eighteen the angel's description of the destruction of Babylon shows it is the result of supernatural intervention, not the hate-spawned schemes of human rulers. In the seventh bowl, the supernatural intervention of God causes an earthquake that devastates Babylon, splitting it into three sections. Then God rains hundred-pound hailstones down upon the city and the surrounding countries. An earthquake large enough to split a whole city into three pieces, while also causing the collapse of other cities in nearby countries, coupled with hailstones roughly the size of a night stand or end table will cause such complete and total destruction that the city of Babylon will literally cease to exist.[71]

As shown in the description of the prostitute in chapter seventeen, and in the destruction of the city in chapter eighteen, the city of Babylon will be three things: (1) the center for military and political power of the whole biblical world (the capitol city of the Antichrist); (2) the commercial center for the biblical world; and (3) the chief or "holy" city of the evil religion that the Antichrist uses to set himself up as a god (NOT the religion of the confederacy, the NEW religion of the Antichrist after the destruction of the confederacy's religion). Thus, the woman is a city, but more importantly, she is the religion that comes to be inseparable from the city.[72]

By the time God destroys Babylon it will have become the habitation of demons and evil spirits, and the resting-place for detestable and unclean birds. Why? Because when God, half way through the seven year tribulation, casts Satan and his hordes out of heaven, the concentration of their wickedness settles upon the city of Babylon (as depicted by the woman in the basket). Babylon, already the headquarters of Satan's number one man, the Antichrist, is the natural choice for Satan's "base of operations" in the biblical world. From there, the wickedness "spills out" into his whole empire.

It is this super-compression of the powers of darkness within the city of Babylon that brings on insanity for those who drink of Babylon's religion, wealth, and power. The powers of darkness will be so strong over this city, and over the religion that is its life's blood, that only sold-out, radical Christians protected by the blood of the lamb will be able to be near her without being seduced into her abominations. In this

---

[71] Hundred pound hailstones dropping from a mile or more high would completely smash everything they strike. Since hail usually comes in a thick, fast torrent, it would obliterate every square inch of the city.

[72] Just as Jerusalem IS Judaism, Mecca IS Islam, Rome IS Catholicism, so the city of Babylon will be inseparable from the religion the Antichrist establishes to make himself a god.

day and age, there will be no lukewarm Christians, because the persecution of believers, coupled with the powerful allure of evil, will quickly either drive them away from Christ for good, or finally into a full commitment to His Lordship.

The deception of the religion that emanates from this city will be powerful enough that Christ Himself prophesied that unless the time were shortened, if it were possible, even the very elect would be in danger of being seduced into Satan's bed of adulteries. This is why God cries out to his people, in Revelation 18:4, "*Come out of her, my people, so that YOU WILL NOT SHARE IN HER SINS, so that you will not receive any of her plagues.*"

WHAT IS THE RELIGION?

We know the great prostitute represents two things: A city that the Antichrist uses as his capitol, and a religion centered in that city.[73] The city we know will be Babylon, but the religion we do not yet know. Do we now have enough information to identify the religion of the prostitute?

Almost, but there are a few peculiar points about this end times religion that still need to be explained: What is the meaning of the prostitute sitting upon ALL SEVEN HEADS of the leopard beast? If she is an end times religion, what connection does she have to the six empires that have all ceased to exist? What is the "religious empire," symbolized by a lamb beast, that deceives the world into worshipping the leopard beast? Could the lamb beast and the prostitute stand as different perspectives on the same religion? If the lamb beast and the prostitute were the same thing, would the Antichrist come to hate a religion that had brought him to a position of demigod in the world's eyes? And why would he destroy a religion that proclaimed him god? First, the seven heads.

THE SIX FORMER RELIGIONS

She sits astride the beast, upon all seven heads, and over many waters. This means she was present in each of the empires represented by the first six heads, and will be present in the empire of the seventh head, and in the eighth empire, that of the whole beast. Her seat upon many waters indicates that she crosses cultural boundaries, national borders, and language barriers. She is not restricted to one nationality

---

[73] Isaiah 14:4; Revelation 17:18; The Antichrist is called the king of Babylon, and the prostitute is described as the great city that rules over the kings of the earth, therefore the Antichrist must control Babylon and it must be his capitol, since HE rules over the kings of the earth.

like Judaism, but is found in every port of call, like the True faith, Christianity.

What possible single religion could have been in Egypt, Assyria, Babylon, Medio-Persia, Grecia, and Rome, as well as continuing on into the Mediterranean Confederacy of Ten Kingdoms and the Antichrist's empire in the future? Each of those empires had a DIFFERENT religion, and although some of their religions where very similar,[74] no single religion can be found in ALL the empires. So if she cannot represent a single religion, what DOES she represent?

The answer is actually quite straightforward: since she sits on all eight empires, each of which had, or will have a different religion, she does NOT represent ONE religion, she represents EIGHT DIFFERENT RELIGIONS! Just as the beast depicts eight separate empires, so she symbolizes eight different religions.[75]

Why would God use one woman to represent eight different religions? For the same reason he uses one beast to represent eight different empires. All eight empires had or will have one important thing in common: they are ungodly empires that rule Mediterranean area, and persecute Israel.

Likewise, the eight religions are all pagan religions that persecute followers of the one, true God. Satan has used or will use all eight empires, and the eight religions that dominate those empires to try and destroy Israel, Judaism, and Christianity.

All of the first six religions had a few things in common. They were all polytheistic, all were religions that were accepted and followed by the government, and all were part of the reason for the persecution of Israel. From Ra, the sun god of the Egyptians, to Ashur/Marduk of the Ayssyrian/Babylonians, to Ahura-Mazda of the Persians, to Zeus/Jupiter of the Greeks/Romans,[76] all of these religions were early incarnations of the Great Prostitute: ruling religions in "world spanning" empires. All were, at one time or other, spread by force to subjugated cultures and kingdoms.

---

[74] The Medio-Persian and Babylonian empires had virtually the same religion, and the Greeks and the Romans had very similar religions.

[75] By modern designations, there are seven different religions. The Assyrians and the Persians had virtually the same religion, and it is identified now simply as the Mesopotamian Religion. The subtle differences (was Ashur supreme or Marduk?) are considered geographic, cultural, and time differences within the same religion, rather than two separate, but similar religions (such as the Grecian and Roman).

[76] I have listed the "supreme god" of each religion. They were NOT monotheistic religions.

THE TWO FUTURE RELIGIONS

Then there will be the religion of the Mediterranean Confederacy of Ten Kingdoms and the religion of the Antichrist's Kingdom. Do we have enough information to discover the identity of the prostitute in her next two forms? Let us start first with the Mediterranean Confederacy of Ten Kingdoms.

We know that the Mediterranean Confederacy of Ten Kingdoms will form in the Middle East, and that it will most likely consist of countries in the area of the Old Eastern Roman Empire. We also know that the modern countries of Greece, Turkey, Egypt, New Syria, and possibly Ethiopia, Sudan, and Libya will be members. Since the angel's "explanation" of the prostitute centered on the identity of the kingdoms upon which she sat, the one criteria that may be more important than any other is that we need to find a religion common to most, if not all of these countries.

As with the previous empires, the religion of the confederacy must be advocated and practiced by the rulers. However, unlike the previous kingdoms, this religion has to be much more widely accepted[77] among the people.

Since the woman was drunk with the blood of the saints, the religion must be violently anti-Christian and anti-Judaism. If currently in existence, it should have a long history of Judeo-Christian persecution. In line with a radical, almost rabid "antichrist" theology, the prostitute religion should be evangelistic and express a strong sentiment that it is the only true faith. What religion fits these facts?

First, the religion has to dominate the region that will be occupied by the ten horns on the beast. From Daniel we know that four of the ten kingdoms will be New Syria, Egypt, Turkey, and Greece.[78] We also know that Libya, Sudan, and Ethiopia may be members of the confederacy. What is the predominant religion in the countries that will probably make up New Syria (Syria and Iraq)? Islam.

What is the predominant religion in Egypt? Islam. What is the predominant religion in Turkey? Islam. What is the predominant religion in Greece? Greek Orthodox Catholicism. What is the

---

[77] All the previous empires had one ruler, and the religion of the empire came from his home country. The masses did not need to fully accept his religion for it to be the official religion of the kingdom. In a confederacy, however, the religion must be accepted by most, if not all of the kings in the council of ten. Such a broad foundation of similar faith among the leaders would seem to suggest that a sizable portion of the populace in each country will adhere to the official religion of the empire.

[78] The four divisions of the Grecian Empire, of which New Syria shall rise up and uproot the other three in the process of overthrowing the confederacy.

predominant religion in Libya? Islam. What is the predominant religion in Sudan? Islam. What is the predominant religion in Ethiopia? Islam.

Of the four countries that will definitely be members of the Mediterranean Confederacy of Ten Kingdoms, three are Muslim, one is Greek Orthodox Catholic. If you include the other three that MAY be part of the confederacy, it makes six Muslim and one Greek Orthodox.[79]

Since Daniel indicates that Persia and Beth Togarmah will be allied with the Antichrist when he invades Israel shortly after having gained control of the confederacy, we could include Iran (modern Persia) and Azerbaijan (roughly the area of Beth Togarmah). Both are Muslim, which makes the count eight Muslim and one Greek Orthodox.

Suppose we take into account any other countries in the region that could possibly be included in the Mediterranean Confederacy of Ten Kingdoms because they were in the Medio-Persian Empire,[80] the Grecian Empire,[81] or the Babylonian Empire.[82] This would include the Russian republics of Uzbekistan, Turkmenistan, and Tajikistan, as well as Afghanistan, Pakistan, Saudi Arabia, and Kuwait. All seven of these countries are Muslim, which makes the count fifteen to one in favor of Islam.

Suppose, just for the sake of argument, we include any countries that were ever controlled by the Old Roman Empire, either East or West. This brings Italy, Spain, Yugoslavia, Great Britain, Albania, Morocco, Rumania, Bulgaria, Hungary, Tunisia, France, and Algeria into our line-up.[83] Of these twelve, Italy, Spain, and France are Roman Catholic dominated (although it may be a stretch to say that France is actually "dominated" by Catholicism); Great Britain is Anglican

---

[79] Since Alexander the Great was actually from Macedonia, and that country is now in existence again, it could be Macedonia, not Greece, that represents the Grecian division. This would make all the countries Muslim, as the predominant religion in Macedonia is Islam. We are, however, in keeping with rule four of interpreting prophecy, reluctant to let current events dictate our interpretations, so we will stick with Greece in our discussion.

[80] The beast had the "feet of a bear" (Revelation 13:2), which is a reference back to the bear in Daniel: the Medio-Persian Empire.

[81] The beast was said to be a leopard, which was the Grecian Empire in Daniel.

[82] The beast had the mouth of a lion, which was the Babylonian Empire in Daniel.

[83] Some historians also include Germany. This seems to be stretching things a bit, since the Old Roman Empire actually only occupied a tiny corner of what is now Germany, and for only about fifteen years out of a total of over fifteen hundred years of Roman rule.

(Protestant); Albania, Yugoslavia,[84] Rumania, Bulgaria, and Hungary must be listed as "none," since no single religion has a majority in those countries (although the war that has been raging in this region between Christian and Muslim ethnic groups since the collapse of the Soviet Union shows there is a strong population of both Muslims and Christians throughout this region), and Morocco, Tunisia, and Algeria are Muslim.

The addition of these twelve countries make three Roman Catholic, one Greek Orthodox, one Protestant, five neither, and eighteen Muslim. If we list all the Christian denominations together it is five Christian, five neither, and eighteen Muslim. If the five that had atheist governments under Soviet rule end up going in the direction of the religion that has the largest majority, the final tally would be roughly eight Christian and twenty Muslim. As you can see, the prostitute is either apostate Christianity or Islam.

No matter how we stretch the boundaries, Islam dominates this region. The Mediterranean Confederacy of Ten Kingdoms will consist of ten countries, and it would be wishful thinking to find even eight countries that could become dominated by apostate Christianity, while we could find ten Muslim dominated countries twice over without too much difficulty.

Thus the answer to our first test: to find out which religion dominates the area where the Mediterranean Confederacy of Ten Kingdoms might arise yields Islam as the dominant religion.

The second test is to find a religion that stands as a "state" religion in the countries of this area. As the world has seen time after time, Muslim countries are frequently genuinely controlled by the Islamic faith. In Muslim countries the rulers, at the very least, profess and outwardly practice Islam, but most of them are genuine believers.[85] This gives the religion extraordinary influence in each of those countries.

Christianity comes the closest to being a state religion in Great Britain, Italy, Spain, France, and Greece, but to say that Christianity actually controls any of these countries except maybe Italy, Spain, and Greece would be stretching the truth in the extreme. In fact, it is very

---

[84] Yugoslavia actually no longer exists, and has been split into multiple countries with shifting boarders. By the time you are reading this book, there is no telling what actual countries will exist in this region. Suffice it to say that there are large populations of both Christians and Muslims here.

[85] Some Muslim countries, such as Turkey and Iraq, officially have secular governments. But one needs only listen to the speeches given by their leaders to see that they STILL use Islam to control and manipulate the people under their authority.

uncertain that Christianity actually has any more influence in these three countries than it does in the United States, and most of us would be very reluctant to actually list the United States as a "Christian" ruled country.

So this test, to find a religion that controls the governments of most of the countries in the Mediterranean area once again yields Islam.

The next test is to find a religion that is rabidly anti-Christ and anti-Judaism, and has a long history of persecuting Jews and Christians. Now, it is true that Catholics have occasionally persecuted Protestants and Jews, but Catholicism is not ANTICHRIST by any stretch of the imagination. Simply pointing out that Catholicism is full of pagan rites and holds to some false doctrine is NOT sufficient to prove it is the prostitute. Christian dogma boils down to salvation by grace, Jesus' death and resurrection, the deity of Jesus, His eventual return, complete repentance and faith in Jesus for salvation, and adherence to the inspiration of the Scriptures, all of which are accepted by the Catholic Church. Catholicism simply does not fit the requirements necessary to be the Antichrist's religion.

Is Islam a radically anti-Christian and anti-Judaism religion? As we shall see in chapter eight, the refutation of most of the dogmas of Christianity, particularly that Jesus is God, is a main theme of the Islamic holy book, the Quran. In line with their theology, the history of Islam is one of bloodshed and persecution toward the saints of God. For much of Islam's early history, the followers of this dark religion simply killed anyone who refused to become a Muslim, which usually meant orthodox Christians and Jews.

REVIEW

The only religion wide spread enough, and with enough governmental influence in the Middle East to be the prostitute is Islam. Only one country that is sure to be in the Mediterranean Confederacy of Ten Kingdoms is Christian, and that could change very quickly through war or coup. The only religion in the region that is anti-Christian and anti-Judaism enough is Islam. Islam has a long history of persecuting Jews and Christians, and of evangelization through the sword.

As we have seen here, Islam is practically the only choice for the Mother of Prostitutes, and as we shall see in the next chapter, she fits that title very well.

THE ANTICHRIST'S RELIGION

In chapter eight we will discuss an amazing tradition in Islam that will allow the Antichrist to gain widespread acceptance among the world's Muslims as a type of savior or messiah. To this end, the Antichrist shall use Islam to gain control of his home country, as well as in many other countries. But Islam will NOT be the religion of the Antichrist's Kingdom, since it would stand in the way of his ambition of being declared a god. The eighth form of the prostitute will be a new religion based on Islam.

After the Antichrist gains control of the Mediterranean Confederacy of Ten Kingdoms, Revelation 17:16 says the ten kings will come to hate the prostitute, and will destroy her. This hatred will be sparked and fanned by the Antichrist and his false prophet, because the Antichrist wants to be worshipped as a god, and Islam would never tolerate a man declaring himself equal with Allah.

From his position as the final prophet of Islam, the Antichrist will radically re-interpret the Quran and spark a regional destruction of Islam as it currently exists.[86] In his new religion, the Antichrist will be a god, and his chief spokesperson will be the false prophet. The full influence of Satan released on the Antichrist's behalf, the frightening supernatural power of his false prophet, the voluntary cooperation of the religious and political leaders,[87] the "persuasion" of military force, including the physical destruction of Islamic shrines and mosques,[88] and finally the psychological effect of wearing the "mark" of this new god ON their bodies will be more than Islam can resist, and within his empire, it will crumble.

---

[86] There will still be hundreds of millions of Muslims around the world (in Indonesia, India, USA, etc.) in countries NOT under his control that will continue to practice the old, unaltered Islam. This "destruction of Islam" is very regional, and only takes place within the countries directly under the Antichrist's control.

[87] Those who don't cooperate will simply "disappear." The Antichrist will be completely ruthless.

[88] While the destruction of Muslim shrines and mosques might sound like speculation, it is based on the solid foundation of the description of the destruction of the Prostitute of the seventh empire. Revelation says ten kings, under the influence and control of the Antichrist, "will bring her to ruin and leave her naked; they will eat her flesh and burn her with fire." At any level, bringing her to ruin, leaving her naked, and burning her with fire is more than just altering the beliefs. The graphic nature of this description clearly implies it will be a VERY physical destruction.

THE WOMAN IN THE BASKET

Further emphasizing the wickedness and abominations of this final version of the prostitute, God gave a vision to the prophet Zechariah concerning her evil nature.

> *"Then the angel who was speaking to me came forward and said to me. 'Look up and see what this is that is appearing.'*
>
> *"I asked. 'What is it?'*
>
> *"He replied. 'It is a measuring basket.* [89] *And he added. 'This is the iniquity of the people throughout the land.'*
>
> *"Then the cover of lead was raised, and there in the basket was a woman! He said. 'This is wickedness.' and he pushed her back into the basket and pushed the lead cover down over its mouth.*
>
> *"Then I looked up, and there before me were two women, with the wind in their wings! They had wings like those of a stork, and they lifted up the basket between heaven and earth.*
>
> *"'Where are they taking the basket?' I asked the angel who was speaking to me.*
>
> *"He replied. "To the country of Babylonia,* [90] *to build a house for it. When it is ready, the basket will be set there in its place.'"* (Zechariah 5:5-11)

Zechariah saw a basket (Hebrew "ephah") with a lead cover. Inside the basket was a woman who the angel said represented wickedness. The woman attempted to get out of the basket, the angel pushed her back into the basket, and replaced the lead cover. Then two women with stork's wings took the basket to Babylonia to build a house for it.

Since the Hebrew word translated "basket" in this verse is "ephah," which was the largest dry measure used in commercial transactions by the Jews, most scholars have concluded the basket represents the commercialism that will be brought to Babylon, and the woman is the inherent corruption that always follows. The use of the word "ephah,"

---

[89] The Hebrew here is ephah, which was the largest dry measure used in commercial trading (about thirty seven quarts, or roughly the size of a ten gallon aquarium tank). It is clear that an actual ephah sized basket would not have been nearly large enough to hold a person, so this basket is not LITERALLY an ephah, it is just called an ephah to emphasize it is very large.

[90] Literally, "to the land of Shinar." The ancient city of Babylon was built on the Euphrates River in the plains of Shinar.

however, is not to bring commercialism into this picture, it is to emphasize the extreme size of the wickedness within.

A real "ephah" sized basket, even if shaped properly, would be barely big enough to hold a new born baby, much less a full grown woman, the use of the word "ephah" should not be taken literally. The angel said "ephah" because it was the largest measure the Jews had, NOT because the basket represented commercial trade. The idea is that there is a gigantic "full measure" of concentrated wickedness inside.

After identifying that Zechariah was staring at a measuring basket, the angel said, "*This is the iniquity of the people throughout the land.*" (Zechariah 5:6). The people throughout the land look to God like this basket. They are all filled with wickedness inside.

This basket does not have a normal lid, but is covered in lead. Lead, being extremely heavy, indicates the strength of the wickedness inside. It takes a very heavy top to keep the wickedness from escaping. The woman obviously wants to get out of the basket, since as soon as the angel lifts the lid he has to shove the woman back inside and replace the cover. She tries to get out before the appointed time.

Next, the prophet sees two women, with the wings of storks, lift the basket above the earth. The stork was listed among the unclean birds in Leviticus 11:13-19 and Deuteronomy 14:11-18, which may indicate the unclean nature of these women. However, since eagles are also listed among the unclean birds, and eagles wings do not seem to imply uncleanness, this is uncertain.[91] Regardless of whether or not the winged women are unclean, the basket and woman inside definitely are. Besides, it is unlikely that clean or pure "women" would be transporting wickedness.

When the two women lift the basket, the prophet is told that they are taking it to the land of Babylonia, where a house will be built for it. In other words, the seat or origin of this concentrated evil will be in Babylon, and from there it will flow outward into the Mediterranean area. The woman of wickedness in this basket, who will have a house in Babylon, corresponds to the prostitute in Revelation whose name is "Babylon the Great," and who represents a wicked religion centered in the city of Babylon. The difference is that the prostitute primarily represents the Antichrist's dark religion, with all its seductive, attractive trappings, that shall be headquartered in the Antichrist's capitol city. The woman in the basket, on the other hand, exclusively represents the

---

[91] Numerous "clean" things are said to have eagles wings, such as the woman in Revelation 12:14, believers in Isaiah 40:31, and the Lord in Exodus 19:4. Since the eagle was considered unclean, just having the wings of an unclean bird did not necessarily suggest uncleanness, although it might.

dark, demonic wickedness that actually underlies his religion. She initially seems very beautiful to behold, but inside beats a foul, rotting, and vermin infested heart. Beneath her beautiful face lurks a bloodthirsty dragon.

This difference is important, because when the Antichrist and the ten kings come to hate the prostitute (Islam) and destroy her, they only destroy the religion, NOT the wickedness. The wickedness continues after the destruction of Islam, and even increases as the Antichrist gains power and influence in the final three and a half years.[92] But the prostitute is not gone. The old prostitute (Islam) has been replaced by the new prostitute (the Antichrist's religion), and it is THIS version of the prostitute that becomes the summation of wickedness. The evil woman in the basket primarily represents the LAST version of the prostitute, which will be the worst, most violent, most corrupt, most evil religion ever.

The theory that identifies the prostitute as Catholicism also interprets this woman in the basket as Catholicism. When the two women lift the basket and take it to Babylon, this theory says it is being lifted from Rome, and represents the relocation of the Vatican to the City of Babylon in the last days. This is pure speculation since there is not the slightest evidence that this basket started, or was ever in Rome. In full fact, there is not the slightest hint as to where the basket started. Why? Because it is not relevant where "wickedness" started, the important thing is that in the last days it becomes concentrated in the city of Babylon.

The theory that Catholicism is both the prostitute and the woman in the basket must also postulate that when Catholicism moves to Babylon, and comes to dominate the region, that it completely displaces Islam. This requires that the Vatican become a military power strong enough to challenge the combined might of all the Arab forces in the Middle East.

Since there are about eight hundred million Muslims in the Mediterranean area alone, the primary religion that would be persecuted by the "Catholic Prostitute" would be Islam, not Christianity. Christians only make up about one to three percent of the population in the Middle East (estimated at less than ten million out of eight hundred million), so this prostitute would not be drunk with the blood of the saints, she would be drunk with the blood of the Muslims.

As can be seen, the "some form of Christianity is the prostitute" approach continues to have no foundation upon which to build a theory.

---

[92] See Revelation 18

THE LAMB BEAST REVISITED

At this point, let us examine the lamb beast in Revelation chapter thirteen again. If you will recall from chapter five, we came to the following conclusions about the lamb beast: It represents the leader of a religion, and as with kings and kingdoms, it also represents the religion.

Of the religion represented by the lamb beast, we know the following:

Number one: since the lamb is a beast, and beasts are representative of empires, the religion must be a type of "empire". This fits Islam since it actually became a literal empire, and today it literally runs the governments of most "Muslim" countries.

Number two: since it appears as a lamb, a symbol of purity and holiness, it must have a definitive set of moral codes. It must recognize the existence of "right" and "wrong," although its idea of "good and bad" will be skewed from God's. As is true of most religions, Islam is legalistic, and has a definite idea of "right" and "wrong." In line with item two, Islam's idea of morality and holiness, to a large degree, has nothing to do with true holiness and purity. Many of the things taught in Islam, as we shall see in chapter eight, are presented as signs of true holiness, and are downright evil in God's eyes.

Number three: since it persecutes those who do not adhere to its tenets, it must be exclusive (present itself as the ONLY truth). As is true with all evangelistic religions, Islam believes that the only way to have any hope of reaching paradise and escape hell is to become a Muslim.

Number four: also since it looks like a lamb, it must portray itself as very righteous and holy. As illustrated almost daily in the fiery denunciations of evil western living, Muslims believe that they are very holy, and that only by becoming a Muslim can one attain true holiness. The Muslim idea holiness revolves around legalistic rites performed each day. All of these "religious" beliefs and actions have the effect of making the flesh feel very pure, spiritual, and holy, while none of them actually rid the soul of sin.

Number five: since it speaks like a dragon (Satan), the words and actions (past and present) of this religion must reflect evil and corruption by God's standards. As we shall see in chapter eight, this fits Islam very well.

Number six: since the lamb beast represents a man who controls or speaks for the religion, it must be so organized that it can be controlled or manipulated by a type of prophet. This we shall also address in detail in chapter eight. Islam, particularly among the Shi'ites, fits this requirement perfectly.

Number seven: since the lamb has two horns, neither of which change in any way, the religion must have two stable divisions within it. Islam has two major divisions: the Sunnis and the Shi'ites. This division developed within a hundred years of the founding of Islam, and there has been very little change in the fundamental beliefs, and differences between these two divisions for well over a thousand years.

Number eight: since the lamb performs miracles on behalf of the leopard beast, it should recognize and accept the existence of "miracles." The Quran is filled with talk of miracles, and the belief in them is fundamental to Islam.

Number nine: since it performs all of its works on behalf of the Antichrist, and it kills those who do not worship him, it must have a very strong "Antichrist" bent. As America painfully experienced September 11, 2001, and as we shall see in chapter eight, antagonism and outright hostility toward Christians (or any non-Muslims), and a complete denial of the deity of Jesus, as well as his death and resurrection is fundamental to Islam. [93]

Number ten: since the lamb beast deceives the "whole" world, it most likely will have a very large following. It is currently estimated that one quarter of the worlds population is Muslim (over one billion people).

Number eleven: it must be in the area where the Antichrist will rule. As discussed previously, the majority of the countries in the Middle East are Muslim.

Number twelve: since it actively seeks to make everyone worship the Antichrist, its theology must be so structured that a physical man

---

[93] Is has become popular today to say that Muslim terrorists are NOT true Muslims, but rather, an extremist, radical minority, because Islam is actually a religion of love, understanding and compassion. The position that Islam is a religion of love, understanding and compassion is not supported in the Quran. It is not supported by the history of Islam. And even more telling, it is not supported by the actions of its founder, Muhammad, who actively used violence and warfare to spread his religion, and promised an instant pass to heaven to any follower who died in a religiously motivated battle. In fact, there is only ONE way to be absolutely assured of heaven in Islam: be killed in a religious battle. Even Muhammad himself admitted that from the way he lived his life alone, he had no genuine guarantee of heaven. Only a few Muslim leaders in the world today actually condemn Islamic inspired terrorism, such as the suicide attacks that occurred on 9/11, or those that Israel has endured for years (in fact, many "moderate" Muslim religious leaders have PRAISED the suicide attacks against Israel). To perpetuate the idea that true Muslims are not violent, they point to the scriptures in the Quran calling for peace. What they do NOT mention is that those "peaceful" scriptures were superceded by the ones calling for violence, and no longer have the force of scripture. Either way, the Antichrist is NOT going to be a "moderate" man of love and compassion.

could be declared a god. Islam does not fit this criterion, and Muslims would violently resist such a declaration. Here, then, is where the Antichrist will make his most far-reaching alterations to the Muslim faith. Since there is probably no more basic fundamental in Islam than the nature of Allah, any change to their understanding of God would essentially cause Islam as it is today to cease to exist. In altering the Islamic faith, the Antichrist destroys it.

We know that Islam in its current form is destroyed three and a half years into the tribulation by the ten kings, who now do anything the Antichrist orders. We know that it is during the last three and a half years that the Antichrist has his full power, and declares himself a god. We also know that during those three and a half years, the lamb beast will be the Antichrist's prophet. From this we can conclude that the lamb beast represents the altered Islamic faith during the last three and a half years of the tribulation. It is this new religion that deifies the Antichrist, which shall be centered in Babylon. Islam will never be centered there.

So the ten kings destroy the great prostitute (Islam), and she is replaced by the great prostitute (Altered Islam, which we shall simply call the Antichrist's Religion). She replaces herself, or more accurately, the seventh form of the prostitute ceases to exist, and the eighth form comes into existence three and a half years into the tribulation. This is really not so wild as it sounds, since it actually happened each time a new empire came along.

If her destruction and reappearance happened six times before, why is not each occurrence illustrated in the scriptures? For several reasons: First, at no other time did any ruler consciously destroy an old religion, and create his own in order to get himself declared a god. Second, at no other time did the ruler or rulers of the previous empire assist the conquering empire in eliminating their own religion. Third, at no other time would the removal of the old prostitute and the installation of the new one play such a crucial role in establishing the credibility of the new emperor. Fourth, this is the final crucial move that allows the leader of the newly conquered confederacy to actually BECOME the Antichrist (by allowing him to be widely recognized as a god in the flesh), around whom most of the events in Revelation revolve. Finally, aside from any of these reasons, we know the prostitute exists in the eighth kingdom, the Antichrist's empire, because she is sitting, not just on the seven heads, but on the whole beast, which represents that final kingdom. This is not hard to accept when you focus on what she represents: the pagan, Christian and Jew hating, government-controlling religions of each gentile empire illustrated on the scarlet leopard beast.

At the time that the Antichrist manipulates the destruction of Islam, gets himself declared a god, invades Israel, sets up the abomination of desolation, and comes into his full power and authority, all half way through the tribulation period, another interesting thing happens: He receives reports from the north and east which anger him, and he charges forth to destroy the source of those undesirable tidings.

As we mentioned earlier, the most likely source for these annoying tidings are the Russian republics, which will most likely be independent by this time, of Uzbekistan, Tajikstan, Azerbaijan, Turkmenistan, Afghanistan and Pakistan. All six of these countries are Muslim, and most of those Muslims are independent minded Shi'ites, tribal members, and radicals. Thus it is very likely that the tidings from the north and east are reports about a rising tide of revolution among these countries against the Antichrist because of his destruction of Islam. These countries will most likely NOT be under his immediate control, will be extremely angry at him for declaring himself a god, and will not tolerate his destruction of their beloved religion.

After conquering the rebelling republics, the Antichrist will return to Israel where he will meet his end at the hand of our Lord Jesus.

SUMMARY

The "Mother of Prostitutes" is not symbolic of one, but of eight religions. Since she existed during each of the previous six empires, and will also exist in the two future empires, she must be eight different religions. She alternately represents the state religions of the Egyptians, the Assyrians, the Babylonians, the Medes and Persians, the Grecians, and the pagan Romans.

During the Mediterranean Confederacy of Ten Kingdoms she will be Islam, and after her destruction at the hands of the Antichrist-controlled ten kings, she will be a radically altered form of Islam that will allow the Antichrist to declare himself a god. The lamb beast depicts this new, Antichrist-deifying religion that will spring from the ashes of the old Islam.

The prostitute also represents the literal city of Babylon, which will be the Antichrist's capitol city, the center of Middle Eastern trade, and the holy city of the Antichrist's new religion. The woman in the basket represents the demonic wickedness that shall be concentrated in Babylon. God destroys the literal city through the earthquake and hail of the seventh vial.

QUESTIONS
FROM CHAPTER SEVEN

1) What does "the mother of" designation mean?
2) What does the woman in the basket represent?
3) How are the prostitute and the woman in the basket similar? How are they different?
4) What are the five things that will not be found in Babylon any longer (after her destruction)? What do these five things represent?
5) What does the prostitute represent? How does she "change" in each of the empires?
6) What is the predominant religion in the region where the Antichrist will reign?
7) What is the one thing about Islam that does NOT fit with the lamb beast?
8) Why do the Antichrist and the ten kings come to hate the prostitute?
9) How is it possible that the prostitute still exists after the Antichrist and the ten kings destroy her? What does this "new" prostitute represent?
10) What is different about the religion of the Antichrist, versus the religion of the Confederacy? What changed?

SECTION TWO
WHO IS BABYLON THE GREAT?

BABYLON THE GREAT, THE MOTHER OF PROSTITUTES:
The Teachings of Islam

ISLAM

For honest, uncompromising and thorough examinations of Islam, its teachings, history, ethics, founder, practices, beliefs, and the major differences between it and Christianity, we highly recommend the following three books: *Unveiling Islam*, by Ergun and Emir Caner;[94] *Islam and Terrorism: What the Quran Really Teaches About Christianity, Violence and the Goals of the Islamic Jihad* and *Islam and the Jews: The Unfinished Battle*, both by Mark Gabriel.[95] These books examine Islam or issues relating to Islam, in much greater detail than it is our purpose to do in this book. All of them ultimately lend more credence to our assertion that Islam is the Great Prostitute of the Mediterranean Confederacy of Ten Kingdoms.[96]

---

[94] Ergun and Emir Caner were raised in Muslim homes in North America, and became Christians as teens. Most of their family still remain Muslims to this day. "Unveiling Islam" ISBN 0-8254-2400-3.

[95] Mark Gabriel was an Imam in Giza, Egypt, and a professor of Islamic History at Al-Azhar University. Almost a year after rejecting the Quran, his search for truth lead him to read the Bible, and to a saving faith in Jesus. His testimony, from his first book, is online at http://www.arabicbible.com/testimonies/gabriel.htm. "Islam and the Jews" ISBN 0-88419-956-8.

[96] As we were about to go to print on this second edition, we were fortunate to find a newly published book that takes a slightly different approach, but ultimately comes to exactly the same conclusion, that the Antichrist will use the religion of Islam to rise to power. This book spends more time discussing Islam, and thus goes into greater detail on the teachings of Islam, and how they relate to the rise of the Antichrist. For those wishing to continue their study of this position, we highly recommend "Antichrist: Islam's Awaited Messiah," by Joel Richardson, published by Pleasant Word (a division of WinePress Publishing). ISBN 1-4141-0440-5.

In order to familiarize you with Islam, we will start with a brief history of the religion from Mohammed to the establishment of the Islamic Empire.

Mohammed was born about 570 AD in the City of Mecca. At the age of forty (610 AD) he received his first visitation from a being who he reports was Gabriel, the chief messenger angel of God. Over the next twenty-two years until his death in 632 AD of a fever, Mohammed received constant revelations.

The Muslim calendar starts in the year 622 AD, when Mohammed and his followers fled from Mecca to Medina to escape persecution. The Muslim calendar uses the designation AH (Anno Hegirae, meaning "in the year of the flight"), and is lunar based, rather than solar based like our western calendar. Thus 2002 AD on the western calendar is 1380 AH on the Muslim calendar.

By the ninth year after the flight to Medina Mohammed was the virtual ruler of the whole Arab peninsula. Over the next several hundred years Islam spread, primarily through war, to rule most of the Middle East. The rule of the Sunni division in the Islamic community was first united in the Umayyad Dynasty in Damascus, later it went to the Abbasid Dynasty in Baghdad, until finally settling on the Ottoman Dynasty in Turkey, which lasted until the end of World War I.

The primary division in Islam, between the Shia and Sunni sects took place very early in Muslim history when a dispute developed over the rightful succession of the Islamic leadership. The Shia sect held to Ali, Mohammed's cousin and the husband of Mohammed's daughter Fatima, while the Sunni division, which encompasses about eighty percent of the Muslim believers, felt no need to stick to relatives of Mohammed.

The Shia sect makes up the majority of the population in Iran, and holds a large percentage of the population in Iraq, Syria and Afghanistan, with substantial populations in a few other countries, such as Pakistan. In every other country, the Shia are tiny, tiny minorities.

The holy book of the Muslims is called the Quran, which means, "That which is to be Recited." The Quran is roughly the size of the New Testament, and is separated into 114 chapters, called Surahs. Traditionally, most English translations give the number of the Surah in Roman numerals (I, II, III, IV, etc.), and the verse designation in Arabic notation (1, 2, 3, 4, etc.), with a comma separating the two. In recent years it has become popular in America to use the same chapter and verse method as used for the New Testament (Arabic notation with a colon between the chapter and verse).

ISLAMIC VIEW OF THE BIBLE

Muslims consider the Bible, which they separate into the Torah and the Gospel (the Old and New Testaments), to be the inspired word of God in their original form. The Quran even states that the Torah and the Gospel reveal that Mohammed is from God, and that the Quran actually confirms the validity of the Bible.

> *"Those who follow the messenger, the prophet who can neither read nor write,*[97] *whom they will find described in the Torah and the Gospel with them."* (Surah VII, 157)

> *"He hath revealed unto thee the scripture of truth, confirming that which was revealed before it, even as He revealed the Torah and the Gospel."* (Surah III, 3)

Of course, the Bible does not confirm that Mohammed is from God. Mohammed is not mentioned in the Bible at all.[98] Not only does the Quran NOT confirm Scripture, in almost every instance in which the same story, incident, or person is described in the Quran and the Bible, they conflict with each other on almost every point. Of the many people that appear in both books about which they disagree are Abraham, Adam, Noah, Mary, Jesus, Moses, Job, Isaac, and Jonah. It would be difficult to find two books covering the same subjects that conflict more than the Quran and our Scriptures.

Muslims are now aware that the Bible and the Quran disagree at every turn, and their only explanation is that the Torah and the Gospel have become extremely corrupted down through the years.[99] Some Muslim clerics have gone so far as to claim that the Old and New Testaments are NOT the Torah and the Gospel. That those books were revealed to Moses and Jesus, and have ceased to exist, and our current

---

[97] It is widely believed that Mohammed was relatively illiterate, and his inability to read or write is occasionally noted in the Quran.

[98] Muslims point to such scriptures as John 1:21, where the priests and Levites ask John the Baptist if he is "the prophet," and he answers, "no," as references to Mohammed.

[99] The irony of this Muslim criticism of the bible is that Islam teaches that the Gospel was given by Allah, and if it has become corrupt, that means the words of Allah can be corrupted, something Islam denies is possible. If Allah's words can NOT be corrupted, then the gospel is true, and Jesus is the only way to God. If Allah's words CAN be corrupted, then Allah is not all-powerful, and the Quran is just as suspect as the Bible. They are caught in their own trap.

books are not inspired in any way.[100] No evidence of the existence of these "other" books has ever been found.

Muslims are aware of modern radical criticism of the scriptures, and have concluded from the many slight variations found among the thirty thousand or more manuscripts of the New Testament that the New Testament is corrupt and flawed. In this they have mistaken obvious scribal errors, such as the absence or addition or words like "the," "and," or "but," the absence or addition of punctuation marks, slight variations in word order (in a language in which words can be in almost any order without affecting the meaning of the sentence much), word misspellings, and duplicate words as major corruptions.[101] The truth is that modern scholars have so many old manuscripts to compare that they consider the modern manuscript of the New Testament to be the most accurate compilation of any ancient manuscript on the planet.

From this base, let us now launch into the meat of our case. Islam is fundamentally opposed to the deity of Jesus, is anti-Christian, anti-Judaism, allows the persecution of the saints of God, and has a strong tradition that will allow for one man to become a type of messiah and rule the Muslim world.

JESUS

Islam firmly denies the deity of Jesus, which is the first foundation upon which Christianity is based.

> *"Say: 'Allah is one, the Eternal God. He begat none, nor was He begotten. None is equal to Him."* (Surah CXII)

> *"The Messiah, Jesus, the Son of Mary, was no more than Allah's apostle and His word, which he cast to Mary: A spirit from Him. So Believe in Allah and His apostles and do not say: 'Three.' Forbear, and it shall be better for you. Allah is but one God. Allah forbid that he should have a son!"* (Surah IV, 169)

> *"The Jews say. 'Ezra is the Son of God'; the Christians say. 'The Messiah is the Son of God.' That is the utterance of*

---

[100] McDowell, Josh, and John Gilchrist, "The Islam Debate," Here's Life Publishers, 1983, Page 38.

[101] Ninety-nine percent of all "variations" are unimportant scribal errors of very little interest except to textual historians. Of the other "variations," not one occurs in a section dealing with a major doctrine of Christianity. Not one doctrine in scripture is suspect because of "variations" (copy errors) in the manuscripts.

their mouths, conforming with the unbelievers before them. God assail them! How they are perverted! They have taken their Rabbis and Monks as Lords apart from God, and the Messiah, Mary's son, and they were commanded to serve but one God; there is no God but Allah; Glory be to Him above that they associate." (Surah IX, 30-31)

It is unclear why Mohammed thought the Jews exalted Ezra to the position of God, or why he thought that the Christians and Jews exalted all their religious leaders to that of God. In any event, he was once again wrong.

"They are unbelievers who say, 'God is the Messiah, Mary's son.'"(Surah V, 76)

"And they say, 'The All-Merciful has taken unto Himself a Son.' You have indeed advanced something hideous." (Surah XIX, 91)

Now contrast this with scripture.

"In the Beginning was the Word, and the Word was with God, and the Word was God. He was with God in the Beginning. Through Him all things were made: without Him nothing was made that has been made. In Him was life, and that life was the light of men. The light shines in the darkness, but the darkness has not understood it. He was in the world, and though the world was made through Him, the world did not recognize Him . . . to all who received Him, to those who believed in His name, he gave the right to become the children of God . . . The Word became flesh and made His dwelling among us. We have seen His glory, the glory of the only begotten of the Father, full of grace and truth." (John 1:1-5, 10, 12, 14)

"If you do not believe that I Am, you will die in your sins." (John 8:24)

"For in Him dwells all the fullness of absolute divinity bodily."[102] (Colossians 2:9)

---

[102] Some translations, such as the King James, read, "…fullness of the *Godhead* bodily." The best translation of theotes is "absolute divinity." When the King James

"And now, O Father, glorify Me alongside Yourself, with the glory which I had with You before the world was." (John 17:5)

Acceptance of the deity of Jesus is not optional in Christianity, and Jesus Himself made it vital for salvation. It is so fundamental that scripture says a refusal to believe Jesus is God in the flesh is the spirit of the Antichrist.

"Dear friends, do not believe every spirit, but test the spirits to see whether they are from God, because many false prophets have gone out into the world. This is how you can recognize the Spirit of God: Every spirit that acknowledges that Jesus Christ has come in the flesh is from God, but every spirit that does not acknowledge Jesus is not from God. This is the spirit of the Antichrist, which you have heard is coming and even now is already in the world." (I John 4:1-3)

We acknowledge that Mohammed received his revelations from a spirit, but as this scripture shows, it was not a spirit from God. He received his inspiration from the spirit of the Antichrist, straight from the pits of Hell, by the authority of Satan.

The Quran lists several "proofs" that Jesus could not possibly be God.

"The Messiah, son of Mary, was only a messenger; messengers before him passed away: his mother was just a woman: they both ate food. Behold, how we make clear the signs to them: then behold, how perverted they are." (Surah V, 79)

"They are unbelievers who say, 'God is the Messiah, Mary's son!' Say: 'who then shall overrule God in any way if He desires to destroy the Messiah, Mary's Son, and his mother, and all those who are on the earth?'" (Surah V, 19)

---

was originally translated, 400 years ago, that is what the word "Godhead" was understood to mean. It means "the divine essence of being God; that which makes God divine."

The idea behind the first argument is that if Jesus ate, He could not possibly be God, because God does not require food. The second argument postulates that if Jesus was divine, then God could not destroy Him if He so desired. Thus Jesus would have overruled God, and since God cannot be overruled, Jesus could not possibly be God. Both of these arguments merely show Mohammed's lack of comprehension for the miracle of incarnation.

The irony of the second argument is that God did desire to have his son die, and that death ensured that the world would not be completely destroyed. Through the death and resurrection of our Lord, which scripture says pleased the Lord because it made it possible to rid the world of sin, Jesus made salvation accessible to each of us. This is the next fundamental of Christianity, after the deity of Jesus: the death and resurrection of Jesus. The Quran teaches that Jesus was not crucified, and if He was not actually crucified, then He could not have been raised from the dead. Speaking of the Jews, the Quran says:

> "For their unbelief, and their uttering against Mary, a mighty calumny, and for their saying, 'we slew the Messiah, Jesus, the son of Mary, the Messenger of God.' Yet they did not slay him, neither crucified him, only a likeness of him that was shown to them. Those who are at variance concerning him surely are in doubt regarding him. They have no knowledge of him, except the following surmise: and they slew him not of a certainty - no indeed: God raised him up to him." (Surah IV, 155-156)

The Quran teaches that Jesus was not killed on the cross, but was caught up to Heaven without ever suffering death. It is interesting that Satan finds the death of Jesus so powerful that he does not just claim that Jesus died, but was never resurrected. This spirit of the Antichrist refuses to admit that Jesus even died. Of course, without his death and resurrection there is no forgiveness of sins, no salvation, no Christianity. This is an Antichrist teaching if ever there was one.

As previous verses from the Quran have revealed, Muslims believe Christians and Jews to be unbelievers. Satan knows the power of the Holy Spirit, so he tried to ensure that it would have no chance to work on his followers.

> "O Believers, take not Jews and Christians as friends; they are friends of each other. Who so of you makes them

his friends is one of them. God guides not the people of the evildoers." (Surah V, 56)

So how are Muslims supposed to react to unbelievers?

"When you meet the unbelievers, smite their necks[103], then, when you have made wide slaughter among them, tie fast the bonds: then set them free, either by grace or ransom, till the war lays down its loads. That is the law. If Allah willed He could have punished them without you, but thus it is ordained that He may try some of you by means of others. And those who are slain in the way of Allah, he rendereth not their actions vain. He will guide them and improve their state, and bring them unto the Paradise which He hath made known to them." (Surah XLVII, 4-6)

Muslims are authorized to slay any of those who do not accept their religion. The last references to Muslims who die in battle ensure that Muslims will not fear to spread their faith through Holy War (Jihad), because they are guaranteed instant access to Paradise if they die fighting for the cause of Allah.

The motivation behind much of the devotional life of a Muslim (praying five times a day, fasting during Ramadan, giving alms to the poor, the pilgrimage to Mecca, reciting the Quran, etc.) is the legalism of merit. There are a large number of traditions in Islam that claim that one's status in Paradise is determined by the amount of merit one has stored up. When Islam was first expanding out into an empire, one of the main methods of gaining merit was to participate in a Holy War (Jihad) for the cause of Allah. Because of the teaching about going straight to Paradise if a Muslim dies on the battlefield against unbelievers with sword in hand, and because martyrs were said to hold very favorable positions in Paradise, Muslims were more than happy to make war on their unbelieving neighbors. This practice is on the rise again, and will find numerous adherents in force in the last days.[104]

---

[103] This is worth noting. Muslims interpret this command to mean "behead" and so, have always used beheading to execute "infidels." Compare this with Revelation 20:4 *"Then I saw thrones, and they sat on them, and judgment was given to them. And I saw the **souls of those who had been beheaded because of their testimony of Jesus** and because of the word of God..."* The Antichrist doesn't just "kill" them, it specifically says they were "beheaded." The only religion that continues to use beheading as a form of execution is ISLAM.

[104] Jeffery, Arthur, "Islam, Mohammed and His Religion"; Bobbs-Merrill Educational

As can be clearly seen, not only is it allowable for Muslims to make war on non-Muslims, it is almost a requirement. This practice has been much curtailed in recent years, but it shall increase as we get nearer the end, when the prostitute shall once again begin to demand blood to fill her golden cup.

THE MUSLIM BELIEFS ABOUT THE END TIMES

Islam teaches that this era will come to an end, and the end is called the Day of Judgment. On the Day of Judgment, the righteous will be rewarded in Paradise, while the evil will be confined to the fires of hell. There are numerous signs of the end.

According to one of the more widely accepted traditions, Mohammed said the end will not come until ten signs have been fulfilled.

The first sign is the rising of the sun from the west. When the sun first rises from where it normally sets, the faithful Muslims will know that the end is near.

The second sign is the appearance of a gigantic beast, made up of parts of many animals, who will brand all men on their heads so that it will be readily apparent who are believers and who are not. This beast seems to parallel the leopard beast in Revelation, that represents the Antichrist. The leopard beast is made up of different animals, and has his mark placed on the heads or hands of everyone in his empire.

The third sign is the invasion of Gog and Magog. Islam interprets Gog and Magog to mean barbarians from the north, who, according to the tradition, will break through the barrier that Alexander the Great set up to keep them out. No Muslims are exactly certain what this means. They will persecute and harass the faithful Muslims, causing great havoc until Jesus, the son of Mary, returns from Heaven to destroy them.

The fourth sign is the rise of a false prophet who deceives many believers. This false prophet will work miracles, perform many wonders, and will pretend he is the Lord, until Jesus, the son of Mary, destroys him when he returns from heaven. This false prophet seems to parallel the False Prophet in Revelation, except the one in Revelation does not declare himself to be god, he declares the Antichrist to be god.

The fifth sign is the return of Jesus, the son of Mary, from heaven to destroy Gog and Magog, along with the false prophet. Remember, the "Jesus" described in the Quran is a prophet of Islam, never died, was never resurrected, and is returning to vindicate Muslims, punish the Christians (who purposely perverted his gospel), and destroy the

Publishing, Indianapolis, 1958, page 212

enemies of Islam. Jesus is returning, but not to accomplish what Satan has told his follower to expect.

The sixth sign is dense smoke that will cover the earth for several days. Along with the smoke will come the next three signs: an eclipse in the West, another in the East, and another over the Arabian Peninsula. Some translators say the word for eclipse actually means earthquake, which would make this a prediction of three earthquakes.

The final sign of the end will be fire that rages up from Yemen to drive everyone to the place where they will await the Day of Judgment.[105]

It is at first startling how closely some of these predictions parallel the prophesies in Revelation and Daniel, until we consider that Daniel had been in circulation about nine hundred years, and Revelation about five hundred years by the time Mohammed made these predictions. Additionally, since Satan is probably aware of at least some of the events that will take place in the last days, he can make predictions of his own that parallel those events closely enough so that when they actually occur, he is able to keep his followers deceived and under his control. Rather than being shocked into reevaluation, they will just interpret the events as Satan says they should be interpreted, and get sucked deeper into the darkness of his control.

THE MAHDI

The Shia, who place much more emphasis on the "prophet/leaders" than do the Sunnis, believe that Allah decreed twelve great prophet/leaders, called "Imams," to guide the Muslims. The last one, the twelfth Imam, disappeared in the year 878 AD (265 A.H. on the Muslim Calendar), and they say he "went into occultation."[106] Just before the Day of Judgment, the twelfth Imam will reappear to lead the Muslims, put down their enemies, and usher in the Day of Judgment.[107] Of the numerous things the twelfth Imam will accomplish, most notable is that he will interpret the dark passages of the Quran, settle the differences between the sects, and vindicate Shia doctrine.

This tradition is worth noting since Shi'ites predominate in the region where the Antichrist shall come to power, and thus he could make use of this tradition to more readily get him recognized as the "ruler of Islam." The Sunnis (forming over eighty percent of all Muslims), however, do not accept the existence of a twelfth Imam,

---

[105] Jeffery, pages 143-144.

[106] That is interpreted by modern Shi'ites as meaning he is still alive, but in hiding.

[107] Some of the Shia believe it was only seven, but the effect is the same, since both expect the coming Mahdi to be the last one.

which would make the area of the Antichrist's influence very limited, hindering his efforts to eventually get rid of Islam in favor of his own religion.

There exists another tradition that is accepted by most Sunnis, about one who will come just before the Day of Judgment, called the Mahdi. While most Sunnis do not accept the tradition of the twelfth Imam, they do accept the Mahdi. The Shi'ites simply claim that the twelfth Imam and the Mahdi are the same person.

Neither the twelfth Imam nor the Mahdi are mentioned in the Quran (which is why some Muslims do not accept either), but both have strong written traditions that are accepted as inspired truth by the Shi'ites. Being much more widely accepted than the twelfth Imam (among Sunnis and Shi'ites), the tradition of the Mahdi is the more interesting and powerful one.

The Mahdi can almost be called the Muslim Messiah. The expectation of his coming among those who firmly believe the Mahdi traditions is something like the expectation of Jesus' return by Christians. His coming is so important that the tradition says that if only one day remained before The Hour, Allah would lengthen that day in order to allow time for the Mahdi to appear and accomplish his primary purpose ("to fill the earth with justice and equity as it has been filled with injustice and oppression"[108]). The primary difference between the Mahdi and the Messiah is that the Mahdi will not be God, just a great leader.

According to the traditions, the Mahdi will be descended from the house of Mohammed, through his daughter Fatima. The Mahdi's name will be Mohammed, and some say his father's name will be Abdallah (the same as the original Mohammed's father). The Mahdi will have a bald forehead, a hooked nose, and most interestingly of all, the tradition states that the world will not end until this man has ruled over the Arabs for seven years, at which time, he will die.[109]

The Antichrist will take advantage of this tradition, which Satan has set in place in preparation for this man of iniquity. At some point a powerful, charismatic religious leader will arise in Syria and become the 'real' leader.[110] The Antichrist will assume the identity of the Mahdi to build a following among the Arabs in and around Syria. From his position as the new spiritual leader of Islam, he will have the

---

[108] Jeffery, page 145.

[109] Jeffery, pages 145-147.

[110] A situation similar to Iran during the 1980's may arise, with the Antichrist assuming the role as spiritual leader, along with the real power, and the "official" king remaining in power, but only as a figurehead.

unwavering support of the Shi'ite Muslims in Syria, what remains of Iraq, and Iran. The "official" king of New Syria will probably retain his position as king (and as a member on the counsel of ten kings in the Mediterranean Confederacy of Ten Kingdoms), but the real power will be in the hands of the Mahdi.

Since the tradition of the Mahdi is not in the Quran, and is not completely accepted among the Sunnis, the Mediterranean Confederacy of Ten Kingdoms will not voluntarily turn the confederate empire over to the Antichrist. The Antichrist probably will have started "re-interpreting" the Quran, presenting radical, blasphemous teachings to the Muslim world. This will only solidify the resolve of the council.[111]

This refusal to accept his authority will "force" the Antichrist to publicly denounce the members of the council as unbelievers for defying the will of Allah. He will then be justified in declaring a Jihad against the Mediterranean Confederacy of Ten Kingdoms, in order to bring them back under the wing of Allah. After three and a half years of war, having conquered three of the countries, and on the verge of destroying the rest, the confederacy will bow to his authority. And the whole Arab world will know for sure that the Mahdi has come.[112]

After his subjugation of the confederacy, the ten leaders of the council will accept the Antichrist's proclamations as coming from Allah himself, and will assist him in getting rid of the old Islam in favor of his new, demon-worshiping, Antichrist-deifying religion.[113] At this point a man will appear who will do awesome miracles, including calling fire down from heaven, and who will claim to have received his power from the Antichrist. His appearance will hasten the destruction of Islam. This False Prophet will become the "high priest" of the Antichrist's new religion, second in command in the empire, and will be a key element in getting the Antichrist accepted as god among the people of the empire.

---

[111] Recall the visions in Daniel where the Antichrist is depicted speaking boastfully from the moment he arrives. He promptly attacks the Mediterranean Confederacy of Ten Kingdoms, uprooting three.

[112] It is only AFTER the conquest of the Mediterranean Confederacy of Ten Kingdoms that the Antichrist has his full power and authority. According to Daniel, he will only have complete authority and power for the last forty-two months (three and a half years) of his reign.

[113] The ten horns come to hate the prostitute, and destroy her. This is the end of the prostitute religion of the seventh kingdom, Islam, and the beginning of the prostitute religion of the eighth. This new religion will be the Antichrist's re-interpretation of Islam. The destruction of Islam within the area under the Antichrist's control is so thorough (as we mentioned in the previous chapter) that it is doubtful he will even retain the name "Islam" for his new religion (although it is "based" on Islam). He will most likely give it a completely new name.

Then will come the rebellion of the countries to the north and east. The Antichrist, with the full support of most of the Arab world, will attack and demolish these infidels. This war will also last about three and a half years. After the subjugation of the tribes in the north and east, the Antichrist will return to Israel, to the valley on the south side of mount Carmel,[114] to await the return of Jesus. The Antichrist will gather all the forces under his command, including any that can be deceived into joining him.[115]

SUMMARY

As we have shown in this chapter, the woman with the title, "Mystery, Babylon the Great, the Mother of Prostitutes and of the Abominations of the Earth" will be Islam during the seventh empire in our progression, the Mediterranean Confederacy of Ten Kingdoms.

Islam has a following that completely dwarfs that of all other religions in the Mediterranean area; it is radically anti-Christian and anti-Judaism; it fervently believes that Jesus is not God, and states that the proclamation of his deity is hideous; it allows for the murder of those who are not Muslims and will not convert; and it has a tradition that shall allow the Antichrist to step in as the new world leader.

But this religion is not the worst.

The Antichrist will destroy Islam as it currently exists, and will replace it with a religion, steeped in demon worship, that will accept him as god. This will be the ultimate Satan can devise.

Islam is the Great Prostitute ONLY in her seventh form: the religion that rules over the Mediterranean Confederacy of Ten Kingdoms. Islam is NOT the Great Prostitute religion of the Antichrist. That religion, the eighth form of the Prostitute, a type of Neo-Islam that is modified beyond recognition, will be much, much worse.

CONCLUSION

So what is the purpose of this book? To better equip the saints of God to prepare for the coming insanity, so that they will not be caught unaware, and unprepared, at the arrival of the man of sin. Unless the church gets its eyes off of Catholicism, Rome, Russia, and the Common Market, the arrival of the Antichrist in New Syria will catch it

---

[114] Armageddon means "the mountains of Megiddo." Megiddo is a city south of Mount Carmel situated at the entrance to the only militarily important pass through the Carmel mountains. The pass forms a valley in which the Antichrist and his grunts shall meet their end.

[115] In Revelation 16:13-16, the Antichrist, the Dragon, and the False Prophet send three unclean spirits out to deceive the nations that are not directly under the Antichrist's control into joining him at Armageddon.

completely off guard, and the deceptive, seductive power of the demons under his control will have an even greater effect, because the church will not see it coming.

Because they have not seen it coming, and have not listened to the Spirit of the Lord warning them to flee, many Christians will be persecuted, and will die in the Middle East. The Antichrist and his religion will show no mercy.

Awaken, 0 Israel, throw off the veils that blind you to the coming events. Shake free from your preconceived ideas about the End, and let the Spirit of the Lord open your eyes to the signs of the times. These things are even now right at the door. Do hide your head in the muddled waters of comforting teachings that promise rescue from all persecution. Seek God for the full power of His Spirit, so that when persecution comes, you will not crumble, you will not be crushed, but you will stand against it, not by power and might, but by His Spirit.

May our Lord and Savior watch over you and your family in the coming insanity. To Him belong all praises and glory forever and ever. Amen.

END TIMES PREDICTIONS
BASED ON SECTION TWO

17) The ruling religion of the Mediterranean Confederacy will be Islam.

18) The Antichrist, along with the ten kings, will destroy Islam as it exists today by declaring himself that Mahdi, and reinterpreting the Quran so that he is recognized as a god.

19) The destruction of Islam will spark a rebellion among some Muslim states to the north and east (the "stans": Afghanistan, Pakistan, Tazikstan, Turkmenistan, Uzbekistan).

20) After beating the revolutionaries in the north and east, the Antichrist will return to Israel, and will send ambassadors around the world to get as many nations as possible to join him there. Many nations will agree to send troops to Palestine.

21) The Antichrist, having interpreted the many plagues thrown upon him correctly (the trumpets, vials, and thunders in Revelation), will know that the return of Christ is imminent, and will actually gather his troops at Mount Carmel to await the return, hoping to defeat him.

HOW CLOSE ARE WE TO THE END?
The Multimetallic Image
and the Return of Christ

"As He was sitting on the Mount of Olives, the disciples came to Him privately, saying, 'Tell us, when will these things happen, and what will be the sign of Your coming, and of the end of the age?'" Matthew 24:3

In our many conversations with people on Bible prophecy, someone will invariably raise the burning, ageless question, "how close are we to the second coming of Jesus?"

As one sincere gentleman phrased it, "We have been taught for years the 'fig tree' concerning Israel becoming a nation in 1948, and we've heard teachings on the great Olivet prophecy. What's your opinion?"

In other words, "I've heard all the traditional answers, and it doesn't really clear it up for me. Do you have anything that can add a little clarity to this issue?"

The best answer we can give to help us understand how close we are to the end, and how soon the Lord will return, is found in Nebuchadnezzar's dream, as recorded in the second chapter of the book of Daniel. We firmly believe that Jesus was pointing to the multimetallic image when He answered this same question, posed by His disciples, two thousand years ago.

*And Jesus answered them, "See that no one leads you astray. For many will come in my name, saying, 'I am the Christ,' and they will lead many astray. And you will hear of wars and rumors of wars. See that you are not alarmed, for this must take place, but the end is not yet. For **nation will rise against nation,***

*and kingdom against kingdom, and there will be famines and earthquakes in various places. All these are but the beginning of the birth pains. **THEN they will deliver you up to tribulation**...*
Matthew 24:4-9

Nations are always rising against other nations, and kingdoms are constantly going to war against each other. If there is one universal thing in human history, it is war. Thus, if this is taken as a general sign of ANY nations going to war, it is not helpful in the least. But we don't believe Jesus ever gave answers that were pointless, or so general they were of no help whatsoever. No, that is not our Lord. His answers were not always easy to grasp, but they were ALWAYS helpful to those who sought diligently to understand.

We believe he was not speaking of ANY nations, but rather, the key nations referenced in scripture as playing a crucial role in the end times, in the rise of the Antichrist, and in marking of the beginning of the seven year Tribulation.

If there is one thing virtually all evangelical Biblical scholars agree on, it is that the only body parts on the multimetallic image in Daniel 2:31-45 yet to be formed are the feet and toes of iron and clay. On this we too agree . . . in part.

Where we differ is that while we understand the historical fulfillment of the first four body parts on the image (and have addressed them in detail in our first chapter), we ALSO believe those body parts are YET TO BE FORMED in the end times. In other words, we believe there is a double reference to both historical kingdoms and future nations within each of the first four body parts (also called a "major" and "minor" fulfillment). The connection between those historic kingdoms, and the future nations, is that each corresponding country will be ruled by the exact same satanic prince.

Historically, as we showed in chapter one, the head of gold represented the Babylonian Empire. It was conquered by the Medio-Persian Empire (chest and arms of silver). The Persians were defeated by the Grecian Empire (belly and thighs of bronze). And finally, the Grecian empire succumbed to the Roman Empire (legs of iron). All we have left are the feet and toes of iron and clay, as well as a problem (the Roman Empire was not overthrown by a "ten kingdom confederacy"). Further, the body parts of the statue did not "crumble away" as each kingdom rose to prominence – they remained.

That would leave the Mediterranean Confederacy to arise independently of the other kingdoms, and on one level, that is true (as those kingdoms are gone, and the confederacy is not yet here). But we believe the fact that there is no depicted "break" at the ankles of the image points to another truth: the statue will be "rebuilt" in the end times. Or to put it another way, the exact same progression that we witnessed in history will repeat itself in the end times, with each kingdom rising to prominence, followed quickly by the next, ultimately paving the way for the rise of the Mediterranean Confederacy of Ten Kingdoms.

Those body parts that were missing, from Babylon to the Roman Empire, must be brought back into existence on the global map to fulfill Bible prophecy concerning the image. The tricky part will be in specifically identifying these countries (remember, they don't have to have the same name, the critical connection is that they must be ruled by the same satanic prince). As we will prove, all four of these nations do exist today, and they are poised to become prominent in global, or more precisely, Arab affairs.

The nations will rise to prominence in the exact same order as they did historically, but there will be some differences. First, they will become prominent in international affairs, but they will not have the time nor the power to create physical "empires." Recall that in Daniel 7:12, in referencing these same satanic princes, we read:

"As for the rest of the beasts, their dominion was taken away, but their lives were prolonged for a season and a time."

They are still around, but they simply do not have the dominion and power they enjoyed in times past.

Second, the duration of the "reign" of each will be greatly compressed, and the time between each nation's rise will be very short in comparison to their historical counterparts.

Why? The answer is found in Revelation 12:12.

"But woe to you, O earth and sea, for the devil has come down to you in great wrath, because he knows that his time is short!"

All Satan needs this time is for each of these satanic princes to do his part to prepare the Arab world for the rise of the Antichrist. Their job is to prepare the region for Satan's ultimate play, to "prep" the economic, political and spiritual stage of the Islamic world so that everything is in place for the Antichrist's entrance.

We know that when the rock strikes the feet of the image, the entire statue is present, and the entire statue is destroyed. As we mentioned previously, this means that some nations will exist in the end times which will be representations of these body parts, and Christ will obliterate all of them at the point of His return.

So which nations will it be?

The head of gold was Babylon, and central place of power within that empire never really moved anywhere. It remained in the city of Babylon, which is located in modern Iraq. So we believe the end times "head of gold" will be Iraq.

The chest and arms of silver was Persia, and while their center of power shifted somewhat, it remained generally located within the region where it arose, which is located in modern Iran. So we believe the end times "chest and arms of silver" will be the nation of Iran.

The belly and thighs of bronze arose in Greece, and then split into four independent "kingdoms," each with its own center of power. So how do we deal with this? Well, scripturally, the focus of all Grecian activity shifts to two of the four divisions: Syria and Egypt. And of those, one of them gives rise to a ruler who will come to represent the end times Antichrist. That ruler was Antiochus Epiphanes, and the kingdom was the Syrian division. Based on this, we believe the end times "belly and thighs of bronze" will be the nation of Syria.

Finally, the legs of iron arose in Rome. As detailed in chapter one, the center of "Roman" power shifted from Rome to Constantinople during the last two thirds of the Roman Empire. Constantinople is currently called "Istanbul," and is located in modern day Turkey. Based on this, we believe the end times "legs of iron" will be the nation of Turkey.

Another way of saying this is that the "major" fulfillment of this vision was in the historic empires of Babylon, Persia, Greece and Rome. The "minor" fulfillment will be in the end times, and will involve the nations of Iraq, Iran, Syria and Turkey. Each of these countries will take their turn becoming prominent in Arab affairs until they are united in the Mediterranean Confederacy of Ten Kingdoms, and ultimately, by the Antichrist himself.

If we are right, it is possible that this progression may have already started. We present the following cautiously, and with full knowledge of how many previous scholars have gone astray trying to fit current events into Biblical prophecy. What we believe without hesitation or reservation is that this progression from gold, to silver, to bronze, to iron will repeat itself in the end times. That, we believe, is definitive, and will happen. What we propose tentatively is that based on this belief, the following "interpretation" of this fact MAY be true.

If we are correct, the world may have already witnessed the rise and fall of the head of gold, Iraq, under insane rule of Sadaam Hussein.

Under his leadership, Iraq dominated regional Islamic politics for a good portion of the last fifteen years, give or take a few. He was brought down by a coalition of more than 70 nations, many of them Islamic, lead by the United States.

If he was the head of gold, then the next nation to rise to regional dominance will be Iran. Just as was true of Hussein, their nation will be marked by malignant cruelty in political affairs and actions, both domestically and internationally. Although they will not conquer it, they will dominate the region through fear, intimidation, and adept diplomatic manipulation. Ultimately, as was true of Hussein, in its quest for more power, it too will seek to gain more territory and influence in order to secure its position as the leader of the Islamic Arab world. As such, Iran will cause civil unrest in Iraq, and will very likely occupy a large portion of that country (as Iraq will now be weak, and unable to defend itself). Iran will only prevail for a short time, however, and just as was true of Hussein, this territorial ambition will lead to its downfall.

The "Iraqi" occupation will cause an uproar of fear and frustration among many Mediterranean Islamic states, particularly the Islamic countries recently liberated from the Soviet Union. These Islamic states will join forces to denounce this occupation, and a new "coalition," again including Islamic states, but this time lead by the rising power of Syria, will ultimately bring Iran to its knees.

Syria will take a leadership role in this coalition (in much the same way that America did in the overthrow of Hussein), and will start by denouncing the Iranian occupation. Together with its Islamic allies, they will succeed in breaking the Iranian strength, and will push Iran out of the major portion of Iraq. Because none of these nations will be true military giants (in the sense that America is), the conflict will not be long or drawn out. Iran will be overextended by the Iraqi occupation, and will break fairly quickly when confronted by relatively small skirmishes from hostile neighbors pressing in on all sides.

At this point, Syria rises to regional dominance, and through diplomatic manipulation and intimidation, they move in to occupy the southern portion of Iraq and will gain control of the prophetically critical city of Babylon. This will result in the formation of the end times nation that will give rise to the Antichrist, the nation we have called New Syria. It is at this point that the stage is set for the rise to power of the Islamic Mahdi and his false prophet.

Next, after the belly and thighs of bronze, comes the legs of iron. In fear of Syria's aggression, strength and dominance in regional affairs, there will be overtures made from Turkey to Egypt, as well as Greece and a few other Islamic states. They will meet, possibly in secret, to form an alliance for protection against the fearsome might of Syria. As the capital of Syria is Ankara, the other nations will agree to allowing their "Council of Ten United Islamic Nations" capital to be located in Istanbul. It will be here that the ten toes in Daniel, and ten horns in Revelation, will form into one semi-unified confederacy, and the multimetallic image will be completed. While the rise and fall of these nations leading up to the formation of the ten were minor fulfillments of the vision from Daniel, the formation of the ten will be a major fulfillment.[116]

When the finished works of Satan are completed in forming the feet and toes on the image, gross spiritual darkness will cover the people, and the Antichrist will rise up among them. That full and completed image will symbolize the final "man of sin," the Antichrist himself!

If we are correct in this interpretation, it is highly likely that the Antichrist, the greatly anticipated Mahdi of the Islamic faith, is somewhere in Syria alive and well at this very moment. He is quietly watching world events, just biding his time as he waits for exactly the right time when he can step onto the stage of world events, and take command of all that he surveys. He lurks in his own world of gross darkness, never dreaming that it will ultimately drive him to his own destruction at the coming of our Lord and Savior, Jesus Christ.

No one knows the very day or hour of His glorious, imminent return, but it is given to those who watch to know the times and seasons in which we live.

We believe that Jesus was referencing this image from Daniel when he stated that nation would rise against nation, and kingdom against kingdom, and that immediately after that, would start the time of the tribulation. Therefore, consider the statue of gold, silver, bronze and iron mixed with clay. If we are correct, we find ourselves in the prophetic times and seasons of "silver" on that image as of this writing.

---

[116] The minor fulfillment of the formation of the feet and toes of iron and clay happened on May 29, 1453 when the Ottoman Turks, an Islamic empire, took the city of Constantinople, and overthrew the Eastern Roman Empire. The city's name was changed to Istanbul, and it remained the capital of the Ottoman Empire until WWI brought about its dissolution in 1922. An Islamic empire conquered the Roman Empire, exactly as the progression in the vision of the multimetallic image predicted. This Islamic empire was not a confederacy of ten kingdoms, and it was not conquered by the Antichrist, but was dissolved, as it was but a minor fulfillment of the prophecy (minor fulfillments do not, typically, fit every detail of a given prophecy). In the major fulfillment, yet to come, the Antichrist himself will overthrow the ten kingdom Islamic alliance that we have tagged "The Mediterranean Confederacy of Ten Kingdoms."

THAT is how close we are to the end; THAT is how near we are to the coming of our Lord and Savior, Jesus Christ. How many years is that exactly? We don't know. But what we believe is that it is unfolding right before our eyes, in events that are fairly easy to observe and track. And we do not believe the remainder of these events will be lengthy or that the time periods between them will be long or drawn out.

We believe they will advance rapidly to reach their final conclusion in . . . this generation!

SHEEP AND GOAT NATIONS
America and the Church in the End Times

"*…and Jerusalem shall be trodden down of the Gentiles, until the times of the Gentiles be fulfilled.*" Luke 21:24

The times of the Gentiles will culminate when the antichrist breaks the seven-year peace pact with Israel in the middle of the week. He enters Jerusalem with force and sets up the abomination of desolation. It is the nations within the boundaries of the great harlot that will persecute and kill the Jews and Christians in the tribulation. (Revelation 6:9-11; 7:4-17). These are the "end times" Gentiles that will take over Jerusalem – NOT the whole world!

All nations will not be evil, goat nations. There are to be both sheep and goat nations even at this time period.

> "*When the Son of Man comes in his glory, and all the angels with him, he will sit on his throne in heavenly glory. All the nations will be gathered before him, and he will separate the people one from another as a shepherd separates the sheep from the goats. He will put the sheep on his right and the goats on his left.*
> "*Then the King will say to those on His right, 'Come, you who are blessed by my Father; take your inheritance, the kingdom prepared for you since the creation of the world. For I was hungry and you gave me something to eat, I was thirsty and you gave me something to drink, I was a stranger and you invited me in, I needed clothes and you clothed me, I was sick and you looked after me, I was in prison and you came to visit me.*

"Then the righteous will answer him, 'Lord, when did we see you hungry and feed you, or thirsty and give you something to drink? When did we see you a stranger and invite you in, or needing clothes and clothe you? When did we see you sick or in prison and go to visit you?

"The King will reply, 'I tell you the truth, whatever you did for one of the least of these brothers of mine, you did for me.'

"Then he will say to those on his left, 'Depart from me, you who are cursed, into the eternal fire prepared for the devil and his angels. For I was hungry and you gave me nothing to eat, I was thirsty and you gave me nothing to drink, I was a stranger and you did not invite me in, I needed clothes and you did not clothe me, I was sick and in prison and you did not look after me.'

"They also will answer, 'Lord, when did we see you hungry or thirsty or a stranger or needing clothes or sick or in prison, and did not help you?'

"He will reply, 'I tell you the truth, whatever you did not do for one of the least of these, you did not do for me.'

"Then they will go away to eternal punishment, but the righteous to eternal life." (Matthew 25:31-46)

In the above passages there are three classes of people mentioned: the sheep nations, the goat nations, and "My Brethren." On the international level, "My Brethren" are the Jews. Because of Satan's deep hatred of Israel, this will be the criterion that separates who will join the Antichrist and who will not. The sheep nations, those who ally with and minister to Israel, will not fight against Christ at Armageddon because they will not ally with the Antichrist against Israel, while many, if not all of the goat nations, those who hate and despise Israel, will. Then again, many people in the goat nations that are unable to help the Jews, "my brethren," but are sympathetic toward them, and have not taken the mark of the beast and have escaped death will be allowed entrance into the millenium at the second coming of Christ as earthly people to populate the earth.

"And it shall come to pass, that every one that is left of all the nations (goats) which came against Jerusalem shall even go up from year to year to worship the King, the Lord of Hosts, and to keep the feast of tabernacles." (Zechariah 14:16)

While Egypt will be one of the future ten kingdoms whose armies will fight with the antichrist at Armageddon, even families that are left in that country will be allowed entrance into the millenium – "*and if the family of Egypt go not up, and come not, they have no rain.*" (Zechariah 14:18). Not only Egypt, but also "*all the families of the earth…*" (Zechariah 14:17).

As Egypt and the people in the territory of Assyria will be under the power and authority of the antichrist during the tribulation, many will escape the mark of the beast also, and be allowed entrance into the millenium.

> "*In that day (i.e. the glorious future, the day of the Lord)[117] shall there be a highway out of Egypt to Assyria, and the Assyrian shall come into Egypt, and the Egyptian into Assyria, and the Egyptian shall serve with the Assyrian. In that day shall Israel be the third with Egypt and Assyria, even a blessing in the midst of the land: whom the Lord of hosts shall bless, saying, Blessed be Egypt my people, and Assyria, the work of my hands, and Israel mine inheritance.*" (Isaiah 19:23-25.)

The goat nations are the nations that will kill the Christians and "my brethren," the Jews, and fight Christ at Armageddon. The ten (goat) kingdoms will be formed within the territory of the great harlot, Islam. Not the common market. If Islam is anti-Christian and anti-Jew, and if claimed by many, the common market in Europe is the ten horn kingdom, and the antichrist comes out of one of them, then who are the sheep nations? How can the antichrist rule the whole world under one world government and literally have all nations and all people submit to him and worship him and take his mark or be killed and at the same time be sheep nations at the second coming of Christ?

These are indeed Christian (sheep) nations for Jesus to call them: "*sheep,*" "*righteous,*" "*blessed of my father,*" and say they are called "*into eternal life,*" and shall "*inherit the kingdom prepared for you from the foundation of the world.*" (Matthew 25:31-46). Therefore, we conclude from these scriptures and other scriptures (as explained earlier in this book) that the common market is NOT the ten horned kingdoms, the antichrist will not and cannot come from Europe, nor will he rule the whole wide world. The great harlot that rides the beast is not the

---

[117] The E. W. Bullinger Companion Bible

new age movement, or any part of Christiandom, and the plagues or the wrath of God does not fall upon the sheep nations or upon anyone within the goat nations that will not bow their knee to the antichrist. Even in that city called Babylon the Great, the headquarters and the center of antichrist kingdom during the last three and a half years of the tribulation period, John writes:

"...and I heard another voice (Christ) from heaven, saying, come out of her, my people, that ye be not partakers of her sins, and that ye receive not of her plagues." (Revelation 18:4.)

Since the saints of God escape the wrath of God in Babylon the Great, and many within the geographical extent of the antichrist kingdom, then it only stands to reason that the Christians within sheep nations, which are outside of his kingdom, escape God's wrath also. God's wrath does not fall upon His people (John 3:36, Romans 5:9, I Thessalonians 5:9). Not only will many escape His wrath but also the wrath and the rule of the antichrist.

The antichrist will not rule America or any other sheep nation. Even as powerful as the antichrist might be, he will still be somewhat fearful of the awesome military and spiritual strength of the United States and her allies at that time. There shall never be a day that a demonic prince will rule America. Nor shall there ever be a foreign king that shall step his foot on America's soil to rule.

If we are truly living in the last days, as most Christians believe, and Israel exists today in fulfillment of Bible prophecy, and the Great harlot of Revelation 17 that will persecute and kill the Jews and Christians even prior to the complete formation of the ten kingdoms is in existence, then does it not stand to reason God is raising up "Sheep" nations for these last days also?

We are not intimating that there will not be sheep (Christian) within goat nations, nor goats (ungodly) in sheep nations, as there will be. Until sin is extinguished once and for all by Jesus after the Millenium, there will always be darkness where there is light, and light wherever darkness lurks. But the sheep nations will be predominately light and the goat nations will be predominately filled with darkness right up to the Second Coming of Christ. We believe the sheep nations are the United States, Canada, Great Britain, France, and some other nations of people that will bow their knee to Christ, and reject alliance with the Antichrist in these latter days. These sheep nations will not be under the authority of the beast. He will not rule these nations, and especially the United States of America.

In continuance throughout these last days darkness will grow darker and the glorious light will grow brighter. The church, the called-out Body of Christ, will shine like the noonday sun.

God did not intend for this nation to be overspread and run by the forces of hell. The church can point the finger of blame for its national sins on our politicians, judges, our school boards for the spiritual wickedness that is rampant in our country. However, much of the blame rests on the irresponsibility of the church. Many of God's people have 'laid back for years by believing the ungodly idea that we must have complete separation of Church and state, in that we must separate our biblical teachings and up-bringing from our political views. Every Sunday they would carry their bibles into churches, live holy, and on Monday vote into political office an ungodly person. Then expect these leaders to do the right thing for our neighborhoods, our states and our nation. Many adopted the attitude: "why should we speak for or against policies, or get involved in politics – after all we're living in the last days anyway, and there's not too much we can do."

With that ungodly and unhealthy attitude we, the church, gave Satan and his hordes a green light to inflict a moral and spiritual cancer on America. All through the course of our history the body of Christ should have been demonstrating that we are the Salt and the Light in this darkened world, pulling down demonic strong holds in high places so thereby freedom can rule. There has been and there still is a clarion call going forth for this nation, and all nations, to repentance. Once again, God is swabbing many nations with His precious blood. God is calling his church, His people, to repentance. It is the Lord's desire to keep America great and strong. Long ago God set this land, America, this continent, apart not to be corrupted, but reserved for a holy purpose. What holy purpose? To be an ever burning light set high upon a hill to other nations and to be an umbrella, a safety for Israel to the end times.

This is the purpose and the destiny of America and the Body of Christ. And the Body of Christ is beginning to hear and answer this call as never before.

God said to Abraham

> "...Get thee out of thy country, and from thy kindred, and from thy father's house, unto a land that I will show thee; And I will make of thee a great nation, and I will bless thee, and make thy name great; and thou shalt be a

blessing: And I will bless thee, and curse him that curseth thee: And in thee shall all families of the earth be blessed." (Genesis 12:1-3).

"And I will make thy seed to multiply as the stars of heaven, and will give unto thy seed all these countries; and in thy seed shall all the nations of the earth be blessed." (Genesis 26:4).

These are the promises God made with Abraham, Isaac and Jacob to promote and spread the gospel to all nations. These promises to and through national Israel will yet be fulfilled in the Millenium age when they will have accepted their rejected Messiah at the Second Coming of our Christ. Jesus said, *"I am not sent but unto the lost sheep of the house of Israel."* (Matthew 16:24).

If Israel would have, as a nation, accepted Christ, He would have used Israel to spread the Gospel to all the world. But national Israel failed in this calling. The spiritual Jews today, the "called out body of Christ," believers, the spiritual seed of our father Abraham are called to carry on the gospel program. Israel, as a nation, rejected the true living Stone, and because of their rejection of Him, Jesus said to them, *"The Kingdom of God shall be taken from you, and given to a nation bringing forth the fruits thereof."* (Matthew 21:43).

The kingdom of God given to a "nation" to bring forth the fruits thereof, we believe, has a two-fold fulfillment: in general, the Church as a whole throughout the world, and in particular, the United States of America. A nation set apart by God for this purpose. The United States is a nation that came into being and was established upon the Word of God and the Christian principles.

Again, God is shaking the nations and will continue to do so. At this same time He is also shaking his church out of their complacency. In this shaking, righteous judgements must first come to the house of the Lord until the church learns righteousness and obedience to God and His word.

And in this shaking, God is forming and putting together all of the glorious parts of the body of Christ as it pleases him. It will not be a holy tabernacle or temple made with hands established upon man's views, his preconceived ideas – but it will be the Holy Spirit that knits together this body. Within this shaking God is raising and calling forth His holy Apostles and Prophets to speak to heads of state to establish and guide this nation and other nations in the way of the Lord for this end-time. No longer will they (including any Christian ministries) feel hindered and intimidated by the faces of clay, of cold church members and pastors who don't want the mighty voice and anointing of the Holy Spirit in their lives. No longer will God's Apostles and Prophets sit idly and receive the finger of accusations pointed at them that they speak falsely and therefore out of order!

God is planting within their spirit a holy anger and a boldness that has never been felt before. The Holy Spirit indwelling his people does not know intimidation – only victory! Their voices are going to be heard. Some in the churches will murmur and complain they don't manifest the "love of God" because of the holy anger and sharp words they will speak. It is the anger of the Lord that they feel, and his words of correction they speak! They feel the Lord's anger well up deep inside their very being against the ungodliness, the unabated lawlessness that is running rampant throughout the world and especially this nation. Against the vile passions of the wicked openly demonstrated, the murder and the wholesale slaughter of the innocent, the unborn who never received into their tiny lungs a breath of fresh air – all because of the stamp of approval by the hideous sound from the gavel of ungodly judges! God allowed them to be in office and unless they repent and stop this madness, God will judge them as he did the ungodly leaders of old.

God's holy Apostles, Prophets, Teachers, Evangelists, and Pastors and many-membered Body of Christ's church are beginning to say, "enough is enough!" They will stand together, and pull down demonic strongholds across this called-out nation. Some will even pronounce prophetic judgements by the anointing of the Holy Spirit upon the ungodly unless they repent. A latter day revival is coming in strength and power of the Lord throughout the world and this land. It's going to be a Holy Ghost, Body of Christ revival the world has never ever seen.

Islam and the Antichrist are going to be a thorn in each other's side. But, the glorious body of Christ is going to be a thorn to both of them. This revival is going to cause havoc and turmoil throughout the world. Multitudes will love to hear the prophetic words and many will repent and accept the Lord as God and savior. However, many will not listen or believe the voice of the Holy Spirit. Their hearts will grow darker and darker. They will be overcome with demonic hatred toward the glorious body of Christ. This Body of Christ in the end times will know no darkness. It will have no shadows lurking in secret crevices of men's souls. It will be a glorious body of light! It will be clothed with the righteousness of the Lamb. It will truly be a body without spot or blemish. This Body will hear no other voice except out from the One that proceeds from the throne of God!

The scriptures declare we are heirs of God and joint heirs with Jesus Christ. This Body of Christ will be clothed with his righteousness, His nature, and will demonstrate the fullness of Christ. This Body of Christ, this great army of the Lord that God is putting together for this end time ministry, shall not be hindered or stopped by the forces of hell.

That burning ember! It is that burning ember that the saints of God feel flickering in their inner most being that will begin to burn and grow brighter and brighter and brighter until all flesh or sinful, carnal traits are consumed by this ever burning ember. This is the fire of the Lord! As this body of Christ marches across this land, in oneness of the Spirit with others across the seas, their voices shall be heard and their every step shall be ordered of the Lord.

No man has ever felt this kind of heavy anointing, this baptism of fire that God is beginning to kindle within His people. They will radiate with the glory of the Lord and speaking the mind from the loving heart of the Lord, demonstrating the fullness of the resurrection power of our Christ. This will be the early and latter rain poured out in abundance. God is going to show forth His glory, His judgement, His love, His anger, His wrath. Everything that God is will be demonstrated to the hell bent ungodly world! Many of the ungodly will run and try to hide in crevices in the earth and in rocks and the mountains from the wrath of Him that sits upon the throne. However, God will always extend and show forth His love and kind mercy to those who are repentant. There will never, ever be a time where the Spirit of the Lord will be withdrawn from the earth. It is His greatest desire that all come to know the Lord, and that none perish.

During the outpouring of the early and latter rain, the body of Christ ministry will not seek her own glory, but rather will glorify the father in heaven. Every single cell in each member in this body of Christ will be radiating life. The fullness of life! There will be no diseases, no sickness, no darkness or shadows in the glorious body. Every cell in our bodies filled and overflowing with the resurrection power of God! The beginning of this glorious ministry will begin with that ever-burning ember growing brighter and brighter until this body becomes a flame of fire! This is that baptism of fire.

This burning ember that will grow brighter and brighter is conditional upon obedience to the Word and the voice of the Spirit. It's going to burn away all destructive forces of hell that try to stand in the way of this latter day ministry. God is going to have His Moseses, Elijahs, Joshuas, and Isaiahs in this Body. This is the Body of Christ for which Jesus returns. But, before that time there must be a powerful ministry raised up to preach the everlasting gospel with a flame of burning fire to an unregenerate world. The prayer that Jesus prayed as recorded in John 17:21-23 was heard of the Father. It will be answered in its completeness and totality in this glorious Body of Christ, the one without spot or wrinkle.

Jesus prayed,

> *"That they all may be one; as thou, Father, art in me, and I in thee, that they also may be one in us: that the world may believe that thou hast sent me, and the glory which thou gavest me I have given them; that they may be one, even as we are one: I in them, and thou in me, that they may be made perfect in one; and that the world may know that thou hast sent me, and hast loved them, as thou hast loved me."*

God himself set this great nation aside and He sanctified it. He called this nation to be a holy nation, a shining beacon of that Glorious light to all nations. This is America's destiny.

There are yet future demonic battles in the heavenlies that the saints of God must battle. The results of these battles in the heavenlies, whether they are won or lost, are played out on earth. It is the prayers of the Saints that cause the empowerment of God's Holy angels to go into battles to drive the demonic forces from off of this land. This is why it's important that every Christian pray daily for this nation and our leaders; and to vote for godly leaders regardless of party affiliation.

Satan has declared and sworn by his wrath that America is going to be a "goat" nation. Well, what Satan has declared and what God has ordained are definitely two different things! Not only is Satan subject unto God and His Holy angels, but also to the saints of Jesus Christ! Christians across this land have declared America for Jesus – and it IS going to be. God's people are rising up everywhere. Again it is worth repeating – God's holy people are beginning to, as never before, pull down and cast out demonic strongholds across this country. Satan's kingdom has already been defeated! That darkened kingdom was defeated on the cross of Calvary!

It is true our beloved nation is in trouble as never before. It is in spiritual and moral bondage. At the birth of our nation, when our founding forefathers wrote and signed that glorious and historical document, the Declaration of Independence, it was adopted to secure America, her people, free from spiritual and political bondage. Through time, however, we have lost much of our heritage and our freedoms by allowing the powers of darkness to over-spread. But we, God's people, see another glorious Declaration of Independence that God's people are beginning to declare as never before. This Declaration of Independence is lifted high above the earth. It will never, ever be cast down by any man or any league of foreign nations of darkness of demonic origin. It was joyfully written for all who will take Jesus into their hearts, and brings gifts, promises, and life eternal to those who accept it, but death and eternal punishment to those who oppose it.

It was signed and sealed by the blood of Jesus Christ. The precious blood that flowed through Emmanuel's veins. This glorious Declaration of Independence that offers faith, hope and love is called the Word of God, and the Gospel of the Kingdom. It was prepared before the foundation of the World, and it offers the only true independence that can be offered: freedom from sin, from the bondage of darkness, from the evil of this world, from the death and destruction that reign here, but will be overthrown soon.

Multitudes and multitudes of Americans are rededicating their lives, their allegiance to the flag, and to the United States of America, and making bold proclamations of their faith and allegiance to the Cross and unto the Lamb!

We have taught for years that America and God's people have a place, a destiny, to fulfill in God's plan in this darkened world and in these end times. She was set aside for a holy purpose to be a beacon of light of that glorious gospel of Jesus Christ to all nations. She started out that way, she can be now, and she can end that way. God has placed the responsibility of her destiny into the hands of His people. Her destiny, her rise to greater heights, or her fall to the lowest valley is contingent upon obedience to God and His word. God desires His people to take back this land for Jesus. His name always lifted high, higher than any hill, or higher than any mountain:

> "*And I, if I be lifted up from the earth, will draw all men unto me.*" (John 12:32,)

> "*and he said unto them, Go ye into all the world, and preach the gospel to every creature.*" (Mark 16:15).

In conclusion, know this: God will always judge sin. Whether it be saint or sinner, one individual, a group, or a nation – unless and until the sin is repented of and washed away by the atoning blood of our savior, Jesus Christ. The judgements of our God toward our nation are forthcoming and will increase each time in severity with divine justice and in proportion to our national sins until our people turn to God and repent. For God's judgments are always for repentance. Then, in God's loving mercy, toward a repentant nation we would hear Him say:

This nation shall stumble
This nation shall weave
She shall stumble and fall to her knees
I will hear a sound
I shall turn and see
A nation of repentance has returned to me
I shall stretch forth mine arm
and extend to her mine hand
I will raise her up and say
Behold, I am healing thy land.

God Bless America!

BIBLIOGRAPHY

Arberry, A. J., "*The Koran Interpreted*," MacMillan Publishing Co., Inc., New York, NY, 1955.

Caner, Ergun, and Emir Caner, "*Unveiling Islam*," Kregel Publications, Grand Rapids, MI, 49501, 2002.

"*Companion Bible*," Zondervan Bible Publishers, Grand Rapids, MI, 1974.

Dawood, N. J., "*The Koran*," Penguin Books Ltd., Harmondsworth, Middlesex, England, 1980.

Gabriel, Mark, "*Islam and Terrorism: What the Quran Really Teaches About Christianity, Violence and the Goals of the Islamic Jihad*," Charisma House, Lake Mary, FL, 32746, 2002.

Gabriel, Mark, "*Islam and the Jews: The Unfinished Battle*," Charisma House, Lake Mary, FL, 32746, 2003.

Green, Jay P., ed., "*The Interlinear Bible*," Sovereign Grace Publishers, Lafayette, Indiana, 47903, 1986.

Jeffery, Arthur, "*Islam, Mohammed and His Religion*"; Bobbs-Merrill Educational Publishing, Indianapolis, IN, 1958.

Larkin, Clarence, "*Dispensational Truth*," P.O. Box 334, Glenside, PA, 19038, 1920.

McDowell Josh, and John Gilchrist, "*The Islam Debate*," Here's Life Publishers, Inc., San Bernardino, CA 92414, 1983.

"*New International Study Bible*," Zondervan Bible Publishers, Grand Rapids, MI, 49506, 1985.

Pickthall, Mohammed Marmaduke, "*The Meaning of the Glorious Koran*," New American Library, Inc., New York, NY, 10019.

Vine, W. E., *"Vine's Expository Dictionary of New Testament Words,"* Evangelical Christian Publishers Association, United States, 1952.

Whiston, William, trans., *"The Works of Josephus,"* Hindrickson Publishers, Peabody, Mass., 1985.

Zacharias, Ravi, *"Light in the Shadow of Jihad: The Struggle for Truth,"* Multnomah Publishers, 2002.

2913194